GLEANINGS FROM AN OLD PORTFOLIO

Gleanings From An Old Portfolio

LADY LOUISA STUART.

PAINTED BY MRS. MEE.

LADY LOUISA STUART.

GLEANINGS

FROM AN

OLD PORTFOLIO

CONTAINING SOME

CORRESPONDENCE BETWEEN LADY LOUISA STUART AND HER SISTER CAROLINE, COUNTESS OF PORTARLINGTON,

AND

OTHER FRIENDS AND RELATIONS

EDITED BY

Alice Georgina Caroline (Strong)

MRS. [GODFREY] CLARK

VOLUME ONE

1778-1784

PRIVATELY PRINTED FOR DAVID DOUGLAS

10 CASTLE STREET, EDINBURGH

1895

TO

WYNDHAM, GODFREY, AND LIONEL

MY DEAR BOYS—

    Most of the following letters belonged to my Aunt, Caroline Erskine, who expressed a wish before her death that they should be privately printed, so that the many descendants of the charming and accomplished Lady Portarlington might become acquainted with her character, and that of her sister and chief correspondent, Lady Louisa Stuart.

    I am glad that the eldest of you will be able to remember the house in Gloucester Place, with its quaint furniture, pictures, and prints, remaining, when it came to me, much as it had been when it belonged to Lady Louisa, and which had descended from her to my aunt, through Lady Anna Maria Dawson, one of Lady Portarlington's daughters, and a favourite niece of Lady Louisa's.

    Trusting that these few words will explain to you how these letters came to be in my possession, and why this attempt to edit them has been to me a labour of love, I conclude with the hope that in after years when you turn over the old books that were once Lady Louisa Stuart's, or look at the clever oil-paintings of Lady Portarlington's, these volumes may serve to remind you of the link between yourselves and these ladies of a past generation, and also recall (if I may add this without undue egoism),

Your affectionate Mother,

A. C.

TAL·Y·GARN, 30*th November* 1895.

CONTENTS

CHAPTER I—1778

WORTLEY LODGE AND LUTON

TO LADY CAROLINE DAWSON FROM LADY LOUISA STUART

viii CONTENTS

CHAPTER II—1778

DAWSON COURT AND LUTON

TO LADY LOUISA STUART FROM LADY CAROLINE DAWSON

TO LADY CAROLINE DAWSON FROM LADY LOUISA STUART

To Lady Louisa Stuart from Lady Caroline Dawson

To Lady Caroline Dawson from Lady Louisa Stuart

b

CHAPTER III—1779-81

LONDON AND EDINBURGH

To Lady Louisa Stuart from Lady Caroline Dawson

To Lady Louisa Stuart from her Brother William

To Lady Louisa Stuart from Lady Carlow

CHAPTER IV—1781

AUTUMN AND WINTER IN IRELAND

TO LADY LOUISA STUART FROM LADY CARLOW

CHAPTER V—1782

DAWSON COURT AND DUBLIN

To LADY LOUISA STUART FROM LADY CARLOW

CHAPTER VI—1783

SCOTLAND AND IRELAND

To Lady Louisa Stuart from Lady Bute

To Lady Bute from Lady Louisa Stuart

To Lady Louisa Stuart from Lady Bute

CHAPTER VII—1784

IRELAND, SCOTLAND, AND ENGLAND

TO LADY CARLOW FROM LORD CARLOW

TO LADY CARLOW FROM LADY LOUISA STUART

LIST OF ILLUSTRATIONS

NOTE

*THE Editor begs to acknowledge here her debt to those who have kindly contributed
letters to this collection, particularly to the Dowager Lady Hatherton, to Mrs.
Morritt of Rokeby, and to Lord Home. She also wishes to express her gratitude
to her father-in-law, Mr. Clark, to Mr. James Home, and to her kind publisher,
Mr. David Douglas, for their valuable help in revising the proofs, and in assisting
her to arrive at correct data in the annotations.*

TO

LADY CAROLINE DAWSON

FROM

LADY LOUISA STUART

DEAR gentle Friend, within whose happy breast
Some fav'ring Planet fixed the cheerful guest,
Oh may contentment long her wonted reign
O'er that mild region undisturbed retain !
Bright as the beam that dries a summer show'r,
May Comfort circle ev'n affliction's hour !
May wayward Fancy ne'er presume to bring
One draught of anguish from a distant spring ;
But when kind Fortune grants the prosp'rous day,
Round present pleasure unaspiring play.

If bliss from worth, if strength from firmness flow,
Such is the fate thy patience sure shall know.
Far diff'rent mine—Each bud of seeming joy
The gloomy Presage can betimes annoy,
Deep to my bosom's inmost folds proceed,
Pluck the weak root, and bruise the little seed,
Or if the transient bloom ere then be fled,
Pour fost'ring drops on sorrow's hateful head,
And lest some ray of adverse sun impair,
Shade the night plant with unabating care.

Then let thy heart ('tis asked in Friendship's name)
Forgive the grief thy Reason ought to blame,
Nor think, uncheck'd by mine its rage allowed
To stretch o'er life th' impenetrable cloud ;
Faint as she seems, her weak attempt's pursued,
Her sober counsels are each hour renew'd ;

Yet She, ev'n she can sometimes tell me too
No cheering prospect glads her utmost view,
That grateful charms, nor winning graces warm
My pensive converse and my faded form,
That past pursuits regret alone supply,
That Hope recedes, and Youth prepares to fly.

Nay, even the Muse, by whose assistance now
These vain complainings may more smoothly flow,
Finds all her arts and all her power defy'd,
Nor feeds my pleasure nor supports my pride,
When sickly spleen no object round can spare
The frequent curse must undeserving bear,
And oft be told that her pernicious hand
Forbade the bliss which Fate might else have planned,
Wove twisted evils Time shall never part,
Or fill'd the cup whose poison slew my heart.

But murmurs cease! nor from my best loved friend
One smiling thought let all your accents rend,
Or if the rent a partial cure bestows,
Take now your last, and here for ever close.
Yes! skill'd to soothe, to soften, and to cheer,
Returning Reason shall again be clear;
Not that her hand may Mem'ry's sigh restrain,
Or stifle Truth when Truth produces Pain.
The Soul let wild Imagination charm
To frantic joy or instantaneous calm,
The sudden flash for one bright moment speed,
Nor care if Night in double gloom succeed,
Her placid torch more steady, more serene,
Can chase no feature from the real scene,
But taught by Her, perhaps my strengthened eye
That real scene shall unappall'd descry.
Be this Her task; to make the wasting fire,
The torturing wish, the groundless hope retire,
Bid good already gain'd in value rise,
And veil the happiness that Fate denies.

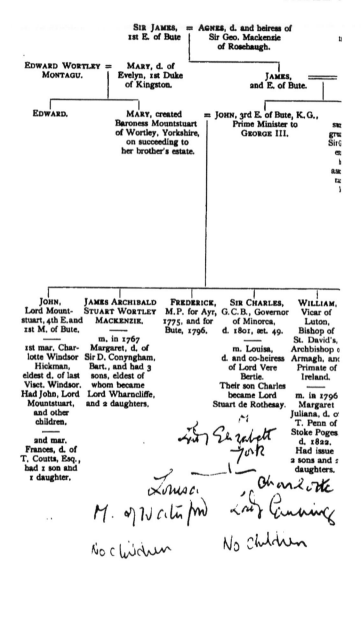

TABLE 0

SIR JAMES, = AGNES, d. and heiress of
1st E. of Bute | Sir Geo. Mackenzie
of Rosehaugh.

EDWARD WORTLEY = MARY, d. of
MONTAGU. | Evelyn, 1st Duke
of Kingston.

JAMES,
2nd E. of Bute.

EDWARD.

MARY, created
Baroness Mountstuart
of Wortley, Yorkshire,
on succeeding to
her brother's estate.

= JOHN, 3rd E. of Bute, K.G.,
Prime Minister to
GEORGE III.

JOHN, Lord Mount-stuart, 4th E. and 1st M. of Bute.	JAMES ARCHIBALD STUART WORTLEY MACKENZIE.	FREDERICK, M.P. for Ayr, 1775, and for Bute, 1796.	SIR CHARLES, G.C.B., Governor of Minorca, d. 1801, æt. 49.	WILLIAM, Vicar of Luton, Bishop of St. David's, Archbishop of Armagh, and Primate of Ireland.
———	———		———	———
1st mar. Charlotte Windsor Hickman, eldest d. of last Visct. Windsor. Had John, Lord Mountstuart, and other children.	m. in 1767 Margaret, d. of Sir D. Conyngham, Bart., and had 3 sons, eldest of whom became Lord Wharncliffe, and 2 daughters.		m. Louisa, d. and co-heiress of Lord Vere Bertie. Their son Charles became Lord Stuart de Rothesay.	m. in 1796 Margaret Juliana, d. of T. Penn of Stoke Poges. d. 1822. Had issue 2 sons and 2 daughters.
and mar. Frances, d. of T. Coutts, Esq., had 1 son and 1 daughter.				

[handwritten annotations:] Lady Elizabeth York

Louisa M. of Watford No children

Charlotte Lady Canning No Children

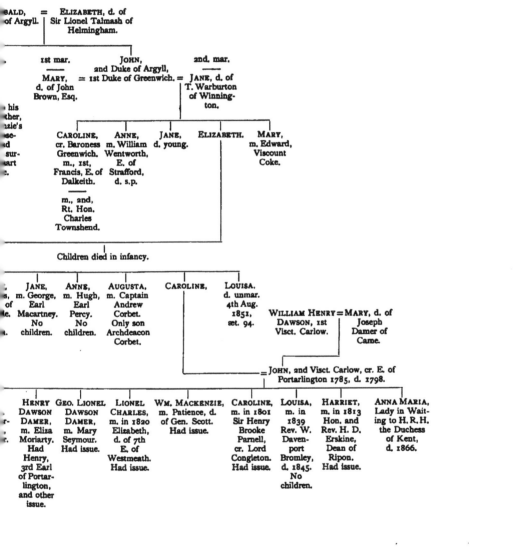

ßALD, = ELIZABETH, d. of
of Argyll. | Sir Lionel Talmash of
Helmingham.

1st mar.   JOHN,   2nd. mar.
——   2nd Duke of Argyll,   ——
MARY, = 1st Duke of Greenwich. = JANE, d. of
d. of John   T. Warburton
Brown, Esq.   of Winning-
ton.

his
ther,
zie's
se-
d
sur-
art
.

CAROLINE,   ANNE,   JANE,   ELIZABETH.   MARY,
cr. Baroness   m. William   d. young.   m. Edward,
Greenwich.   Wentworth,   Viscount
m., 1st,   E. of   Coke.
Francis, E. of   Strafford,
Dalkeith.   d. s.p.

m., 2nd,
Rt. Hon.
Charles
Townshend.

Children died in infancy.

JANE,   ANNE,   AUGUSTA,   CAROLINE,   LOUISA,
m. George,   m. Hugh,   m. Captain   d. unmar.
Earl   Earl   Andrew   4th Aug.
Macartney.   Percy.   Corbet.   1851,
No   No   Only son   æt. 94.   WILLIAM HENRY = MARY, d. of
children.   children.   Archdeacon   DAWSON, 1st   Joseph
Corbet.   Visct. Carlow.   Damer of
Came.

= JOHN, 2nd Visct. Carlow, cr. E. of
Portarlington 1785, d. 1798.

HENRY   GEO. LIONEL   LIONEL   WM. MACKENZIE,   CAROLINE,   LOUISA,   HARRIET,   ANNA MARIA,
DAWSON   DAWSON,   CHARLES,   m. Patience, d.   m. in 1801   m. in   m. in 1813   Lady in Wait-
DAMER,   DAMER,   m. in 1820   of Gen. Scott.   Sir Henry   1839   Hon. and   ing to H.R.H.
r-   m. Mary   Elizabeth,   Had issue.   Brooke   Rev. W.   Rev. H. D.   the Duchess
m. Eliza   Seymour.   d. of 7th   Parnell,   Daven-   Erskine,   of Kent,
. Moriarty.   Had issue.   E. of   cr. Lord   port   Dean of   d. 1866.
Had   Westmeath.   Congleton.   Bromley,   Ripon.
Henry,   Had issue.   Had issue.   d. 1845.   Had issue.
3rd Earl   No
of Portar-   children.
lington,
and other
issue.

GLEANINGS FROM AN OLD PORTFOLIO

CHAPTER I

LADY LOUISA STUART,[1] at the time these letters begin, was only twenty-one years old, and probably much resembled the sketch on the opposite page. She had never been as much admired as her youngest sister, Lady Caroline Dawson (then lately married, and settled in Ireland); but though without the latter's good looks, spirits, or accomplishments, she possessed superior powers of mind, which made themselves felt in conversation or in correspondence, and have preserved her name among the cultivated women of the latter end of the last and the beginning of the present century.

Lady Louisa was, even in youth, an omnivorous reader and a fair classic scholar ; whilst in later life one of her greatest pleasures was to collect curious editions of Portuguese or Spanish poets, from which she would translate extracts with great facility and accuracy.

Her love of versifying showed itself when quite a child, and continued all her life, the earliest specimens

[1] For further information on the family see table on preceding page.

still extant being written in a large childish hand, followed by others at intervals, down to the last lines written when over ninety years of age. A tragedy in prose, called *Jugurtha*, evidently written at an early age, is probably the one mentioned by Lady Mary Coke in her *Journal*.[1]

In maturer life she excelled in the vigour and precision of her English prose, of which examples may be seen in the *Memoir of John, Duke of Argyll*, and the introduction to her grandmother, *Lady Mary Wortley Montagu's Letters*.

It was a good thing for her that she had acquired this early taste for self-cultivation, for at this time she appears to have led a lonely life for a girl of her age and position.

Her father had retired from politics, a disappointed and embittered man, seeking consolation less from his family than from his favourite botanical and horticultural pursuits :—Lady Bute was already a sufferer from the gouty and other disorders which were to make her, a few years later, a complete invalid :—the four elder daughters had all married early, and the youngest, Lady Louisa's particular friend, had lately followed their example, leaving her very much thrown on her own resources. Fortunately for us, it may be said, one of the most engrossing of these was the attempt

---

[1] "I stay'd with Ly Bute till two O'clock, and was much entertain'd with her youngest Daughter, a child of ten years of Age, who shew'd us the begining of a French Novel wrote by herself, and inform'd us She was going to write a play, that the plan was fixt, and was to be taken from a Roman Story. She is a very extraordinary Girl, and has certainly a great genius."— *Journal of Lady Mary Coke*, vol. i. p. 174.

to preserve, by means of pen, paper, and ink, that intercourse with her dear companion which she so much missed.

———

LADY CAROLINE DAWSON from LADY LOUISA STUART

Wharncliff, 3rd July 1778.

I HAVE this moment received your dear, delightful, long letter, and in the transports of my gratitude for it, cannot help being angry with myself for grumbling so much in my last. Thank you a thousand times; I wish I had anything to say which would repay you; but though I foresee this will be an immense packet, I fear it will not give you the pleasure yours has done me. You have no notion what a delight only one day of your company would be to me just now, or how it would increase my enjoyments; I want nothing but you to share them with me, and I think you could to the full extent.

Never tell me of your Welsh scenes. What a view might Mr. Dawson or you take from this window! This spot is really a paradise, and I only regret that I cannot possibly find words to describe it well enough to give you the least idea of its beauty, or to justify myself for talking a little wildly upon the subject; but you have so often seen me in raptures at the idea of such scenes as these, that you will not wonder if the reality almost turns my brain. This dear little cottage is placed, like an eagle's nest, upon the very summit of a steep rock, which is entirely covered with wood, and the trees grow almost close to the walls; we are

not four yards from the edge, and if we should tumble
out of our uppermost window, might have a good
chance for rolling down the whole way.   I cannot tell
you what the prospect is, it extends so far and has such
variety, but the most striking beauty consists in two
valleys, one cultivated and divided into small fields
with patches of wood intermixed with farm-houses,
the other covered on both sides to a vast height with
woods, the river running in the bottom, of which you
only catch a glimpse here and there as the trees will
let you.   My mother tells me it falls in cascades in
several places; beyond these valleys, and the hill that
divides them, the vast moors rise one above another.
But remember I have yet only seen everything faintly,
for we arrived here yesterday after lying at Sheffield,
and it has rained to-day as hard as it could pour.   A
gleam of sunshine invited us out after dinner, but
when we had rambled to a good distance from the
house, the rain began again, and by the time we got
home we were wet to the skin, and met all the family
coming here to meet us, on foot and on horseback, with
every kind of cloak and covering you can conceive;
you never saw so droll a scene.   I am in such haste,
and have so many things to say, that I believe I am
very incoherent; but no matter, I am almost as pleased
with the house as the place.   My mother talked of it
as such a wretched hovel that I was surprised to find
it so well as it is.   We have each a bed-chamber, and
there is a room decently hung with old tapestry to dine
and sit in.   What can one desire more?   To say the
truth, it is a farm-house, and has very little furniture,

but yet the old housekeeper keeps everything so
nicely clean and neat that it puts me in mind of descriptions in romances where you meet with cottages
belonging to shepherds and shepherdesses. I do
assure you I never saw any place like it in this
respect, and I would sooner lay my cap upon the floor
here than upon a chair at Luton. All my mother
has told us of Yorkshire cleanliness seems to be true.
She laughs at me for my raptures, but I am much
mistaken if you would not join with me in preferring
this cottage and situation to any great house and fine
park we know. I had pictured the rocks and hills to
myself so often that they only answer my expectation ;
but the woods surprise me most ; they are immense
beyond imagination, and besides the greatness of the
scene, the whole country looks so much more fertile,
more *riant* than any I have ever seen ; it seems so
populous and the inhabitants look so contented, that,
in short, what would I give to have you here !

We went (in a chaise) to the Hall House[1] this
morning. It is a pretty place, and I should have
thought the view very fine if I had not come from
hence. The house is ill contrived, but might be made
comfortable. I forget to tell you about our journey.
We lay two nights on the road in vile inns, but I
persuaded my mother to go and see Hardwicke, where
Queen Mary was confined so long, and where there
is a room furnished with her work. It is a noble old
house, everything remaining in the state it was in her
time, and the old magnificence preserved with great

[1] Wortley Hall.

care; think how I was delighted, and not less with the park, though that seems neglected; you look down from a steep bank of wood upon a noble river. Our first day's journey was through a frightful country in general, but we passed by several pretty parks. Nottingham is beautifully seated upon the Trent, which runs through lovely meadows, and the Duke of Newcastle's castle[1] stands upon a high rock. The road from Mansfield here was delightful.

4th July.

I TOOK such a ramble this morning! over hill and dale, rock and cliff, and I may add through mud and mire, but attained my end at last, and got down to the river, which I found a broader stream than I could have thought; but, indeed, it may well look narrow from hence, for I suppose we are three or four hundred feet above it. Most of my way was through the wood, and much like a steep staircase to go down, for I stepped and sometimes jumped from one great stone to another (by the help of a good stick that I had the wisdom to buy at Sheffield). The river roars among a noble collection of these stones, and upon one of them I sat down at its brink, and began wishing for you once more. I could have stayed there for ever, but I found it was time to wade and clamber up again,

---

[1] Nottingham Castle, a fortress of the first class, with a fine Norman keep, was dismantled by Colonel Hutchinson, under the Commonwealth, but restored and made habitable by the Cavendishes, Dukes of Newcastle. It was burned down by a Reform mob in 1830, when Henry Pelham-Clinton, Duke of Newcastle, succeeded in imposing a heavy fine upon the Hundred. He then sold the ruins, which have been restored and converted into a museum by the Corporation of Nottingham.

so came home heartily tired, to give an account of my travels to my mother, who had had her people of business. We have been at Wentworth House this evening, and dine to-morrow at Wentworth Castle. You shall have an account of both. My mother told you how Mrs. Charles Stuart left us. She has had two letters from her, the first thinking her mother at the point of death, but in the second she says she is better. I fear she is not well herself, poor thing. She told me she intended to send your picture by means of Mrs. H. Hobart, but I daresay her present distress allows her no time to think of it.

My mother is exceedingly well, and not the worse for last night's expedition. Adieu, and God bless you! I have hardly any ink, and can scarce scratch out even this vile scrawl. When shall I write you a decent common sense letter? Adieu once more.— Yours ever affectionately,   L. S.

Mrs. Charles Stuart mentioned in the foregoing letter was the wife of Lord Bute's fourth son, and daughter and co-heiress (with her sister Albinia) of Lord Vere Bertie, son of the first Duke of Ancaster. Her sister had married in 1757 George Hobart, afterwards third Earl of Buckinghamshire. Her mother, Lady Vere Bertie (Anne Casey), whose lingering and painful illness lasted till the following November, was then being nursed by her daughter, who had only been married in the previous April, her husband having since gone to join General Howe's army in America. Mrs. Delany says in her letters: "Mr. Charles Stuart still abroad waiting the events of war, separated from his bride in a fortnight after they married. Both worthy, amiable, and tenderly attached to each other, and besides her terrors for the hazards he runs and uncertainty of his return, she has been for six months past attending her dying mother and is ready to lye-in. Lady Bute has been her great support, and a wonderful woman she is, and bears up under such complicated misfortunes that nothing but true Christian philosophy could support."

Charles Stuart had been given a Commission, as was the custom of that day, when sixteen years old, and in 1777, when twenty-four, was full Colonel, commanding the 26th Regiment. He served in America in 1778; in 1798 he was made a General, K.C.B., and Commander of the Forces in the Mediterranean; and in 1800 appointed Governor of Minorca. He then submitted to the Secretary of War a plan for the formation of an efficient and seasoned army to act against the French at Toulon and Genoa. Sir H. Bailey speaks of it as a masterly project, but the Cabinet proposed to cut it down to a degree fatal to its success. Sir Charles took great offence and threw up his Commission. He died in March 1801, aged forty-nine, at the lodge[1] at Richmond, of which park he was Deputy Ranger. He was M.P. for Poole.

His son, the well-known Ambassador at Paris, was created Lord Stuart de Rothesay, and repurchased his grandfather's place—Highcliffe, in Hampshire: the house built by Lord Bute had, however, been previously pulled down owing to the encroachment of the sea.

THE SAME from the SAME.

Wharncliff, 7th July 1778.

DEAREST SISTER—I hope now to give you a plainer account of myself than I did in my last piece

----

[1] Called Thatched House Lodge, now occupied by General Lynedoch Gardiner.

of incoherent nonsense, which was written by scraps
at different times, almost always in a violent hurry,
and when I had no great plenty of materials.   I write,
you must know, upon a chest, for I am not worth a
table, but I have no less than three chairs, and there
are window seats besides, so that article is nobly supplied.   However, I would give up all these conveni-
ences to stay here a fortnight longer, for I find my
mother talks of returning next Monday, and as she writ
to my father yesterday, I suppose she fixed herself as
usual to a day, so you see you was mistaken in fancying
our stay was to be prolonged.   I fear this excursion will
prove to me what a journey to London is to a country
miss, whom it spoils for all enjoyment of the place she
goes back to.   It is impossible I can ever like Luton
after being accustomed to such glorious scenes as these,
but (by the way) I had a hint given me last night that
I was to keep my sentiments upon that point to myself, and not seem too much delighted with this country
when I returned.   *Entre nous*, I suspect I shall not
be the only person who will have occasion for reserve,
for I am much mistaken if my mother would not, by
giving way to her secret inclinations, be extremely
fond of this place, I mean of Wortley,[1] for she is not
partial to a wild scene as I am; she likes very much
to talk over the situation, and form plans to make the
house comfortable, and is always saying with how
little trouble the grounds might be laid out in a pretty
manner, and how she could manage it if she lived

[1] Wortley Hall is distinct from Wharncliffe Lodge.   The one is outside the
Chase, the other within it.

here. I need not add that she is in exceeding good spirits.

I received a letter from Mrs. Stuart last night; her mother, she says, is still in the same dreadful condition, lifted in and out of bed by four people, and wishes so much to be released herself, that she (Mrs. Stuart) is almost forced to wish it too. She seems very miserable indeed, yet appears to hope that Gen. Howe [1] has brought good news with him, of which I heard nothing, though Lord Strafford told us he was certainly arrived. We dined at Wentworth Castle,[2] as I mentioned we should in my last, and were received, as you may suppose, with every kind of civility. I owe you a list of my remarks upon that place and Lord Rockingham's, and you shall have them, such as they were, made on the spot, though you will not think my opinion good for much perhaps. Wentworth House,[3] upon the whole, disappointed me; I had so often heard of it as one of the noblest houses in England, that I did not think it answerable to that idea. It is, I dare say, one of the largest, and the front is most magnificent, whether beautiful or not I am no judge, but I thought it striking altogether; but for the inside, it really does not seem answerable. Except a very fine hall, adorned with a composition that imitates marble of all colours,

[1] Sir William Howe left America for England in May 1778, and landed at Portsmouth on 1st July, after retaking Long Island, which was lost previously by Sir Peter Parker and General Clinton.

[2] Wentworth Castle then belonged to the Earl of Strafford, who had married Lady Anne Campbell, second daughter of John, Duke of Argyle and Greenwich.

[3] Wentworth House, built by the Marquis of Rockingham, at that time held by his son. After his death in 1782 it descended to the Fitz-William family.

and two or three more rooms which are quite unfinished, I saw no fine spaces. The rooms on the ground floor are low and dark, and the furniture by no means magnificent. The worst of all is the situation. Should you think it possible that in this country of *prospects*, where one would think it required uncommon care to pick out a spot without one, anybody could build so vast a house directly behind a huge hill ? This hill the present lord has half cut away, and is going on, but a great deal more must be done before the view is opened. I saw no more of the place than what appeared from the road leading to the house, and that seemed to be very formal and old-fashioned. Wentworth Castle is not so large, but looks more convenient, and there are some very fine rooms in it (a gallery of 180 feet, for example), all very handsomely furnished, and it commands an exceeding pretty view. I have no time to enter into particulars of the place, but altogether it pleased me extremely, though I did not like the water, which, though *serpentine*, does not look natural ; and then there is a kind of canal that comes across down to it that has an ill effect. At Lord Rockingham's I saw no water, but a string of fishponds. Both places have a vast number of ornamental buildings, pyramids, ruins, temples, etc., which adorn the whole country, and are finely seen from Wortley. I forgot to say we were at church on Sunday, and had a very good sermon from an honest, plain man, just the right kind of country clergyman. Well (as Miss Mure[1] says), what else

[1] Daughter of William Mure, one of the Scottish Barons of Exchequer.

shall I tell you ?   Instead of being less delighted as the
novelty wears off, I am more and more charmed with
this country every day, and really think I was made
for it.   If you did but see me rambling over the rocks !
I take delightful walks when my mother has business,
and we generally drive out once a day, but for my
misfortune, we have no equipage except the great
rumbling coach and four, and as we go as slow as
possible, this would be a bad diversion if the views
were less beautiful.   Yesterday we were at the forges ;
I cannot say I took so much pleasure in seeing them
as their situation, which is lovely indeed, upon the
bank of the river, under a hill covered with wood.
The park here is all covered with vast stones, and yet
the turf may vie with any garden, and, neglected as it
is, you very seldom see a thistle or a nettle, though
quantities of ferns and heath ; there are no flints,
which makes the walking very good.   We have had
the finest warm weather imaginable, so I am no judge
of that point, but I am tempted to suspect this country
is not so cold as Bedfordshire, though perhaps it may
be pretty sharp on the ridge of this rock.   I believe
the fruit is forwarder, for when we first came we had
very good cherries, and yet there was not one ripe in
the garden at Luton.   I have got yours of the 28th,
and delight in your descriptions ; but I would not for a
hundred pounds have your letter intercepted, and your
wicked remarks upon your country neighbours shown
to the world—good people who, I daresay, are as civil
and as friendly as one could desire, and try to cram you
with their feasts, and have all their love and kindness

repaid thus. Fie upon you! Yet I must own your description of the *temple by the waterside* is admirable, as well as that of Lady Jane's two friends, Mrs. C. and Lady M., in your former letter. Pray tell me how you like Miss Dawson,[1] for when you get this letter you will have had time enough to know. I am sorry you have so great a neighbourhood, and that you find it the custom to be *good neighbours*, as they call it! but it certainly is a judgment upon you for your intolerable yawnings at Luton; it has been decreed that since you wanted company you shall have enough. I suppose Lady Lothian and Lady Emily[2] will come to that dear place when we go back, and probably Mrs. Charles Stuart again, if Lady Vere dies. The other Mrs. Stuart[3] is at Southampton, and for Lady Mary Lowther[4] God knows what she is doing, for she has not writ to either of us these three weeks. Indeed, we hardly hear from anybody, and have no newspapers, so that it is just the peaceful retirement you read of in romances, and we both agree that we feel as if we had been settled here for six months, and did so before we had lived here two days. My mother is now employed with her steward, who has dined with us two or three times, and is the most stupid, disagreeable fellow you ever saw. He seems

---

[1] Sister of Lord Carlow, married later to Major Metzner.

[2] Lady Caroline D'Arcy, only daughter of Robert, sixth Earl of Holdernesse, married in 1735 William Henry, fourth Marquis of Lothian. They had one son, William John, who succeeded as fifth Marquis, and two daughters, Louisa, married Lord George Lennox, and Wilhelmina Emilia (always spoken of as Lady *Emily*), who married in 1782 Major-General John Macleod.

[3] Margaret, daughter of Sir David Conyngham, wife of James, Lord Bute's second son, the heir of Wortley.

[4] Mary, eldest daughter of Lord Bute, married in 1761 Sir James Lowther, afterwards first Earl of Lonsdale.

to put her out of all patience. I never mentioned two Vandykes at Wentworth House, of which there are copies at Wentworth Castle, both of the great Earl of Strafford, one whole length in armour with a dog, the other sitting in a black gown and dictating to a secretary. This last is a famous picture. Both have expressive countenances. Lady Mary has sent a letter to my mother at last, where she says she was at liberty to come to Luton just when we left it, and for news, madam, Sir George Osborn[1] is to marry Lady Heneage Finch, with a long story that *she* proposed to *him;* this I take to be trumped up by the *sisterhood* in order to account for his being so soon comforted after Mrs. Lockhart's cruelty, as it seems Lady Heneage refused him long ago, and now sends a message to say she has been enamoured of him ever since, which is a probable story. I am as usual ashamed to send such a heap of nonsense, but it has been scrawled by three or four lines at a time, in as many days, so it is little better than a paper of memorandums ; and your Ladyship must also excuse the inequality of *size*, in consideration of my poverty. I shall write no more till I get to Luton. I am sorry to say we set out on Monday (this is Friday), and bid farewell to this lovely place, where, besides its beauty, we have lived in as *comfortable* a manner as you can conceive. There is a bookcase among other things, so we are at no loss in an evening, and the weather has been glorious ; you would have enjoyed

---

[1] Sir George Osborn of Chicksands Priory, Beds, married Lady Heneage Finch, daughter of David, seventh Earl of Winchelsea.

it extremely.   Adieu, my love ; pray continue to write
me full accounts.—Your ever affectionate,

L. STUART.

Luton Hoo, so called from the Lords Hoo and Hastings,
its owners, down to the fifteenth century, and afterwards
inherited by the Boleyns, was purchased in 1763, the park
enlarged, and the house partially built by the Minister Earl
of Bute.   The grounds were laid out by Capability Brown,
and the house designed by Adam, also the architect of the
house begun by Lord Bute in Berkeley Square, but sold to,
and completed by Lord Shelburne, and now called Lansdowne
House.   Luton, though never completed, was nevertheless a
place of great pretensions.   The principal rooms were on a
grand scale, and the library 146 feet long.   The house was
partially burned down in 1844, and the estate finally sold.

Luton seems never to have been popular with the family.
Lord Bute passed much of his time at Highcliffe, the seat near
Christchurch, to which he removed his well-known botanic
garden.   Lady Louisa always disliked Luton, which nevertheless possessed in its fine library and gallery of pictures many
attractions.   Mrs. Delany, an old friend of Lady Bute's, was
there with the Dowager Duchess of Portland in 1774, and
gives a very pleasant description of the place in letters to
Lady Andover and Bernard Granville.   " It is," she writes, " a
very fine house, a very fine park, fine situation (the house
not finished).   It is very capacious and elegant, and after
walking through a grand apartment with a delightful saloon,
and a magnificent and most agreeable library, nobly furnished,
your Ladyship must please to go up 42 steps to a very long
gallery, which conveys you to at least four complete apart-
ments of large and lofty rooms, all elegantly furnished without
ostentation, but well suited.   As to *pictures, vases, marbles,*
and a long *et cetera* of curiosities, it would be *endless* to

recount them." [1] Her other letter gives fuller detail, and adds, " They have opened a view to the river, and the grounds and plantations are fine." [2]

———

THE SAME from the SAME

Luton, 15th July 1778.

DEAR SISTER—The first thing I have to tell you is that we returned to this place yesterday evening (lying only one night upon the road, which was at Leicester), and found everything as we left it, or a little altered for the worse, for the country is quite burnt up, and half the flowers are gone, so that it has but a dismal appearance ; indeed, I believe I look upon it with an evil eye, but I shall talk more of that when I have thanked you, my dear, for yours of the 5th, which I found here ; they told me they had sent one letter to Wharncliff; I hardly think it can be from you, so shall patiently expect its return. I do acknowledge that you are very good to me, very good indeed, but my complaints were reasonable when they were made, so I do not deserve to be scolded. I think you seem in a way to grow very comfortable, and am happy to think it ; I am glad too (by the way) to remember your cold constitution; for they give most dreadful accounts of the heat at London, and even here, though we have felt no more than was agreeable in the temperate regions where we have been. I think I understand pretty well how you stand with regard to Miss Dawson. I was sorry when I heard she meant to stay in Ireland, and had a dispute about it with my mother, who fancied it would be pleasant to you to have somebody who

[1] *Corr. of Mrs. Delany*, 2nd series, i. 542.   [2] *Ibid.* ii. 34.

knew the neighbours, but I insisted that Mr. Dawson
(my love to him) was a sufficient introductor. I rejoice
to find the ghosts are departed, or, if you will, laid, for
though they may be peaceable, they can't be pleasant,
and now you have the house to yourselves, you may
perhaps make it comfortable; at worst, it surely is not
such a scene of inconvenient melancholy magnificence
as another[1] that shall be nameless, or else every unlucky
fatality attends you; the place you describe is very
agreeable and pretty. Pray let me have a full description of your *fête champêtre*.

When I came in last night they gave me three
etters from Lady Jane Macartney,[2] but I was very much
disappointed to find two of them only copies of another,
with duplicates of a bill for fifty pounds upon Coutts,
and the third a vast packet filled with letters to other
people, and but a short one to myself, dated 22nd of
April, all about business. It came by Evans, whom she
has sent over, and desires me to recommend; seven
guineas and a half are for her, to be due on the 1st of
November, thirty for Nurse Spence, and three for the
woman at Copthall, which I shall not pay, but do as
you did last year.

The rest is to pay you, if she owes you anything, or
else to be kept till another opportunity; therefore, my
dear sister, will you send me your bill, for, if I remember

[1] Luton.
[2] Jane, second daughter of John, third Earl of Bute, married Sir George, afterwards Earl Macartney, the well-known Envoy Extraordinary at St. Petersburg and Ambassador to China.

She was in Grenada with her husband, who was at this date Governor of the Caribbee Islands, which were threatened by the French fleet under D'Estaing.

right, you paid a good deal. She sends a very good
character to be given Evans, but desires that none of
us will take her (particularly Lady Mary Lowther), and
that we will not believe anything she says about her or
Grenada. I am glad she is rid of her. Now I must
indulge myself in talking a little of my beloved Yorkshire ; I hope you are not quite sick of the subject, for
you must not expect to hear the last of it this great
while, though it appears at present more as if I had
had a very pleasant dream, than as if I had really been
a hundred and fifty miles from this place. But you
cannot conceive with what dislike I return to it. You
yourself never hated it more heartily, and never despised
it so much ; you have no idea how little it appears to me,
and how compleatly uncomfortable I feel in this great
house, after being so much the contrary in our dear
little clean, neat cottage at Wharncliff, where we really
lived in quite a pastoral manner. I never think of it
but as the abode of peace and content, for it is exactly
the retirement you sometimes see described in a
romance, where travellers driven in by a storm find a
happy family and a place that they think a paradise.
'Tis true we are quite solitary and quiet enough here,
but it is with a mixture of melancholy and stateliness,
while there we seemed to be in a retreat from all care
and anxiety, just what poets are always talking of,
though I never saw their descriptions realised before.
I doubt you will laugh at my style of admiration and
delight, but I will defy you and go on. I could scribble
for three hours upon the beauty of that place. I believe
I used to sit for as long every day upon the edge of the

highest rock eating up the prospect, and never took my
eyes away without difficulty, such a scene of wood as
you look down upon, such variety in the shape of the
hills, such cultivation in the valleys, such a cheerfulness in
the whole! and then such an extent of country as comes
at once under your eye, and everywhere such an appearance of fertility, quantities of cottages, all neatly
built of stones, and seeming clean and comfortable
within, the children playing about them, not the miserable, pining, ragged, poor little creatures you see in this
country, but looking fat and healthy, and their fathers
and mothers strong, handsome people, in general neatly
dressed, and always employed.

I made many acquaintances among them in my
rambles, and diverted myself very much, for they have
a great deal of character, an original simplicity, and yet
an awkward sort of shyness, that makes them very
entertaining. There I could travel about without any
fears, for you meet nobody but these honest people;
no London gentry, no sturdy beggars. I cannot help
saying a word of my dear Rocks; those at Wharncliff
are beautiful, especially where the cleft is, which they
call the Dragon's Den;[1] they are tumbled about in
the most romantic confusion, the bushes of birch,
hazel, holly, mountain ash, etc., growing among
them, and really upon them, and all these great stones
twined round with the finest wild honeysuckles I ever
saw. Under this rock there is a green walk about a
yard wide upon the edge of another covered with wood

[1] "Dragon's Den," see the ballad in Percy's *Reliques* relating to the Dragon
of Wantley.

to the bottom, and this noble wood can't be less than
two or three miles in length. It is chiefly oak and ash,
but there is fine birch intermixed, and some old
yews, good deal of holly among the underwood,
which has a good effect as you look down; even the
quantities of fern and heath add to the beautiful wild-
ness. My mother has another vast wood called Softly,[1]
which joins to Wharncliff, another beautiful bank
opposite to that, called the Forge Rocker, where the
tin mill and forges are placed, the river running in the
bottom, and fronting to it a vast hill without trees, the
rocks towering over it. I shut my eyes and delight
to fancy I am up on the spot. I am a fool for trying
to describe it, but it is a pleasure to me to think it all
over again; I daresay I shall never like any place so
well. You may believe I was sorry enough to leave
it. I got up at five o'clock, and walked to all my
favourite places. It was a lovely morning, and I
thought everything more charming than I had ever
seen it (for I always found I liked it better and better
every day). At last my mother sent for me, and a little
after six we set out, she laughing at me for looking
doleful, and advising me to choose a Yorkshire
husband. Now the Luton influence has seized me,
and I am half in the vapours already, what with the
place itself and the politics I hear talked. My father
has got a bad swelled face, and keeps his room. My
mother is very well, but still a little tired. She was not
the least so when she went, but coming back the heat
was excessive, and the dust, for the four or five last

---

[1] 'Softly Crags,' part of the wood in Wharncliffe Chase.

stages, intolerable. We dined at Derby the day before yesterday, where the river Derwent is very beautiful, and runs among fine meadows. We went to see the silk mill and the great church, which is very handsome, with several tombs of the Devonshire family, particularly Bess of the Hardwickes. Leicester, where we lay, is a large ugly town in a frightful flat country. Northamptonshire is almost as bad, and the part of Bedfordshire you come through worse than either, though you go by Woburn, which seems a fine place.

My mother does not seem to think my father's complaint anything but a swelled face ; he sits in the library with all the windows and doors close shut, which in just such weather as this would even suffocate you, and I daresay makes him worse. She says it quite overcomes her. Frederick and William [1] came here about five minutes after we came, and the latter looks much better, but I only see them at meals.

Pray, my dear sister, let me have a very, very long letter from you, for it will be a great comfort now I am forlorn and peevish in this. But I will make no more invectives. I assure you I feel as far from you as you can do from us, and have great reason to feel it, for your letters are an age in coming ; yet I am happy to think you are much more comfortable than you would be here. Pray mention if you have heard anything of poor little Stuart. Adieu, my love, the post waits.

---

[1] Lady Louisa's brothers, the third and fifth sons of Lord Bute ; Frederick was M.P. for Ayr in 1775, and for Bute in 1796 ; William was subsequently Archbishop of Armagh and Primate of Ireland. See *post*, 1780.

These frequent allusions to 'little Stuart' refer to the writer's nephew Stuart, afterwards Archdeacon Corbet, son of Captain Andrew Corbet and the writer's sister, Lady Augusta, who died the previous December.   The boy was at this time at Lady C. Dawson's house in London being treated for lameness, and was apparently under the charge of Mrs. Middleton, bedchamber woman to Princess Amelia.   Mrs. Middleton had had either the same or another house in Kensington before Lady Caroline's marriage, and it was of her Lady Mary Coke had written in her *Journal* in 1774: "I went to Mrs. Middleton at Kensington to meet the Duchess of Beaufort and Lady Bute and their young ladies. Lady Caroline Steúart sang to us.   Did you ever hear her? I think I never heard a more pleasing voice, nor a better manner." [1]

THE SAME from the SAME

Luton, Tuesday, 21st July 1778.

DEAREST SISTER—You need not be at all afraid that I should think your journal an odd composition.   I am so much charmed with it that I long for the second part, and want to see the characters you have painted in action ; but I pity you for being forced to spend so much of your time in visiting and playing at cards by daylight; however, I know you can make everything afford you some diversion or other, and I hope you are attended by your usual good spirits.   I wish you would explain yourself a little more about the illness you talk of, for you are not apt to consult physicians for nothing, and you do not say whether

[1] See *Lady Mary Coke's Journal*, 17th October 1774.

the bath has been of service to you. I wish to hear a
good reason for all this. I am not at all surprised at
your horsemanship; I always thought you would take
the first opportunity to ride, and as Mr. Dawson seems
to be your only companion, I suppose it is the most
comfortable time you have. How do the rest of the
family go on? are they grown fond of you? Does
Mr. Joseph [1] open his lips oftener than he did in town,
and is he kind or cruel to the lady who admires him?
For my part, I am sufficiently accustomed to dumb
people, for here are Frederick and William who speak
about six words a day, and instead of being any company or comfort, only serve to give me the vapours
by walking up and down the room without ceasing;
don't think I mean my room, for I assure you they
never deign to visit that, but after tea, as my father
and mother always retire to the library, I have brought
down my work and sat with these two gentlemen to
try if any acquaintance could be made with them, and
as I tell you, I am entertained with their eternally
walking backwards and forwards, or now and then fling-
ing themselves upon the couch, yawning, and asking
me questions as 'When we go to London?' 'When
you come back?' 'Whether the Duchess of Portland
comes here this year?' and so forth. Sometimes, indeed, they have got into a dispute, but otherwise I give
you an exact description how our evening passes till there
is a joyful acclamation at the sound of the supper bell.
The rest of the day is employed as usual in trailing to
the farm and dawdling to the flower garden; but bad

[1] Joseph, a younger brother of Mr. Dawson, born 1751.

as it is, it will be worse when they go, for they at least enliven our meals a little.   My father still complains of a pain in his face, is out of spirits, and has not dined with us since we came back.   Poor William, too, after looking ill these three days had a return of his headache yesterday, though before he seemed better than I had yet seen him.   My mother is well and in very good spirits, considering the *ennui* that I believe is insepar- able from this house, and which I own has at last infected me.   I have often told you, though you knew it pretty well, you could not conceive it thoroughly except you could conceive the family too, without yourself. There is a journal in return for yours.   Lady Mary writes that she is kept in town (heartily sick of it) waiting for Sir James Lowther.   Poor Mrs. Stuart is still in the same way ; she tells me she never goes to bed without expecting to hear Lady Vere is dead when she gets up, and what with the melancholy scene, and want of sleep in a hot, close room, her spirits are sunk to such a degree that she can hardly write.   It is now very near a month since poor Lady Vere has been lying in this manner between life and death, which is really dreadful. I flatter myself, my dear sister, you will continue to write as often as you can, for it is, I assure you, a charity.   You never mention any of your English friends.   Do you often hear from Lady Frances, Lady Lucy, Mrs. Legge, Miss Herbert, and what are they doing?   If you still think of coming back through Scotland, pray let it be part of your plan to go and see Wharncliff, which by the bye I have not forgotten, though the wise old proverb ' You cannot eat your cake and have your cake ' ought to silence me.   Lady Lothian, I fancy, means to pay us a visit soon.

Luton, 26th July 1778.

I AM charmed with your play and ball, and still more so to find you were in such health and spirits as to begin all again at four in the morning. I assure you that article surprises me, for it was out-doing yourself; yet, my dear sister, I could have liked very well to hear you had not danced at all; do you understand me? Sure your jovial neighbours must adore you. But you are a great enemy to particulars, for you say you dined at Mr. Archdale's[1] (who, I con-clude from that, lives near you), without mentioning anything more either about him or his wife; however, I see you are almost hurried out of your senses, so I forgive all omissions. Have you no hopes that this tumult of company and diversions will subside? I should pity myself very much in your place, but as you are a more sociable creature, I do not know whether you want my compassion, so I will not risk throwing it away; indeed, my chief apprehensions regard your pocket, for between giving entertainments and managing your farm I fear you will be undone. Well, I hope Providence designs to take care of every-thing, therefore I quit this subject, which I should think much too earthy to be talked of if I was in a

[1] Probably Mr. Mervyn Archdall of Castle Archdall, who had married, 1762, Mary Dawson, daughter of Vis-count Carlow, and sister of Lord Port-arlington. They may have been staying at a small place called The Grove, often lent in later years by Lord Portarlington to his nephew, General Archdall, when he was master of the Queen's County hounds.

Paradise, or anything like one; but since I came down from the mountains I am grown very worldly-minded, and have lost all inclination for descriptions. Your journals are the comfort of my life. I hear and see you while I read them, and talk to you while I answer them. I dance with you, laugh with you, and ride with you; though when out of such reveries I am as sober and as serious as becomes an inhabitant of Luton.

My father and the men went away yesterday, so we are left quite alone, and are likely to remain so this week, unless Lady Lothian and Emily come, which would make us very comfortable. As it is, I like it better than when the men are here, but my mother does not.

Monday.

I wrote so far last night after supper, so lose no time; but I have twenty more things to say. Lady Betty and Mr. Mackenzie[1] are either arrived or expected every moment, which will please my father very much. He did not hear it when he left us. I daresay we shall have them here for some time; if not too long, it will do very well. You must know my mother attacked me one day last week for looking melancholy, and said she was sure I fancied *he* neglected me, and had been fretting about *him*. There was something of truth in it, but I cannot tell how the thought could enter into her head; however I would not own any such thing. She said no more, and appeared offended, which I was sorry for; but I had fifty reasons for not entering into explanations.

[1] Lord Bute's brother, Mr. Stuart Mackenzie, and his wife Elizabeth, third daughter of John, second Duke of Argyll.

An allusion probably to Lady Louisa's romantic affection for Colonel William Medows, her second cousin.   He was the youngest son of Philip Medows of Thoresby, Notts (Deputy Ranger of Richmond Park), and Lady Frances Pierrepoint, sister of the first Duke of Kingston.   Lord Bute would not hear of an engagement, and the disconsolate hero afterwards married a Miss Hamerton, who predeceased him.   William Medows was later appointed Governor of Madras, and distinguished himself there.   He became a General and K.C.B., and died in India in 1813, when the news of his loss greatly affected Lady Louisa.   This will explain many allusions to an unhappy attachment which are scattered through these pages.

Charles Medows, eldest brother of William, had married in 1774 Anne Orton, youngest daughter of John Mills of Richmond.   He succeeded ultimately to the estates of his uncle, the second and last Duke of Kingston, and was created Earl Manvers in 1806.   It was he, apparently, who was then living with his wife and family near Luton.   William Medows was then with General Howe's army in America, and Lady Louisa would thus hear from his brother both of him and also of Charles Stuart.

The entertainment (or 'Mischiánzā,' as it was called) mentioned in the following letter was given to the General before leaving America.   In the *Century Magazine* for March 1894 there is an account illustrated and written by the unfortunate Major André, who took part in it.   This is the list of knights as given by him :—

Knights	Shield	Motto	Lady
Chf. Knt.: Lord Cathcart, 17th Drns.	Cupid on a Lion	'Surmounted by Love'	Miss Achmuty
Esqres. { Capt. Hazard, 44th { Capt. Brownlow, 57th			
Hble. Mr. Cathcart, 23rd	A Heart and a Sword	'Love and Honour'	
Esq.: Capt. Peters, dsd.			
Mr. Bygrave, 16th Dra. .	Cupid tracing a Circle	'Without End'. .	Miss J. Craig
Esq.: Mr. Nicholas			
Captn. André, 26th . .	Two game cocks fighting	'No Rival' . .	Miss P. Chew
Esq.: Mr. André, 7th			
Capt. Horneck, Guds.	A Burning Heart	'Absence cannot extinguish It'	Miss N. Redmond
Esq.: Mr. Talbot, 16th Drag.			
Captn. Mathews, 41st .	A Winged Heart .	'Each Fair by Turns'	. Miss Bond
Esq.: Mr. Hamilton, 15th			
Mr. Sloper, 17th Dra. .	A Heart and Sword .	Honour and the Fair [1]	
Mr. Brown, 15th			

[1] See also *Gentleman's Magazine* for May 1778, p. 353.

THE SAME from the SAME

At Night.

WE went to see the Meadows's this morning, and found them at home like a comfortable couple, as they are, with a fine fat boy (their youngest), whom they reckon like General Paoli. Think what a face that would make for a little child! but it did not strike me. They showed us an old newspaper with a full account of the entertainment given by the officers at Philadelphia to General Howe. Have you heard of it? There was a carousal, and the names of the knights and their mistresses, as Lord Cathcart, knight of the Burning Mountain, defending the beauty of Miss Polly Chew against Captain Watson, knight of the Golden Sun or the Silver Moon, I forget what, who asserts the charms of Miss Nancy Barton, with their squires, and all are published at length; they will be put in the Ballads, at least they deserve it. Mr. Mackenzie knows no news, for though we hear from Mrs. Charles Stuart that young Hobart has written his mother word that the army is removing to New York, Colonel Meadows has not mentioned it, and he is better authority.

Tuesday, 28th July.

I have read over your letter again; you will have had descriptions enough by this time, but how come you to think of our making another journey when my father goes to Highcliffe?[1] I cannot conceive such a thing possible. My mother talks of going to Bulstrode,[2]

[1] Lord Bute's villa on the coast of Hampshire.

[2] The residence of the Dowager Duchess of Portland. See p. 64.

but that is no party of pleasure; in my opinion we are very comfortable *tête-à-tête*. We are both tumbling over Swift's works, and they furnish conversation enough. I do not feel half the *ennui* I did when I wrote last. What a different life you and I are leading! I do not envy you, and I dare answer you do not envy me; yet perhaps you could part with some circumstances, and I with a great many. By what you say of your neighbours, one would think you were among your own countrywomen (I beg your pardon, you are so—I forgot myself)—you know whom I mean—but I suppose there are the same sort of people to be found all over the world.

I must tell you a ridiculous story the Meadows's were mentioning yesterday, which I had heard before, but not with particulars.

When the Commissioners embarked, a violent quarrel arose between Mrs. Eden and Antony Storer. He could not go without his pianoforte, and chose to insist upon placing it in her cabin, but she rebelled, and after squabbling some time, they appealed to Governor Johnson, who, seeing both in violent wrath, advised them to keep the *piano* and leave the *forte* behind. However, they were not in a humour to taste his wit, and the dispute continued, till the surly old Captain, her uncle, came and settled everything by swearing that if either of them said another word the subject of debate should be tossed overboard.

We have just met with a grievous misfortune— breaking the key of the library, and as every press had been carefully locked first, we must bid farewell to the books.   Alas! we looked very blank after this exploit.

This tardily-appointed and fruitless 'peace' Commission consisted of Lord Carlisle, William Eden (afterwards Lord Auckland), Sir Henry Clinton, and Governor Johnstone, with the celebrated Dr. Adam Ferguson as Secretary.   It sailed for America in April, and returned in December, having issued its manifesto to the American people in June.

George Johnstone was third son of Sir James Johnstone of Westerhall, Bart., and a younger brother of Sir William Johnstone-Pulteney.   As Captain R.N. in 1763 he was appointed Captain-General and Governor-in-Chief of the Province of West Florida.   He was in Parliament, and occasionally spoke in the House.   On one occasion he had a violent quarrel with Col. Barré, and on another fought a duel with Lord George Germain.   He also was an East India proprietor, and at a meeting in 1773 proposed General Monckton as Commander-in-Chief in India.   In 1778 he was appointed one of the Commissioners, as already mentioned, to quiet the American rebels, but in 1779 Congress charged him with having offered a bribe of £10,000 to General Read, and declined any negotiation so long as he remained a member of the Commission.   In consequence he resigned, and in 1784 was appointed as Commodore of a naval squadron, which Comte de Grasse was dispatched to intercept.   His success seems to have been moderate.   In 1782 he sent two French transports home.

A quarrel with Captain Sutton led to a suit at law, in which Johnstone was cast in £10,000 damages.   The cause was carried through the Courts of Appeal, and the verdict was finally set aside by the House of Lords in 1787.   In 1783 he became an East Indian Director, and in 1785 stood for Ilchester, and was beaten.   His last years were spent at Portsmouth.

The Mrs. Eden mentioned was Eleanor, daughter of Sir Gilbert Elliot, who had lately married William Eden. Many pleasant reminiscences of Eleanor Elliot are preserved in Lady Minto's family *Memoirs*. Lady Louisa also writes of both her and her husband very affectionately :—" Mr. Eden was in 1780-1782 the Secretary and real master of Ireland, she the daughter of Sir Gilbert Elliot and sister of Lord Minto, the most gay, jovial, and good-humoured, free-hearted of women, almost a proverb for uninterrupted prosperity and happiness, adoring her husband, delighting in her children, having a countenance always lit up with sunshine. Alas! she lived to be a picture of silent misery most affecting to behold : her daughter, Mrs. Nicholas Vansittart, died of a lingering decline ; her eldest son was found drowned in the Thames (1810); Lord Auckland himself died suddenly in 1814, and grief brought on her some seizure of the muscles that gave her the stiffness of a statue, immovable, and to appearance nearly insensible, till a hollow voice proceeded out of the form." [1]

The other hero of the quarrel about the piano, so amusingly narrated, was Anthony Morris Storer, M.P., a Jamaica proprietor and diplomatist, and Minister at the Court of France 1783. He was one of the dandies or maccaronies of the day, and a friend of Mrs. Eden's brother, Hugh Elliot. ;

The 'surly old captain' was Admiral John Elliot, who had, eighteen years earlier, distinguished himself by vanquishing Thurot in the naval engagement off the Isle of Man.

<hr>

THE SAME from the SAME

Sunday, 2nd August 1778.

MY DEAREST SISTER—Though writing to Lady Jane Macartney and Charles Stuart has em-

[1] Notes to Lady Frances Scott's *Irish Journal*.

ployed me all day and I am quite tired, I must say
a few words before I go to bed to thank you for the
charming long letter I received this morning; indeed,
you are very, very good, and I wish I could repay the
pleasure you give me, for your journals are really
more entertaining at this distance than you can conceive. I am only afraid you should grow indolent, or
think you have done enough, and leave off the custom.
It is a foolish fancy, but I am just now pleasing myself
with the notion that you may be going on with it at
this very moment; but, on second thoughts, you are late
people, and perhaps have not done supper; I may be
dreaming of you by the time you begin. Is it not hard
that your unreasonable hours should shut one out from
all intercourse with you, either in the same town or a
thousand miles off? Well, at any rate pray remember
your promise of looking at the moon and thinking upon
a friend of yours. I have always omitted putting you
in mind of it, and if this is not very long in going, she
will be in her highest glory when you get it; I assure
you she shall be looked at with the same purpose on
this side the water. I am almost ashamed of writing
such very silly stuff, but (as you will conclude from it)
I have little or no matter of fact to discourse upon,
and I must say something. Good-night, however, for
the present. I am too sleepy to talk any more.

                                                    Monday.

My father is come, but I have not yet seen him, so
shall go on with my remarks upon your letter. I knew
very well you would laugh at my rapturous descrip-

tions, but pray no more of the Muse, she and I have had no such intimacy this great while. I do not deny that I am much better pleased than if I had not been in Yorkshire. It is a great entertainment to me to think it all over again, and now I am grown peaceable and reconciled to this place. Thank you for your good matronly advice, but there is an ugly old proverb that talks of going 'out of the frying pan into the fire,' which will, I think, always hinder me from acting upon the motive you mention, and, except by the way of comparison, as when I am just come from something much better, I do not hate it quite as bad as you do. I should have liked to explore your old castle with you extremely, and I see the Spire-hill[1] as plainly as possible, which Mr. Dawson is very good to leave open for the nobility and gentry of Port Arlington. Pray is that a large town, or is it the neighbourhood that makes your ball so brilliant, for you describe it as much superior to a country assembly here? You continue dancing, I see. Parker, to whom I delivered your message faithfully, lifted up both hands and both eyes when she heard of it. You young giddy creature! *Apropos* of Parker—Frederick told us that Lord Lyttelton lodged this summer in her friend's (Mrs. Stuart of Bond Street) house, at Brighthelmstone, and one day thought fit to send for her, and told her he had promised to go and read to Lady Derby in the evening, so if she had ever a play in the house, he desired she would lend it him; but the good old gentlewoman, highly shocked at his prophaneness (for it was Sunday),

---

[1] Near Emo, upon which Lord Carlow erected an obelisk.

after rebuking him with a great zeal, brought him
Hervey's *Meditations*, which she assured him would
tend more to his edification than any play in the world.
Do but imagine Lord Lyttelton reading Hervey's
Meditations to Lady Derby!

The Lady Derby alluded to was not Miss Farren,
as might be supposed, but Elizabeth Hamilton, daughter
of the sixth Duke of Hamilton, and the second wife of
the twelfth Lord Derby.   She was a fine lady, and
the last person who would care to listen to Hervey's
Meditations.

Thomas, second Lord Lyttelton, died on 27th November 1779.   His well-known dream or vision of the spectral
woman is related in the *Scots Magazine*, vol. li. p. 650.
There occurs also in *Lady Mary Coke's Journal*, 30th
November 1779, the following passage corroborating the
story of his death: "*Tuesday.*—I went to town to buy
a couple of gowns.   Lady Bute carried me to the shop, and
from her I heard of Lord Lyttelton's death.   He dreamed
the preceding night he was to live only three days after that,
and added that although he was not a person to have much
faith in such sort of things, he had a heaviness upon him he
could not shake off.   On Thursday he went to the House of
Lords, and spoke violently against the Government, and on
Friday he went to a small house he had at some small
distance from London, and had some company with him.
On Saturday, in the evening, he said, ' This is the third day,
and I am still alive ' ; he went to bed and ordered his servant
to bring him his rhubarb, which he took every night.   When
his servant returned he found him sitting up in his bed, his
head leaning on one hand.   He spoke to him, and Lord
Lyttelton not answering or moving, he touched him and
found he was dead.   What can one say to such sort of

things? Mr. Fortescue told all this to Mr. Ross, who mentioned it to Lady Bute, from whom I had it."

THE SAME from the SAME

At Night.

MY father seemed very well, and dined with us. He has brought my mother a new key (I told you our mischance in my last), so we shall get some books, I hope. William has sent me Chatterton's works,[1] which is very kind and attentive in him. Chatterton was supposed to be the real author of those poems published under the name of Rowlie, as written in the time of Edward the Fourth (you remember them, I daresay, for we read some of them together), and poisoned himself at eighteen years old from despair at being neglected, joined to great poverty. They say he first applied to Mr. Walpole, who treated him as an impostor, and advised the booksellers not to buy the poems. I think if I were that gentleman I should feel a little remorse at the reflection of having contributed to deprive the world of such extraordinary genius, should not you? What they have now published consists chiefly of pieces he wrote for the newspapers and magazines, quite for bread, and a few poems; I can't say they please me, but I have only cast my eye

[1] A small octavo volume, *Miscellanies in Prose and Verse*, had just been published. Chatterton died eight years earlier. Walpole's defence appeared in 1779, in the form of a *Letter to the Editor of the Miscellanies*, printed at the Strawberry Press. See also Cunningham's *Walpole*, vol. vii. p. 102.

over them.   He seems to have been but a profligate boy,
notwithstanding his astonishing talents; but what do you
care about all this ?   I wish I had something more entertaining to tell you.   As I have not, I just talk of what
is most in my head.   My father seems pleased with
Mr. Mackenzie's arrival.   They come here next week,
and are not certain whether they go to Scotland or not.
Lady Betty is delighted with her travels.   You may
believe we have fifty ridiculous stories of her already.
She has brought my father two Roman teeth, right
ancient and wonderfully curious, but he begged leave
to refuse them, under pretence that he did not collect
antiquities, and that in the way of natural history a
Consul's tooth was not so valuable as a shark's.   I
don't find, however, that she has got names for them.
though the person who sold or gave them to her might
as well, when he was about it, have done the thing
handsomely and told her they came out of Cæsar's or
Cicero's jaw at once.

My father talks of sending for young Mure,[1] who
is quartered in this country, when his uncle comes.
I have a mind to fall in love with him *pour passer le
temps*.   What do you think of it ?   Adieu, and God
bless my dear sister.

Mr. Mackenzie was Lord Bute's only brother, James
Stuart, who had assumed the additional surname of Mac-
kenzie on inheriting his great-grandfather's (Sir George
Mackenzie's) estates.   He married his cousin, Lady Elizabeth
Campbell, fourth daughter of John, second Duke of Argyll
and Greenwich.   He was Minister at Turin, 1758-1762, but

[1] Probably Colonel Mure, son of Baron Mure of Caldwell.

had been recalled by Lord Bute to take the direction of the
Government in Scotland, and to assist the latter in the Cabinet
in the negotiations for peace. After his brother's resignation
he took little part in politics, and died in 1800, at the age of
eighty-one—it was said of a broken heart—a few months
after his wife. Dutens, his secretary, writes of him as 'well
versed in the sciences, particularly in mathematics, algebra,
and astronomy'; and even Walpole, who was always bitter
about any of Lord Bute's relations, adds his testimony to
Mr. Mackenzie's worth. At his death the estates passed to
his brother's second son, James, whose son was created Baron
Wharncliffe. Lady Louisa, in her *Memoir of John, Duke of
Argyll*, gives a most amusing account of Mr. Mackenzie, to
whom his brother's children never appeared to grow any
older: 'At eighteen you were five years old; at thirty, nay
forty, not above twelve; assailed with jokes and nursery
stories, enough, as Miss Hoyden says in the play, to make
one ashamed before one's love.' The romantic story of his
attachment when only nineteen to the 'Barberini,' a celebrated opera dancer at Venice, and how his intention of
marrying her was frustrated by the Duke of Argyll, was a
tale to which the circle of curious nieces and nephews at
Luton were never tired of listening, when a certain Abbé
Grant, a witness to these tragic scenes, came to stay there in
after years. James Mackenzie eventually married the Duke's
third daughter, Elizabeth, who seems to have persuaded him
that her 'fervent passion,' as Lady Louisa puts it, deserved
more than a cousinly regard, and won from him a grateful
return. The marriage appears to have been a very happy
one. Lady Louisa thus describes her uncle's wife: "Lady
Betty Mackenzie's figure, though always too thin, passed for
fine in her youth; her face was even then plain, but not yet
seamed and disfigured, as we saw it, by the confluent small-
pox. The older she grew, the stronger those who had

known her mother thought the resemblance between them in features, manners, and mind. Like the Duchess [1] she was honest, upright, well-meaning, and good-natured; like her, ill-bred, positive, and anything but wise. She did not, however, inherit her Grace's insensibility; there they were very dissimilar, for Lady Betty had a warm heart, and most assuredly the power of loving. I defy a more devoted attachment to exist than she had to my uncle; and being love of the genuine sterling kind (marked by a sincere preference of another to self), which always ennobles the character, it raised her above the folly of hers wherever he was concerned. Her constant attention to his wishes, and visible delight in his presence, were not debased by any silly fondness unbecoming their age. If through youthful flippancy one sometimes simpered at the looks of affection exchanged between the ugly, wayward old woman and the good man in a bob-wig, one's heart presently smote one, since, in sober earnest, one could not but allow that their steady, cordial, perfect union was a sight beautiful to behold." [2]

The 'Dutens' just mentioned, and often alluded to by the sisters, was a certain Louis Dutens, who was born at Tours in 1730, and had taken orders in the Church of England. He was secretary to Mr. Mackenzie when the latter was British Minister at Turin, and, in his absence, *chargé d'affaires*. He had travelled as tutor to Lord Algernon Percy, a son of the first Duke of Northumberland, who had given him the living of Elsdon. He was also Historiographer to the King. Mr. Dutens was one of Mr. Mackenzie's executors, and a residuary legatee. He died in 1813.

---

[1] The Duke's second wife 'Jenny Warburton,' maid of honour to Queen Anne, and afterwards to Caroline, Princess of Wales.

[2] See Introduction to *Lady Mary Coke's Journal*.

THE SAME from the SAME

Luton, 16th August 1778.

YOU make me think Sunday quite a fortunate day, my dear sister, though I was very near fancying it the contrary this morning, as they assured me I had no letters. At last it proved a blunder of George's, and I got yours with an additional pleasure, which made me actually caper about the room; 'twas well I happened to be alone. I have read it only four times, and am diverted beyond measure with the misfortunes of the Coote Cavalcade[1] and the account you give of Miss Cary. Such a character must be extremely entertaining. By your description she is just such another as we remember Mrs. Eden, but with more accomplishment and more beauty, and that always makes one like people better. I would have given a great deal to see your neighbours set out on their journey. I assure you I am acquainted with them all now, and feel as if I understood the *carte du pays* perfectly; but how pitiful descriptions of our dull doings must seem to you after all your gaieties! However, you have them by heart, so you can't be disappointed. The Mures left us this morning, and Lady Lothian (who is perfectly well) goes on Wednesday. We have rubbed on this week as we could. The weather was charming. We went out very often (we young ladies, I mean), and did what we might in the evening: sat below and behaved properly one night, went upstairs and played at Cross

---

[1] The family of Dean Coote at Shanes Castle, where Miss Cary was then staying. See introduction to Chapter II.

Purposes and Questions and Commands another, and my father fixed us all at Commerce the two or three last. He brought out the Mississippi Table,[1] too, one day when it rained, and that helped off some tedious moments. Thus ends the list of our festivities. As I had two ladies upon my hands to entertain, you may suppose I could not be very comfortable with either; Miss Mure was very merry and completely good-humoured, would be a delightful person in a gayer house than this, but I fancy grew heartily tired here, though you may be sure she said everything to the contrary. I like her very well, but her cousin best. By the way, I received a letter from her this morning, where she says she is very much pleased with her Duchess[2] and Miss Burrel,[3] that the ladies admire their brother extremely, and that Lord Graham and he are in constant attendance upon Lady Wallace, the Duchess of Gordon's sister; so much for Scotch news. I take it for granted the newspapers have told you before now all that has happened at Grimsthorpe; I mean the shocking accident of young Lindley's being drowned before the windows, and the Duke of Ancaster's death a few days after, which Mrs. Stuart mentions in a letter my mother had from her to-day, and seems much shocked at. It seems he has been long in a very bad way. Lady Vere is surprisingly better, but she is not well herself. I am sorry for the Duchess of Ancaster and Lady Priscilla, though perhaps when their affliction

[1] A sort of bagatelle board.
[2] Douglas, eighth Duke of Hamilton, married, April 1778, Elizabeth, daughter of Peter Burrell.   [3] Duchess of Hamilton's sister.

goes off, they may lead a more comfortable life than they did before.

Peregrine, third Duke of Ancaster, died 12th August 1778, his eldest son having predeceased him in 1758. Robert, the second son, succeeded, but died in the following year. Priscilla Barbara Elizabeth, the elder sister and co-heir, was allowed the Barony of Willoughby d'Eresby, after a short abeyance, and married Peter Burrell, whence by heiresses descends the present Baron, who is also by a recent creation Earl of Ancaster. The dukedom passed to Lord Brownlow Bertie, brother of the third Duke, as male heir, on whose death the dukedom became extinct, and the earldom of Lindsey passed to General Bertie of Uffington, a distant cousin. The Duchess mentioned in these letters was Mary, daughter of Thomas Panton, master of the King's race-horses at Newmarket. She was Mistress of the Robes.

The lad who fell out of the boat and was drowned at Grimsthorpe a few days before the Duke's death, was Thomas Linley, a celebrated violinist, and son of one of the proprietors of Drury Lane Theatre. He was brother to the beautiful Miss Linley, who married Richard Brinsley Sheridan. There is a portrait of the brother and sister by Gainsborough at Knole.[1]

THE SAME from the SAME

Monday Night.

THESE two days have been pleasant enough. Lady Emily and I trot about together, and talk nonsense, and moralise, and now and then dispute. Lady Lothian and my mother play at Cangiomento. My

[1] *Annual Register* for 1778, also Lord Dufferin's *Memoir of Helen, Lady Dufferin.*

father has been, or seemed at least, in very good spirits ever since they came. All this company have told us no news that would interest you, so do not expect a livelier letter than usual. I will tell you one of our amusements, that you may try the experiment and astonish your family if you choose it. My father one day began telling a story I daresay you remember, that some of his friends enchanted a cock by drawing a line with chalk down his beak and continuing it upon the floor, which took from him all power of motion. This was received with a violent laugh, but at last he offered to have it done, provided a bet was laid upon it. Lady Lothian and Mrs. Mure laid a guinea, and Robertson had orders to chalk the cock's bill accordingly, when, behold, we were all thunderstruck to see the creature lie as if he were dead, but with his eye fixed upon the white line before him. I could never have believed it if I had not seen it, so one should not be too incredulous. Young Mure dined here twice ; he is not so handsome as he was. Martin came to dinner to-day, but went away very soon after. Good-night to you now, for it is late and I am sleepy. Do you know I did nothing last night but dream of poor little Stuart. I thought I had him in my arms, that he looked beautiful as a little angel and not at all lame. You were with him. Once more good-night, and excuse this nonsense.

Tuesday.

My mother and I had letters from Lady Jane this morning, as I suppose you will have too. Mine is of May the 19th, but she has one of the 7th June. She seems to keep up her spirits very well, and to be very happy with the thought of your settlement—in short, says to me much what I told you she did to my mother in a letter that came by the packet, only more at large. Adieu, my dearest sister; always think me yours,

L. S.

———

The whole country was by this time tired of the mismanagement and expense of the American War, which was denounced in the House of Commons as 'unholy and suicidal.' The Duke of Richmond in the House of Lords, supported by what was called the Rockingham party, advocated the acknowledgment of the independence of the thirteen rebellious states, and was anxious to recall His Majesty's forces to the protection of the mother country, and of her nearer dependencies; the new alliance of the French with the Americans had driven consternation into the country, and the neglect of the authorities to protect Gibraltar sufficiently to prevent the French fleet from slipping through, had suddenly awakened many to a sense of personal danger. Admiral d'Estaing, the clever commander of the Mediterranean fleet, had, after passing through the Straits, crossed the Atlantic, and was now threatening to bombard General Howe at Sandy Hook.

Admiral John Byron, the poet's grandfather, was despatched to America in June 1778 in charge of a fleet wretchedly manned and equipped; and on the 9th of July Admiral Keppel sailed, in anticipation of a Declaration of War from the French, in pursuit of their fleet, which, however, he did not discover till the 27th, when the battle was fought, for the mismanagement of which he was afterwards tried by court-martial, but honourably acquitted.[1]

[1] See Sir Erskine May's *Constitutional History of England*.

THE SAME from the SAME

Luton, Tuesday, 26th August 1778.

I WAS extremely disappointed, my dear sister, at not receiving a letter from you on the usual day, but the packet I got to-day made ample amends ; however, before I say any more of it I must tell you the news just come from America.   Frederick brought the *Gazette* about two hours ago, and there are letters both from General Clinton and Lord Howe.[1]   General Clinton is at New York ; the 28th June he was attacked upon his march there from Philadelphia by Washington's army, whom, however, he drove off, and saved all his baggage and artillery.   His letter is very clearly written and spirited ; you will see the *Gazette*, I suppose, but I just give you the heads.   Lord Howe writes in spirits too, but is in great measure blocked up by D'Estaing's fleet, which is much superior in strength to ours (however, accounts are received from Byron that his squadron did not suffer so much from storms as had been reported, and that he had ten ships safe).   The packet, which narrowly escaped being taken, sailed on the 18th of July.   Poor Colonel Monckton[2] is killed.   This will seem but indifferent news to you, but we have been so frightened that we received it with exultation.   Mr. Mackenzie received a letter on Sunday from Mr. Dutens, who writ word that Mr. Crawford,[3] who had seen one of the officers come

---

[1] Vice-Admiral Viscount Howe in command at Sandy Hook.

[2] Hon. Henry Monckton, fourth son of first Viscount Galway. His death is mentioned in the *Annual Register* for 1778.

[3] John Craufurd, commonly called *Fish* Craufurd, was the grandson of

over, told him that Lord Howe was blocked up,
and that Clinton and his army of 16,000 men were
invested by General Washington with 32,000, and
their retreat cut off, and that they had provisions only
for three weeks. To be sure, it was impossible that
Charles should be arrived at that time, but it really
put me into an agitation of spirits that I have not
yet recovered, and I do not know I ever felt more
unhappy. I believe living alone and brooding over a
thousand disagreeable fancies depresses one's mind.
Instead of growing used to your absence, I find it
more and more heavy upon me every day. Well, I
hope in God there was no reason for anxiety, since we
should certainly have heard from him if he had been
arrived, and this *Gazette* seems to have quite enlivened
my father and mother. She has been telling me all
the while that she had no sort of apprehension, and yet
I could see in her eyes that she was as uneasy as
possible. You know there is nothing so unpleasant as
that. Now the chief hope or fear seems to be that
Byron should drive away D'Estaing and join Lord
Howe, or that he should not arrive in time, or be
defeated, and the blockade continued. Keppel is gone
out again, but it is supposed the French will not meet
him, so that he has lost the opportunity of bringing
them to action.

My father has had another swelled face, but it is
quite gone and he is now well, though I cannot say he

Mr. Middleton, founder of Coutts's Bank, who left two daughters, one of whom married the fifth Lord Stair, and the other Peter Craufurd, Esq., father of John and James Craufurd.

looks so.   I mention this particularly because Lady Mary [Lowther] tells me they reported in London a week ago that he was very ill, and it may reach your ears and alarm you.   He complained, as I wrote you word (just before Lady Lothian came), a little more than usual, and seemed very low - spirited, but there was nothing serious in it, and my mother did not seem uneasy.   Lady Mary has had a violent bilious disorder, and looks pale and thin, but seems very chearful.   She came this morning, and I assure you I was most extremely glad to see her.   I have not seen any of my brothers and sisters in a comfortable way for so long, that it is quite a relief to me.   She means to stay three or four days and then return to London, and lie here a night next week in her way to Lowther, where Sir James is gone.   She says they are mighty good friends.   Mr. Mackenzie and Lady Betty came on Saturday, and Dutens was to follow with William to-day, but he came alone, which disappointed me extremely.

Now, my dear, let me thank you for all the pleasure your letter has given me, and for the shades,[1] though Miss Cary has given you a sharp nose I am not at all acquainted with.   I gave one to Parker,[2] who received it with great joy.   I am delighted to see you are so comfortable, but pray do say a little about yourself, and tell me whether you feel quite strong and well, and whether you are grown fat, for Lady Mary says she heard that when you was in Dublin you seemed very ill and quite weak from overfatigue ; she mentioned,

[1] Silhouettes.   [2] Lady Bute's maid.

too, having heard from one of your friends that you might perhaps stay till after Christmas in Ireland, which you may believe does not enliven my thoughts and prospects. As for us, I find my father talks of going a progress after this company has left us ; I hope he will, as it is likely to do him good ; and then my mother thinks of going to Bulstrode, but she heard yesterday from Mrs. Stuart that Lady Vere .is much better. She intends going for ten days to Lord Robert,[1] and will spend one or two here in her way back, which may perhaps hinder our moving. I had two letters from Lady Jane by the West Indian fleet, one of the 19th of May, the other the 7th of June, both in good spirits. Lady Mary is worse to-day (Wednesday), and talks of leaving us to-morrow.

P.S.—My father asked four or five questions about Lord Carlow's coming to London, and seemed to think it will be proper to show him civilities, so hope it will please him.

Luton, Monday, 31st August 1778.

DEAREST SISTER—I am afraid I shall tire you by repeating over and over again how much your letters please me. I do not know what I should do without their assistance, but while you continue punctual there is at least one day in the week I look forward to with pleasure ; yet I begin to be very anxious about our meeting again, and am often really astonished when I think of the long, long time that has past since I have seen you and enjoyed the full pleasure of friendship and confidence which I never do but with you ;

---

[1] Lord Robert Bertie, afterwards for a few months fourth Duke of Ancaster.

however, I have the satisfaction of believing you happy and comfortable, so ought not to complain. Indeed, though my spirits are very apt to sink when I feel so much alone in the world, yet I am ashamed to mention it as a grievance when I see people much more deserving of happiness than me oppressed with so many miseries. Poor Mrs. C. Stuart came here to-night in her way from Lord Robert Bertie's back to Lincolnshire. She looks tolerably, though grown very thin, means to stay two days, and I am glad of it, for we are entirely alone, as my father went to London this morning and the company left us yesterday. Lady Vere is astonishingly recovered, but Lord Robert very ill, that is to say, oppressed with excessively low spirits, and to all appearance in a decay. She herself seems rather better than when I saw her last, and begins to flatter herself with hopes of hearing news very soon. I hope in God we shall, and that they will prove pleasant. Lady Mary (Lowther) came down here on Tuesday and left us on Friday, for not finding herself well, she went to town again to see her doctor, and if she has not a sour letter from the North, will stay two or three days more in her way to Lowther, where he chooses she should go. However, she expects to come back by the meeting of Parliament. She was perfectly agreeable and unaffected while she stayed here.

I mind news so little that I had almost forgot to tell you her friend Mrs. Lockhart is to be married this week to Colonel Harcourt,[1] who has made

---

[1] He married Mrs. Lockhart of Craighouse, 21st September 1778. He was afterwards third Earl Harcourt.

acquaintance with her at Southampton, where she was with Mrs. Stuart. They go directly to Nuneham. This has broke out very suddenly, but does a little better than Prince Boothby, or even Sir George Osborne. Lady Betty speaks very affectionately of dear Car, and is in perfect good humour and good spirits, as well as Mr. Mackenzie. I am still a great favourite.

Lady Emily has wrote me two letters (which, by the way, I must think of answering) since they were here. The last was from Lord Waldegrave's,[1] near Warley Camp, where, she tells me, she dined in my brother's tent, but he did not make his appearance ; they, and Lady Louisa Lenox with them, are going to the music meeting at Salisbury, and they mean to spend three weeks or a month with your relations in Dorsetshire.

Mrs. Stuart means to leave us to-morrow or next day, and if Lady Mary does not come, my mother talks of going half-a-day's journey with her for amusement. She (Mrs. S.) is very low-spirited this morning. Adieu, my dear sister, I am rather hurried to make up this letter, as we send our packet to Lady Jane to-day. Believe me, my love, ever your   L. STUART.

Tuesday, 8th September 1778.

I HAVE been looking in a map for Waterford and Kilkenny, and endeavouring to trace your whole route, but it seems much more than forty miles from Port Arlington ; however, I suppose you like it the better for being a long journey, and your accounts really

---

[1] Navestock, in Essex ; it was pulled down in 1811.

are delightful enough to make one sick of all the
tours and elegant descriptions they publish.   You
know I keep all my letters, or if I did not I certainly
should yours, and it will be a vast entertainment to
read over these charming journals in a series.   I need
not tell you the 'screaming stone' and terrible
'Queen' take my fancy, but I hope you made further
inquiries about both, for I should like to know their
whole history, and whether the last was a descendant
of Fingal.   Your descriptions make me almost tremble
for the honour of my beloved Yorkshire, which certainly
can boast of no such rivers, though as your forte is
water, ours is wood, and I think you are very silent
upon that, so we may conclude that all countries excel
in something.   You see, my love, your letters are not
thrown away, and so much as they themselves amuse
me, I have still more pleasure in thinking of the
kindness you show in writing them, when you have
so little time, and so many employments you like
better.   I wish any chance could possibly throw Miss
Dawson in my way, for I should delight to ask a million
of questions, and hear your praises from one of your
new relations.   I am sure she must be fond of you.

I believe I writ to you on Tuesday while Mrs.
Stuart was here.   She left us the next day with great
reluctance, and we carried her as far as Hitchin.   We
have been quite alone ever since till Lady Mary
Lowther came this evening, and found ourselves very
comfortable; you know I always tell you a *tête-à-tête*
does best. We both read the same book, and it furnished
us with a great deal of conversation; it was *La*

Nouvelle Héloïse,[1] with which I am charmed, perhaps
more than I should be, yet I do not think I feel the
worse for it, though Rousseau says in his preface,
' Toute fille qui en ose lire une seule page est une fille
perdue;' and indeed I believe it might be very dangerous to people whose passions resemble those he
describes. But I have nothing to do with love, so
it is safe for me, and I do think it, notwithstanding
several absurdities, the most interesting book I ever
read in my life. I can hardly believe some of the
letters to be feigned, and am thoroughly convinced he
must have felt a great deal of what he describes; but I
can talk no more of it at present, for it is between two
and three in the morning. Do not scold me for raking
at this rate. God bless you, and good-night.

Wednesday.

Lady Mary is now quite well, and means to pursue
her journey to-morrow. She tells us there are no
political news of any kind, and for tittle tattle she
seems to have none; she has not seen poor Miss
Monckton.[2] Miss Mure writes me word that she is
very happy to hear a certain family mansion[3] in
a certain island is repairing and fitting up, as she
thinks it must mean something; I believe this is true,
but cannot imagine what the master of that house can
have in his head (this is *entre nous*), for I hear on all

---

[1] Originally published in 1759. The
author died in July 1778.

[2] Mary, daughter of first Viscount
Galway, who married, in 1786,
Edmund, Earl of Cork, and died

1840. She was sister of the Col.
Monckton mentioned before as killed
in the American War.

[3] Mount Stuart, her father's place
in the Isle of Bute.

sides that he is building and doing a great deal in Hampshire.[1]   Don't take any notice of what I tell you in your letters for fear they should be seen, for it seems a very displeasing subject to my mother, and when anybody asks questions she always says (short) that she knows nothing of the matter and never inquires. I guess we are likely to stay late here, and everybody plagues me with saying that you will not come till after Christmas, so, for my own part, I do not care.   My father is now at Highcliff, but we expect him every day.   Lady Mary says she had a melancholy visit from Lady P. Bertie while she stayed in town, and that she gave a very indifferent account of the Duchess.[2] They are going to Bath as soon as the season begins. Mentioning Bath makes me remember that the Mr. Malone I once met at your house married somebody there this summer, and Lady Mary says he jilted Miss Jane Boughton and used her very ill.   Mrs. Pitt is come to England, and by this time must be in London, for I fancy, and indeed hope, we shall soon have her here; we expect Queen Mary Coke next Tuesday. Did you hear of her scolding poor Lady Frances Scott into hysterics before they left London?   Lady Greenwich, as Mrs. Pitt told Lady Emily, scolded her in her turn, and both were so furious, it almost came to a battle.   I suppose she is not in very good humour now, for she writes with great resentment at some neglect of Lady Betty's; however, my mother desired she would fix her coming when my father was here.

[1] Highcliffe.   [2] The Duchess of Ancaster, see *ante*, p. 41.

Lady Mary Coke was the fourth and youngest daughter of John, second Duke of Argyll, and had married Lord Coke, eldest son of the Earl of Leicester.   In Lady Louisa Stuart's charming *Memoir* of the Duke (who was her great-uncle) she tells the curious tale of the quarrels of the pair after their marriage, eventually ending in a separation, which lasted, however, only three years, as Lord Coke died young, leaving Lady Mary a widow when only twenty-four.   She seems, after narrowly escaping another loveless marriage with Lord March (the Duke of Queensberry's next heir), to have led a busy life in society, curiously blending the card-playing and other foibles of the day with a serious and decidedly Scotch love of sermons and good books.   The great events in her life were her friendship for the Duke of York and her two journeys to Vienna.   ·Edward, Duke of York, was a boy in his teens when he first began fancying himself in love with Lady Mary, who was some dozen years older.   She, however, took it all *au grand sérieux*, and when he died, a few years later, was much disgusted at being treated as an object of mild derision, instead of receiving the sympathetic respect she imagined her due.   After this unfortunate episode she visited Vienna, and at first was loud in her praise of the Empress mother, Maria Theresa, and of the Emperor Joseph, who, she persuaded herself, had a great admiration for her.   Some unlucky meddling, however, in court intrigues, during a subsequent visit, seems to have deprived Lady Mary of Imperial favour, and she returned to England through Italy, pursued, as she fondly imagined, by the vindictive persecutions of the great Empress Queen.   She lived to a great age, and died at Chiswick in 1811.   Lady Louisa describes her appearance as follows: "Her beauty had not been undisputed like Lady Strafford's (her sister) Some allowed, some denied it; the dissenters declaring her. neither more nor less than a *white cat*, a creature to which her

dead whiteness of skin, unshaded by eyebrows, and the fierce-
ness of her eyes, did give her a great resemblance.   To
make amends, there were fine teeth, an agreeable smile, a
handsome neck, well-shapen hands and arms, and a majestic
figure." [1]

[1] Lady Mary Coke kept the volum-
inous Journal which has lately been
privately printed by the Earl of Home,
and very ably annotated by his brother,
the Hon. James Home.   The descriptions in it throw a vivid light on the
life of the latter half of the eighteenth
century, and bring the society of that
time before us with almost microscopic
accuracy.   The Journal is privately
printed by Mr. David Douglas, Edinburgh.   4 vols. 8vo, 1889-1895.

CHAPTER II

LADY CAROLINE DAWSON was the fifth daughter of Lord Bute, and had married on 1st January of this same year (1778) John, eldest son of Viscount Carlow, and she and her husband were then living with his father at Dawson Court, Queen's County. Mrs. Delany thus describes her shortly before her marriage : " Lady Caroline is a genius in painting and musick, and has made a great progress in both ; she has a clear, sweet voice, under good management, and less of the *fashionable yell* than most of her contemporarys. She is extremely good-humoured and sensible, but is one in whom many pleasing accomplishments are a little hurt by an awkward habit : she has no *affectation*, but a *trick* of a laugh at whatever is said or that she says herself."[1] She was the pivot on which most of the affections of her own family were centred. At this time Lady Caroline was a bride of a few months' standing, and Louisa, her youngest and favourite sister, was only twenty-one years old.

The following, which is the first letter we have from Lady Caroline Dawson, describes a visit to Lord De Vesci at Abbeyleix, in Queen's County. Lady De

---

[1] *Letters and Autobiography of Mrs. Delany* (Mary Granville). Edited by Lady Llanover, in six volumes, 8vo, 1861. See vol. v. p. 168.

Vesci (Selina Elizabeth, eldest daughter of Sir Arthur Brook) is described by Lady Louisa Stuart as 'a very beautiful and accomplished woman,' and her intimacy with Lady Caroline was a great solace to the latter in what she sometimes called her 'exile.' Another friend, Miss Charlotte Cary, mentioned in this letter, seems to have been a constant visitor either at Dawson Court or the neighbouring Shanes Castle, where Dean Coote lived, who was connected with the Cary family through her father's first marriage with the widow of Mr. Chidley Coote. Charlotte was the youngest daughter of Archdeacon Cary of Killala, and granddaughter of Bishop Mordecai Cary. She never married, and is reported to have lived to an old age in the town of Portarlington, from whence she corresponded with the Dawson children long after they were married and settled in England.

LADY LOUISA STUART from LADY CAROLINE DAWSON

Tuesday Morning, 15th September 1778.

I AM just setting out for Lord De Vesci's, and I was determined to begin this first, in hopes I may have something entertaining to relate while I am there. My dinner yesterday that I told you of turned out better than I expected, as the most disagreeable of the ladies did not come, being afraid to venture, which I don't wonder at, as so long ago as my ball I expected she would have been brought to bed here, she is such an enormous size, so I had only Miss Cary and her mother and a Miss Bunbury, a fine girl of about four-

teen; and to make it as pleasant as I could, I carried
them into the little study, instead of the great drawing-
room, and as soon as the men came out I sat the old
lady down to cards with three of them, and I remained
chatting with the girls, who entertained me very much.
Charlotte Cary painted the feelings of the Coote family
so ridiculously, and she says they are always scolding
her, and thinks she has no soul because she laughs
when they cry at some nonsense or other.   Mr.
Scawen[1] continues mighty fond of her, and pays her
visits at Portarlington.   You must know that tho' she
is but seventeen, she is the strongest, largest girl you
ever saw, and always romping and full of spirits.   It is
a common trick of hers to take up her mother, or any
other old woman she can lay her hands upon, in her
arms, and carry them about the house as if they were
nothing; so the other day somebody bid her do so to
Mr. Scawen, whom she accordingly whipped up, to his
great astonishment.   I think I should have died with
laughing if I had seen the poor little mortal quaking
and trembling, with his poor little legs dangling in the

[1] The Scawens were from Mollenick
in Cornwall. Sir William, a wealthy
merchant, and M.P. for Surrey, was
of Carshalton Park. He died 1722,
and has a fine monument in the church
there. He and his brother, Sir Thomas
of London, were useful to William III.
when pressed for money. Sir Thomas
had many children, of whom Thomas
had Carshalton, and Maidwell near
Northampton, and was M.P. for Surrey,
and Robert had a villa in Reigate. Of
Sir Thomas's children, James was
M.P. for Surrey, and probably the
admirer of Miss Cary. He died single,
and Thomas was drowned. The three
sisters thus became co-heiresses, of
whom Tryphena married Earl Bathurst,
and Martha married the Rev. Edward
Dicey. Robert of Reigate also left
daughters, eventually co-heirs, of whom
Winifred married Samuel Blunt of
Crabbet near Chichester, and was
grandfather of the well-known Rev.
Henry Blunt of Chelsea, and of the
Scawen Blunts of Crabbet. The name
of Scawen is supposed now to be
extinct.

air, for I suppose he was as much frightened as Gulliver was when Glumdalclitch first seized him in the same manner, and expected, I daresay, to be thrown down when she was tired.   We are all in great hopes here that this news is true of Byron taking nine ships of the French fleet ; there are so many private letters of it, and all of them agreeing in their accounts.   I don't know if Lord Howe's death [1] will be any loss excepting to his family, as I believe he wasn't particularly qualified for a commander.

Abbeyleix, Thursday Morning.

I have never got a pen and ink till now, therefore could not pursue my history, and now I am not in a good humour for writing, as the play last night did not answer my expectation, and lasted till past two o'clock, by which means we did not get home till past four. The play was *Julius Cæsar*, and they left out the women's part entirely, so that it could not be very amusing even suppose the men had been good actors, which was not at all the case, most of them being terrible, so that instead of laughing, which was the least I expected, I was more tired and more inclined to sleep than ever I was in my life.

Saturday Morn.

We left Abbeyleix on Thursday, and I was really so overcome with the fatigues of the foregoing night that I could not write any more, and yesterday Charlotte Cary spent the day with me, which gave me no leisure

[1] A false report.   Admiral Lord Howe did not die till 1799, and Byron did not take the French fleet.   The engagement with D'Estaing off Grenada was a drawn battle.

for writing. She rode with us in the morning, then I set her to write some music for me, and in the evening made her play at whist, so you see one may do what one pleases with her ; but after that she would insist upon my going and dancing with her in the great hall. By that time it was ten o'clock, and she wanted to ride to Shane ; but I insisted upon her staying here, and had a great piece of work to get her to bed, she was so afraid of sleeping alone. I am to carry her to Shane this morning. Now I must return to give you an account of Lady De Vesci's. I am quite in love with her and with their state of living. It is entirely without form, everybody doing as they please, and always a vast number of people in the house. Lady Knapton,[1] his mother, lives with them, and seems no restraint upon anybody, she is so good-humoured. We were about six or seven ladies and as many gentlemen, divided into different parties about the room, some working, some reading, some playing cards, and the room being large and very full, it had a most comfortable appearance. It opens into the library on one side and the dining-room on the other. As it rained most of the time I was there I did not see much of the grounds, but the park is not laid out, as they have employed all their time and money in making a comfortable house first, which I think the most sensible plan. Lady De Vesci was very loth to let us go so soon, but Mr. Dawson had business at home that prevented our staying longer. However, we go again

---

[1] Elizabeth Brownlow, daughter of William Brownlow, Esq., of Lurgan, widow of Lord Knapton, and mother of the first Viscount de Vesci.

into their neighbourhood the end of next week, as Sir
Robert and Lady Staples[1] have been very pressing with
their invitations, and insisted upon our naming the
time, which we accordingly did, and Lady De Vesci
begs we will come to her again after that, to meet
Lord and Lady Tyrone,[2] so you see we have enough to
do ; besides we have a ball to go to on Wednesday
next, which a distant neighbour has invited us to, and
when all this is over we meditate a trip to Dublin, to
buy some things we have occasion for.

Saturday Night.

Here is my time drawn to a conclusion, without my
letter being so, for it rained so much all day it was
impossible for Charlotte to go away, so here she
remains, and has been chattering the whole day, for she
is no worker.   Now I must thank you for your letter
I received yesterday, and tell you how much we were
disappointed at our return on Thursday, for as our news
(if we get any) generally comes in on a Wednesday,
we expected a fine budget, so you may judge of the
disappointment when I found no letter from you, and
that the newspapers did not mention a word of our
fine news that everybody so firmly believed in here,
that before we left Abbeyleix all the men were offering
bets, and could find nobody that would lay against the
truth of the report.   However, your letter comforted

[1] Sir R. Staples of Dunmore, Queen's County, married, as his third wife, in 1776, Hon. Jane Vesey, sister of Viscount de Vesci.

[2] Lord Tyrone, Beresford by name, was afterwards Marquis of Waterford. Lady Tyrone's mother, Lady Bell Monk, was sister to the Duke of Portland's father.

me, and I am very glad to hear my journals entertain you, and that you have had some new books also that have diverted you. I think Anne Pitt's coming will be a charming thing, as she will have so many new storys to tell, they will last a great while. Pray remember my best compliments to her; I hope I am not out of favour, though I fear 'twas I dropped the correspondence. I had a letter from Miss Dawson, who has been some time in Harley Street. They like our house of all things, but she tells me Lord Carlow grumbled at the size of our bed, which he thought himself lost in. I foretold that, for he is used to any little dirty hole he can find. I assure you his bed here is hardly fit to put a housemaid in, and the housekeeper says he would not lie in any other upon any account. I am mightily pleased to find by Miss Dawson's manner of writing that she really does like me, and I shall believe it now as Charlotte Cary told me she said a thousand fine things of me to her. God bless you, my dear. I am come to my last minute, and so must hasten to conclude. Remember our affectionate duty to my father and mother. I am sorry to hear Lady Mary is gone to Lowther, just at the time she should be coming away from it.—Ever your   C. DAWSON.

Give my love to Parker.

Miss Dawson says Middleton is highly delighted with doing the honours and showing the Lions at our House.

_____

The Mrs. Anne Pitt expected by the family at Luton seems to have arrived the day after Lady Caroline's letter

was written, but to have left again in a few days. She
was a daughter of Robert Pitt of Boconnock and Harriet
Villiers, sister of John, Earl of Grandison. She is said to
have resembled her famous brother, Lord Chatham, as much
in her talents as in her features, and was remarkable for her
conversational powers and decision of character. Horace
Walpole, when asked by Monsieur de Caraman if Pitt was
like his sister, answered, 'Ils se ressemblent comme deux
gouttes de feu.'[1] She had been made Privy Purse to
the Dowager Princess of Wales, and was a well-known
figure in the society of the day. Her illness seems to have
been coming on for some time, for as much as ten years
previously Mrs. Delany had written : 'Yesterday morning
the Duchess [of Portland] insisted on my going with her
to Kensington Gore or Knightsbridge (I don't know which)
to see Mrs. Anne Pitt's little improvements, as out of a very
ugly odd house, and a flat piece of ground with a little dirty
pond in the middle of it, she has made an uncommon pretty
place ; she says she has *hurt her understanding* in contriving
to make it so.'[2] She apparently had quarrelled with most
of her relations, and Lady Bute was begged to use her
influence in trying to arrange matters for her with them.

Her eldest brother, Mr. Pitt of Boconnock, created in
1784 Lord Camelford (which title died with his only son),
had married a daughter and co-heiress of Mr. Williamson
of Burnham in Norfolk, and it was apparently there that
Mrs. Anne Pitt wished to go when her brother thought her
unfit to accompany him abroad. Mr. Williamson, however,
objected to receiving her, and she seems to have gone to
London, where she was placed under the care of the celebrated doctor, Sir William Fordyce. She died, out of her
mind, 9th February 1781. The note below will explain

---

[1] See *Quarterly Journal of the Berks Archæological Society.*
[2] *Mrs. Delany's Corr.* vol. i. p. 150.

the relationship of the various members of the family
mentioned by Lady Louisa.[1]

LADY CAROLINE DAWSON from LADY LOUISA STUART

Luton, Friday, 18th September 1778.

MY DEAR SISTER—I received your letter on
Tuesday, but have delayed answering it from day
to day, both because I felt anxious and uneasy, and
because I was in hopes to send you some news ; but
though the New York mail must have arrived in
London the day before yesterday, my father has had
no letters, and we know nothing but from the newspapers, where I see no mention of the June packets.
I suppose the *Gazette* will reach you as soon as this.
It contains no accounts but of some trifling advantages
obtained (in spiking up the enemy's cannon, etc.) by a
detachment from Rhode Island. Lord Howe writes
that the French fleet have left Sandy Hook and sailed
towards the Delaware, and that he, with two or three
ships which have joined him (it does not appear they
are of Byron's squadron), is preparing to follow, in

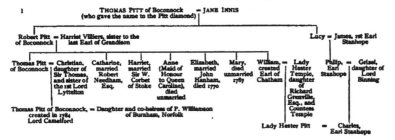

hopes of engaging them.   He mentions the May
packets being taken, and I saw an article in the newspaper that the *Duke of York* packet was taken by
three French frigates.   I am in hopes that was between
Falmouth and Lisbon, not New York.   It is very
strange we should have heard nothing yet.

When I wrote last week, you know, we were alone.
We heard from my father in a day or two. He had been
so ill in Hampshire, he was obliged to return to London,
and came here on Monday.   He said he had had the
jaundice, but he did not look at all yellow, though
rather pale and thin.   He seems much better now, yet
(which is the worst of it) not in spirits ; almost everybody has had some bilious disorder.   He has no men
here, but we have had Mrs. Pitt and Lady Mary Coke,
who leaves us to-morrow.   The first was ill, and left us
on Wednesday.   She was so low-spirited and restless
while she stayed (except the day she came—Sunday)
that it was quite misery to see her.   As for Lady Mary,
she is in great good humour, but you know the general
turn of her conversation is so much to melancholy
stories, or else the wickedness of the world or the
wretchedness of the times, that she is not an enlivening
companion.   In short, it is determined that nobody
who comes here this summer shall be of any use or
comfort to us.   My mother is tired of her, and was also
very glad when Anne Pitt took the resolution of going
away.   She is not much altered, but talks a vast deal of
being neglected, out of society, alone in the world, etc.,
and has made a sad piece of work with her nephew
and niece.   Mrs. T. Pitt's father was to have gone

abroad with them, but when they were upon the point of setting out, changed his mind, and his daughter was forced to agree to staying here too, which was a great distress, as they had designed to settle for some years in Italy, and Mr. Pitt was in a sad state of health. Just then Mrs. Pitt arrives in England, very miserable to find them going, will not accept his house, which he offered to lend her, and insisted upon going abroad again with him ; he refused ; then she said she would go into Norfolk with Mrs. T. P., which the father swore she should not; and, in short, Mrs. Delany wrote to my mother to beg she would invite her here to make all even.

You see I write in a hurrying way.   I have been in expectation of news every moment these four days, and you know there is nothing so disagreeable.   Thank you, however, ten million of times for your letters ; I have no other pleasure.   I was reading the other day some letters written from Spain by a friend of Madame De Sévigné's, Madame Villars, and I could not help being struck with this passage : " L'ennui du palais est affreux, et je disais l'autre jour à la Reine en entrant dans sa chambre qu'il semble qu'on le voit, qu'on le sent, qu'on le touche même, tant il est épais." Apply this sentence where you please.[1]

---

[1] " L'ennui du palais est affreux, et je dis quelquefois à cette princesse, quand j'entre dans sa chambre, qu'il me semble qu'on le sent, qu'on le voit, qu'on le touche, tant il est répandu épais."—*Madame de Villars et Madame de Coulanges, Lettres*, etc., p. 128, ed. 1868.

This application is evidently to Luton.

[Thursday, 1st October 1778.]

AFTER all I said in my last, the Duchess's pressing
messages forced my mother to go to Bulstrode [1]
for a day, and we accordingly went on Monday and
came back on Wednesday. At my return I found your
letter, which is so entertaining that I ought to make no
complaints; yet I must take notice that it falls short of
my due quota by two pages and a half. You certainly
paint as well with your pen as with your pencil, for I
actually see everybody you describe. Charlotte Cary
is exceedingly entertaining, and I wish Mr. S. would
bring her over with him; but her name sounds so like
a novel that I could almost fancy you invent the
character.

I hope you are in the humour to like a long letter,
for I have so many things to say I shall detain you a
great while, and I do not know with which to begin.
I suppose as my mother wrote to you this day se'n-
night, she acquainted you with everything relating to
poor Mrs. Pitt, whose dreadful misfortune is, I fear,
past a doubt, at least F.[2] thought it so much so that
he refused to attend her any longer, and insisted upon
putting her into the hands of her relations. You know
she has only two sisters, one of whom she has hated
for several years; the other, Mrs. Needham, she has at
last been persuaded to go to. My mother went to

[1] Purchased from the Bulstrodes by
Judge Jeffreys, who rebuilt the house in
1686. His son-in-law sold it to the
first Earl of Portland, whose son, the
first Duke, sold it to the Duke of
Somerset. The Duchess mentioned
was Lady Margaret Cavendish Harley,
widow of the second Duke, and well
known as the friend of Mrs. Delany.

[2] Sir William Fordyce, M.D.

town last week on purpose to see her. You see how far her return has been from providing the pleasure you expected. It is really shocking, and my mother has not yet recovered her spirits, which were extremely affected; indeed, it was quite impossible for anything to happen at a more unlucky moment, and all last week we were as melancholy a set of beings as ever met together, quite alone, and both my father and mother out of spirits. To compleat it, I had a letter from Miss Hobart to tell me Mrs. Stuart was too ill to write; however, she is now much better, though she seems excessively dejected, and Lady Vere is to undergo the operation again this week.

I wished to have stayed longer at Bulstrode, and I did not like returning from the Duchess's comfortable apartment to these magnificent barns. The Duchess told us that Lady Pembroke and Miss Herbert were at Weymouth when she left it, the former quite miserable about the King and Queen coming to Wilton, and the want there would be of everything necessary to entertain them, which people would charge to her, though she knew no more of her own house than anybody she met in the street. She said they had no plate and no furniture, that the State Room, which was hung with red damask, had no bed; but that want, I hear, his Lordship has supplied (to their Majesties' use) by hiring a green one at Salisbury. I do pity the poor woman; but the Duchess (who, by the way, has been entertaining them and all their children) insists that they give so little trouble, and are so easy, that in half an hour all difficulties will be over. When they visit Warley Camp they are to lie at Lord Petres's, and at Wilton the Bedfordshire Militia is to mount guard, which, I suppose, James will like very well. Mrs. Walsingham [1] dined at Bulstrode on Monday, and the next day came a Mr. and Mrs. Cole,[2] two friends of the Duchess's—the man a very odd, original character, with a great deal of drollery and humour, but a tongue that could outtalk the whole Capel family together. His wife seems a well-behaved, good kind of woman, and does not often interrupt him. As for poor Mrs. Delany, I believe I writ you word she had been ill. She does not seem quite recovered, and I think her broke this year. She desired a thousand loves to you, and begged I would tell you she should be impatient to talk Ireland over with you. Her chief works to be seen since we were at Bulstrode are a chimney board for the Duchess's dressing-room, and a frame for Lord Mansfield's print—both beautiful, but there was so much fancy in the last it charmed me. At the corners she has put four medallions with the heads of Horace, Virgil, Demosthenes, and Cicero, four other emblems on the sides, and a bee-hive to represent eloquence, a sphinx for philosophy, columns for fortitude, and a group, or what do you painters call it, with the caduceus, the scales of justice, a torch, etc. You never saw anything more compleatly pretty. . . . I was extreamly

---

[1] Charlotte, second daughter and co-heiress of Sir Charles Hanbury Williams and Frances, second daughter and co-heiress of Thomas, Earl Coningsby. She married in 1759 Admiral Walsingham, fifth son of the first Earl of Shannon. He was lost on board the *Thunderer* in 1779.

[2] Mr. C. Nelson Cole and his wife Ann Hester, great friends of the Duchess Dowager of Portland and Mrs. Delany, and constant visitors at Bulstrode.

delighted at Bulstrode with reading a manuscript of Prior's[1] which he left in her (the Duchess's) father's care. It contains heads for a treatise on learning, an essay or opinion, and four dialogues of the dead, all admirably written (though not, I suppose, quite finished), and with as much wit and humour as any of his works. There are some noble lines intermixed, but I had only time to run the book over hastily, and the said Mr. Cole did talk so unmercifully fast all the while that I could have killed him.

I MUST sit down and write to you, my dear sister, just as I would talk to you when I have any uneasiness. I am frightened to the greatest degree. Lady Lothian and Lady Emily came this evening, both seeming very well, but when I took the last out to walk and entered into conversation, she told me she had had a great alarm about her mother, that this day three weeks, dining at Princess Emily's,[2] she was taken with a sort of hesitation in her speech, and appeared confused and not to know what she said; that Lady Mary and the Princess attributèd it to the smell of some flowers she wore, made her lie down, etc., and in about three or four hours she was perfectly well and in excellent spirits (both before and after); that

[1] Matthew Prior published a poem in 1719, called 'Verses spoke to the Lady Henrietta,' the Duchess of Portland's mother. Lady Henrietta Cavendish Holles was the only daughter and heiress of John, Duke of Newcastle. She married Edward, second Earl of Oxford, to whom the country is indebted for his collection of the Harleian Manuscripts, purchased from his widow by the British Museum in 1754. Their only daughter, Margaret, married in 1734 William, second Duke of Portland, and was now his widow.

[2] Princess Amelia Sophia, generally called Princess Emily, daughter of George II., born 1711, died 1786.

she (Lady Emily) was exceedingly frightened, but finding her continue well, began to think it might have
been nothing, yet on last Monday, dining with Lady
Holdernesse[1] at Sion, it returned again in the same
way without there being any cause they could possibly
perceive, only lasted a less time.   They saw no
alteration of countenance, and what seems to alarm her
most, and, indeed, looks very suspicious, Lady Lothian
herself had not the smallest notion of it, and did not
know (nor does not at this minute) that anything had
been the matter with her.   Lady Holdernesse was very
kind, and a sort of physician happening to be there, consulted him ; he said he thought it might be nothing, but
could not say.   However, Lady Holdernesse agreed
with her to invite Sir J. Pringle[2] to meet them at dinner
another day, and they sent for Lord Lothian, who found
his mother perfectly well, as she was when she met Sir
John, and has been ever since.   Sir John told Lady
Emily not to alarm herself (but those, you know, are
words of course), that it might never return again, and
he had known it happen so, but that it was impossible
to tell whether it would or not, and that in case it was
of a serious nature, nothing could be done to prevent

[1] Mary, daughter of Francis Doublet, Member of the States of Holland, and wife of Lady Lothian's brother Robert, fourth and last Earl of Holder-nesse. He died in 1778. Their only daughter, Amelia, Baroness Conyers, married in 1773 Francis, Marquis of Carmarthen, afterwards fifth Duke of Leeds. This marriage was dissolved in 1779, when she re-married Captain John Byron, eldest son of Admiral Byron, and had a daughter, Augusta, subsequently Mrs. Leigh, half-sister of Lord Byron, the poet.

[2] Sir John Pringle, Bart., M.D., was fourth son of Sir John Pringle, Bart., of Stichel, by Magdalene Eliott of Stobs. He was a very eminent military physician, and President of the Royal Society. He died in London 1783, aged seventy-five.

it; that she need not prevent her coming here, and
must not on any account give her the least hint of it,
nor if it returned in the same slight degree take the
least notice.   This she desired me to tell mamma; she
cried, poor girl, and was in great distress, which indeed
is very natural, for it seems to me quite alarming, and
really I can do nothing but watch the poor woman's
words and looks, and shall be in dread and terror every
instant while she stays.   I durst not ask Lady Emily
how long that would be, out of delicacy, but think if
she should have a stroke here how very dreadful it
would be to my mother.   It might hurt both her spirits
and her health more than one can foresee, and besides,
my father is still complaining, and, I think, seems low.
I daresay it will affect his nerves very much too.   This
is all if it should happen here, but God knows I would
not have it happen anywhere for a great deal, for there
is no imagining what a misfortune it would be to Lady
Emily.   Lady Lothian was as well as I ever saw her
to-night, and (for I observed every word she said)
talked just as she used to do; her face was hid by a
great bonnet, so I could not see how she looked.   I
dread to tell my mother, and yet I must.   I am a fool
to scribble so, but, my dear sweet sister, you are the
friend I always think of and my heart always applies
to in any anxiety, or, for that matter, in any joy either—
it is the same; and though you can't answer as I write,
it is some satisfaction to tell you everything, and indeed
when my thoughts go about the world, as they are
terribly apt to do every now and then, and dwell upon
all the friends I have so scattered in it, it is the greatest

comfort to fancy you are contented and happy; it makes up for everything else. God bless you, my dear love, and continue all the comforts of your situation. Pray do not be uneasy at anything I say here, for I may have talked nonsense, and I think I shall not send this perhaps for three or four days, certainly not till I hear from you (which I hope to do to-morrow, for your letters always come on a Sunday), so I shall have time to see how things go.

Sunday, 18th October 1778.

I AM disappointed at not hearing from you to-day, because I now have no chance of it sooner than Wednesday, as we go on Tuesday, and I take it for granted it will be at an early hour. I write notwith-standing, that you may have the earliest notice of our hearing from Charles.[1] My father received two letters yesterday, and finds he has lost another (written first), one of the 21st of August, which I saw. It says nothing about himself, and gives but a melancholy account of public affairs, particularly as to the likelihood of our losing Rhode Island, which, however, we are so far from having done that Sir H. Clinton was going to reinforce the troops there, made us conclude that Charles was gone with him, which made his safety less certain, and my father was confirmed in this opinion by another letter (brought by the coach last night) dated, as he thought, the 4th August last. Upon reading it again he found it dated the 4th of September, and that he was *come from* Rhode Island, where he had been to

---

[1] Charles Stuart, Lady Louisa's brother, mentioned before (page 7) as having left for America.

carry a message, and in this he says he has hopes of
being able to come home. I wonder how my father
came to miss so many particulars at the first reading.
I hoped news from Charles would have put him in
spirits, but it has not, and I will give you a key to the
reason of all his complaints this summer, which have
certainly been altogether of the mind, or owing to it.
You certainly must see a great deal in the newspaper
about Lord Chatham and him, and a narrative adver-
tised of a transaction that passed in the beginning of
the year 1778, and an account of the correspondence
between Dr. Addington and Sir J. Wright. I have
not read it, for my mother carried off the paper yesterday, but the names caught my eyes first, and Lady Bute
had told me enough before Lord Chatham publishing
this ; and a vast number of lies will oblige him, it seems,
to publish an account of the same business in his turn.
Do you not remember William's telling you he found
him one morning enraged at the reports of his coming
into the Ministry ? I find this now all hangs to the
same thing, and is the true reason why he has never
been in spirits the whole summer. Not a word of it
in your letters to me, for my mother does not know
that I know of it, and if she tells you, you know it
between yourselves; and in case she has not, I think, as
you will see the newspapers, you may like to have this
explanation. She does not see most of your letters, but
I hate to have an anxiety about it when I receive them,
so it is best to keep clear of such subjects.

Lady Louisa's explanation relates to a supposed attempt
by Lord Bute to assist Lord Chatham in forming an ad-

ministration in which he was to take a part. The so-called negotiators between the two parties were Sir James Wright for Lord Bute, and Dr. Addington for Lord Chatham. The immediate result was a dispute between Sir James and the Doctor, reflecting seriously upon the truth of one or both. The letters were published, and gave rise to a statement by Lord Mountstuart, Lord Bute's eldest son, dated 23rd October 1778, in which, while omitting that message of politeness proper between his father and Lord Chatham, he denies that the former had any intention of returning into public life. This produced a rejoinder of great length from Mr. Pitt, who, while commenting upon some parts of Lord Mountstuart's statement, seems to admit that no overture had been made by Lord Bute. The dispute was an exceedingly unpleasant one, and although the only discredit attached to Sir James, Lord Bute was extremely annoyed by being thus brought before the public and placed in opposition to Lord Chatham immediately after his death, which had occurred on the 11th of May preceding. The letters are given at length in the *Annual Register* for 1778.

THE SAME from the SAME

London, Tuesday, 20th October 1778.

WE came here this morning, and the first thing I did was to run to poor Lady Lothian's door in hopes of getting some account of her. I find it has been worse than even I thought, and entirely paralytick, but they told me they hoped on Saturday she was out of danger.

Wednesday Night.

The Duchess of Portland is in town for a day or two, and my mother is gone to her, which I am

very glad of, for, indeed, she wants some comfort. She
went to Mrs. Pitt for a quarter of an hour last night,
and found her tolerably well, but this morning she was
quite wrong. It certainly cannot go on so, she must be
confined. Mr. Dutens was here to-day, and told us
that she sent to him a few days ago and begged him
to get her a lodging, as Fordyce advised her to leave
the house she was in; he did accordingly, and came to
attend her to it; she talked with him reasonably enough
for a great while, put on her cloak and hat, and let him
lead her half-way downstairs, then stopped and said
she would go no further, in short, continued upon the
staircase, talking wildly, going up a few steps and then
down, till he said he was so fatigued and so affected he
was forced to sit down upon the steps, upon which she
screamed out to her maid that she had killed him. He
could not get away from her till eight at night, and had
gone at three. She is more in awe of my mother than
anybody, and never till to-day showed signs of raving
before her, but by this means she will give her infinite
vexation. Two of her oldest friends, you see, gone this
year. And this vile business of Lady Chatham, etc.,
keeping both my father and her constantly upon the
fret, it is too much at once. I am in the wrong to
write all this, but cannot help it. Mamma begins to
say she repents of coming to town; we were certainly
quieter at Luton, though melancholy; the winter has
a most unpromising beginning. Your coming, my
dearest love, is the only pleasant thing I look forward
to, and I feel a thousand fears and anxieties about that.
I am cruelly disappointed at not receiving a letter to-

day ; you never used to be later than the Tuesday.   It
will be a dreadful long month to the end of November.
I had fancied if we came to town at this time I should
at least have Lady Emily's company, and be comfortable with her ; poor girl, we shall never be so again.   I
wish I may hear from you to-morrow, or else I shall be
quite uneasy ; perhaps you have been in Dublin, and
that has delayed your letter.

Thursday.

They had carried it to Frederick, and he sent it me
this morning.   I have read it over four or five times,
with great pleasure and comfort.   You will know before
now the last news from America.   There is a report that
grows very strong and seems believed (which, if true, is
the most unpleasant for people who have friends there
that I have yet heard), that Government means to
send twelve thousand men there immediately, instead
of recalling the troops, as we hoped.   Poor Mrs.
Charles Stuart (I have just heard from her) knows
nothing of this, and is highly pleased with his assurances
that he will embark to come home in December.   I
pray God he may.   She desires her love to you.   My
mother has been out all the morning, and is quite worn
out and *abattue*.   She carried the poor woman (Mrs.
Pitt) to a lodging very quietly, but when she got there
she insisted upon going back again, and she said she
was near consenting, for fear she should have run into
the street and raised the neighbourhood.   She kept
her almost by force (for she begins to have the amazing strength usual in those unhappy people), as she had
done Dutens.   Parker is just come in.   She says the

landlady has been here, and ever since my mother went she has been sitting screaming upon the stairs ; a servant of Lady Lothian's came also and said that she was entirely given over. I am in such distress I hardly know what I write, but I will go to my mother and persuade her to see this poor woman no more.

At Night.

Fortunately, my brother Mountstuart [1] is just come to town. I have left them together, and I hope his company will do her good. I am quite afraid she should be ill with such a variety of uneasiness. I said nothing of Lady Lothian, but the caution was vain, for George came and told us the servant was here. We had him up, and, alas ! he gives us as bad an account as possible ; she does not suffer, however, speaks little, and is always inclined to sleep, just sensible enough to know her daughters and the people about her ; she may live some days, but they have no further hopes. My poor friend is breaking her heart. Do you know every room in this house puts me in mind of them, as if it were their own, and this makes it more melancholy than even Luton. We have had a dismal evening, for my mother stayed at home alone, and indeed I thought her right, as she went last night to Madame Welderen's,[2] and she told me she was so much oppressed she did not know

[1] Lord Bute's eldest son, afterwards created first Marquis of Bute. He married first, in 1766, Charlotte, eldest daughter of the last Viscount Windsor of the Kingdom of Ireland ; secondly, in 1800, Frances, second daughter of Thomas Coutts, Esq. He died at Geneva, 1814.

[2] Madame Welderen, sister of Sir John Griffin, wife of the Dutch Minister, Count Welderen.

what she was about. My brother is gone, so I must
go back.

Why am I depressing your spirits, my sweet sister,
by writing all these melancholy details in return for
your cheerful, comfortable letters ? yet, believe me,
nothing unpleasant ever happens that I am not glad
at heart you are not in the way of suffering from it.
How I love Mr. Dawson for his fondness and attention! But how differently have this summer and
autumn been to last year! Well, I will hope the
winter may be as different the other way.

I have a great mind to write to Miss Damer to
inquire after Lady Emily, as for her poor mother, all
one has left to wish is that she may end her existence
easily and without pain. We were considering how
long ago Lord Lothian died—but about three years
and a half—and now, when they were living in perfect
comfort and happiness together, all is ended at once.
I think her likely to be calm at first, and not get the
better of it for a great, great while ; but I will dwell no
longer on the subject. Good-night, my dearest sister.

Miss Damer (afterwards Lady Caroline) was the only
daughter of Joseph Damer of Came, in Dorsetshire, created
Lord Milton in 1762, and Earl of Dorchester in 1792. He
married Caroline, only surviving daughter of Lionel, Duke
of Dorset, and had three sons, of whom the elder, John,
married General Conway's daughter Anne, the well-known
sculptress, whose pretty figures of a wax composition are
still to be seen and admired. Her husband committed
suicide in 1776, in a Covent Garden supper-room, because
his father refused to pay his debts, which amounted to

£70,000. The second son, George, succeeded his father in 1798, and died unmarried in 1808, when the peerage became extinct. The youngest brother, Lionel, married, earlier in the year (1778), Williamsa, daughter of William Jannsen, brother of Sir Stephen Jannsen, Bart. He predeceased his brother by one year, dying in 1807, without children. Lady Caroline, who never married, kept house for her brother till his death. She survived him till 1829. Both Lady Caroline and Lady Emily Kerr, who was a great friend of hers, sat as young women to the painter Romney, the portraits afterwards being exchanged. At this time, however, poor Lady Emily was absorbed by her mother's alarming illness, of which we have just read the account given by Lady Louisa to her sister, dated the same day as the following letter from Lady Carlow describing a visit paid by herself and her husband to the Duke of Leinster's place in Kildare. Their host had married in 1775 Emilia Olivia, daughter and heiress of Lord St. George, and of Elizabeth, only child of Christopher Dominick of Dublin.

By 'the Duchess's grandmother' Lady Caroline probably meant Lord St. George's mother, Mary, the only child of a Lord St. George of a previous creation. She had married a Mr. Usher, M.P. for Carrick, and their son, St. George Usher, was created Lord St. George in 1763, and died in 1775. The Duke's sister, Lady Charlotte Fitzgerald, was then living at Kildare. She married in 1789 Colonel Joseph Strutt of Terling Place, Essex, and was created Baroness Rayleigh, in consideration of her husband's public services.

LADY LOUISA STUART from LADY CAROLINE DAWSON

Carton, 19th October.

AT last we have left Dublin, and are arrived at this place, which I find more agreeable than I expected,

though I don't think I should like to stay long;
but for a couple of days it will do very well, as there is
a good deal to see.   I can't say much for the entertainment within, as the Duchess is not more agreeable in
her own house than she was in mine; however, I am
not sure but what I should grow to have some liking,
or at least esteem, for her, as I am convinced she is
perfectly good and well meaning.   The Duke seems
very fond of her, and being stupid himself, does not, I
daresay, find out that she has any deficiency of understanding.   Lady Charlotte, who is really sensible, seems
to do what she pleases with them both.   You will be
surprised when I tell you there are at present four
generations in the house, the Duchess having her
mother and grandmother paying her a visit, which,
with her children, makes up four, and the great-grand-
mother is a very good-looking woman, not older than
most people's mothers, and the Duchess's mother,
Lady St. George, one would take to be fifteen.   I
must describe her to you, because she is so remarkable.
She has a very pretty little figure, with a face not
handsome, but well enough, and her dress in the
afternoon is a polonaise trimmed with gauze; upon recollection, I am telling you wrong, for it is a Circassian,
all over loops and tassels (like the one Mrs. Stuart
brought from Paris last year), and a little black Henri
Quatre hat upon her head, with her hair dressed up to
it behind.   In a morning she wears an orange-coloured
habit embroidered, or rather embossed, with gold, and
a great rich gold stuff waistcoat, with broad laced ruffles,
and a little white beaver hat with a bunch of white

feathers upon the top, and a black stock, so that she looks the finest French figure you ever saw. Everything seems to go on in great state here. The Duchess appears in a sack and hoop and diamonds in an afternoon, French horns playing at every meal, and such quantities of plate, etc., that one would imagine oneself in a palace ; and there are servants without end. There was no other company the day we came besides the ladies I have mentioned, together with a quantity of Scrub men, who I take to be the Duke's hangers-on. To-day we had the addition of four young ladies, amongst whom was Lady Catherine Skeffington,[1] which you may imagine was not unpleasant to me. That morning they drove us all over the park, which is really very fine, though all done by his father, therefore no wood of any growth, but there is a fine river with rocks, etc.

———

The following account of Mr. Conolly, referred to in the next letter, is taken from Lady Louisa's *Notes* to Lady Frances Scott's Journal, and may be of interest here :—

" Mr. Conolly was the only son of Lord Strafford's eldest sister, Lady Anne Conolly. His sisters were Mrs. Byng, Mrs. Staples, Caroline, Countess of Buckinghamshire, Fanny, Lady (and latterly Viscountess) Howe, and Mrs. Fitzgerald. The hospitality and kindness of him and his wife, Lady Louisa, made their house an asylum for the nieces of both, whenever they wanted protection. Miss Staples chiefly lived with them, and they took the orphan daughter of Mrs. Fitzgerald after the catastrophe of her father, which was

[1] Lady Catherine Skeffington, youngest daughter of the first Earl of Massereene, married, 1784, the Earl of Landaff, died 1796.

subsequent to her mother's death. Mr. Fitzgerald, the son of Lady Mary Fitzgerald, Lord Bristol's sister, by a wild and ruffianly husband, from whom she was separated, had been bred up by her in England, and seemed apparently an entire Hervey, remarkable for the softness and almost effeminate delicacy that for some generations distinguished that family. But after his marriage he went to Ireland, and immediately took up a new character, became as lawless and violent as his father, with whom, however, he was at constant feud. Losing his wife, he [fighting Fitzgerald as he was called] herded with a savage set of people little different from banditti, and, assisted by them, perpetrated an outrage and murder for which he suffered death."

THE SAME from the SAME

Dublin, Monday Morning.

I HAVE not been able to resume till now, and you'll be surprised to hear I am again in Dublin, but Mr. Dawson's business obliged him to leave Carton on Saturday morn; however, he returned to dinner, but found it necessary for us to come back here again, which we did yesterday, and return to Dawson Court (or at least go part of the way) to-day, for I don't believe we shall get away in time enough to get through the journey, but must lie at Kildare, for it is thirty-four Irish miles, which makes above forty English, and is a tolerable long journey for our poor old blind and lame cattle. I must now finish my account of Carton. On Saturday they asked if I should like going to Castletown, Mr. Conolly's, and upon my answering in the affirmative we set out in the coach and six with all due state. I was very much entertained, as it is a very pretty place, though a flat (which you will not credit, I suppose); but there's very fine wood, a fine river, and views of mountains from every part of it, so the flatness does not strike one so much, and I never saw any place kept so neat and nice. They first carried me to the cottage, for you must know it is quite the fashion in Ireland to have a cottage neatly fitted up with Tunbridge ware, and to drink tea in it during the summer. We then went to the house, which is the largest I ever was in, and reckoned the finest in this kingdom. It has been done up entirely by Lady Louisa, and with a very good taste ; but what struck me most was a gallery, I daresay 150 feet long, furnished in the most delightful manner with fine glasses, books, musical instruments, billiard table, in short, everything that you can think of is in that room, and though so large, is so well filled, that it is the warmest, most comfortable-looking place I ever saw ; and they tell me they live in it quite in winter, for the servants can bring in dinner or supper at one end, without anybody hearing it at the other, in short, I never saw anything so delightful, and I am sure you would have been in raptures. Lady Charlotte is so fond of it that she would have me go into every hole and corner of that great house, and then made me walk all over the shrubbery, so that by the time we had finished I was compleatly tired. When we returned home we found a Lord Inchiquin [1] (I don't know how to spell it), and he

---

[1] Murrough O'Brien, fifth Earl of Inchiquin, and first Marquis of Thomond, an original Kt. Companion at the first installation of the Order of St. Patrick. He married, 1753, Lady Mary O'Brien, Countess of Orkney in her own right, and daughter of his uncle, the last peer. They had several

brought a Mr. Orme with him, son to the famous Mr. Orme.[1] One should have expected him to be handsome, as his mother was such a famous beauty, but he is quite the reverse. It is not the fashion at Carton to play at cards. The ladies sit and work, and the gentlemen lollop about and go to sleep, at least, the Duke does, for he snored so loud the other night that we all got into a great fit of laughing and waked him. They asked me if I liked cards, and I pretended I did, much more than I really do, for the sake of getting a card table, for when there is a good many people sitting in that manner it's very tiresome, so I had a party at whist every night; but they seemed to think it very odd that a young woman should like cards. Yesterday, before we set out, we went to church with them. They have a very comfortable gallery with a good fire. I forgot to mention to you the Duke's chaplain lives in the house with them, and reads prayers every morning, which all the ladies of the house attend very devoutly, but I can't say so much for the gentlemen. I think it a very proper custom in a large family, but then I think the master, as well as the mistress, should attend. They were very civil when we left them, and expressed their regret at our going. They wanted me to have staid and Mr. Dawson to come and fetch me, after he had done his business in town, but this I would not agree to. I have been dreaming to-night that I was returned to London and amongst you all. I wish

children, who died young, and one daughter, Mary, Countess of Orkney in her own right, who married the Hon. Thomas Fitzmaurice, from whom the present Lord Orkney descends.

[1] Probably Robert Orme, author of the *History of Military Transactions in Hindustan*, published in 1763.

it was a reality. Pray remember my most affectionate duty to my father and mother. I would write to the latter, but have exhausted all my subjects in this. I hope you'll allow these two last letters have made up for the omissions in one or two former ones, but three sheets is more than your quota, so you must not expect it always. God bless you, my dear Louisa. Ever yours, C. DAWSON.

Mr. Dawson desires to be remembered to you.

Tuesday Morn.

It's Charlotte's fault that I have not begun this before, for she will come and sit with me while I undress of a night, and keeps me laughing at all the droll things she says till Mr. Dawson comes up. She would be very angry with me if she knew I told you this, as she'll think you will hate her from henceforwards, and by the description I have given her of you she says she is quite in love with you. She leaves me to-morrow, as the Abbeyleix and Dunmore people come then or Thursday, and she would not be obliged to sit still and behave well to the King, I believe. However, I shall send for her again soon, as Mr. Dawson thinks he shall be obliged to go to Dublin again, and I won't go with him, for I only hinder him. I am very impatient for the post to-morrow, for I think as your last letter was in a melancholy strain, you will write again directly, and I hope things are better.

Wednesday Morn.

I fear this will be a very short and a very dull letter, for I find, now that we have been at home and alone for some time, I literally haven't a word to say. Mr. Dawson is out all day and defies the weather, and I have painted a good deal lately. This is the whole history of our lives at present. I hear the wind has been contrary, so I must not expect letters to-day ; that is very provoking, isn't it, when I am in a state of anxiety about you.

Saturday Night.

Only think of my being come to the end of the week and have never had time to write any more I fear you will fall short of your due, but you must excuse it on account of some long ones which I sent you lately. On Friday I had the pleasure of hearing from you, and am better pleased with your accounts than I was with the last, though I can't help being very uneasy at all the spiteful things that are in the newspapers about my father. I do think Lady Chatham must be very ill-natured, for what she has published can be of no service to her husband's memory, and it seems as if it was mere malice that induced her to do it. I wish my father would never suffer a newspaper to be brought to him, for I think it shocking that he should be vexed with every non-sensical ill-natured thing that they throw out against him upon all occasions. I hope he will go and divert himself by making the tour you mention ; not that I know what it is, for you did not tell me where he was going ; however, I think a jaunt of any kind always does him good. I am glad to find there are some acquaintances of my mother's in town, as I hope it will prevent her from being much with either Lady Lothian

LADY CAROLINE DAWSON.

LADY CAROLINE DAWSON.

PAINTED BY HERSELF.

or Anne Pitt. I think by the description you give me
of them the only thing to be wished for the former is
that she may be soon released from her misery, and
for the latter that she may be entirely deprived of her
senses, for the most shocking part of her disorder is
her being sensible of her misfortune ; indeed, I hope
somebody will take upon themselves to shut her up,
for it must be trouble to my mother, and I think must
affect her spirits very much to see her so.

I am very sorry for poor Lady Emily, but I hope
that instead of suffering yourself to be dejected by her
misfortune that you act the part of a comforter.

I am glad to hear Madame Welderen is so constantly at home, as my mother is sure of a good whist
party there. I had a letter from Miss Herbert, who is
gone back to Highclear, but she says if she had known
you had been in town, she should have been afraid of
coming to you, as though she likes you, she is not sure
you do her.

I think I told you in my last letter that we shall
not stop at Bath on our way, but go there for a few
days afterwards. Lord and Lady De Vesci and Sir
Robert and Lady Staples have been here since
Thursday, and I think them very pleasant people to
have in the house, as they don't require to be entertained. The gentlemen went a-hunting this morning
with Mr. Archdale's hounds, which are kept here close
to the house ; as to us ladies, the weather, though fine
was so cold that we contented ourselves with sitting
over the fire, and working ; but we have a fine riot in
the house, for they have each of them a son at school

at Portarlington, and we sent for them to remain here as long as they stay, and the children are so happy that they make noise enough to stun one.   Miss Cary got leave to stay, and so in the evening we have a very good whist party, and a working party at each side of the fire, which is comfortable enough.   I really believe some time or another I shall get Lady De Vesci to sit to me, for I think I never saw so regular a beauty as she is, and therefore would be a charming study.   I must now bid you adieu, my dear, for I am quite tired of writing, and I have been obliged to steal this time from my rest, and here is my husband, who has been asleep this hour, but before he went to bed charged me with his love to you, as I charge you with every-thing that is dutiful and affectionate to my dear father and mother.   I am charmed to think there are some hopes of Charlie's return, and I am sure I heartily wish Lady Vere Bertie was released and that Mrs. Stuart could enjoy a little comfort in town with you.   God bless you.—Yours,   C. Dawson.

Lady Caroline Dawson from Lady Louisa Stuart

[London], 23rd October 1778.

Fordyce came here this morning.   It seems he had made Mrs. Pitt go into her room last night by absolute force.   My mother sent the coach about 12 o'clock (to-day), and they carried her back to her nephew's; then she went herself to her, and with the utmost difficulty made her go to bed, and the poor maid too.   The first thing she said was that she must

return to the lodging. I hope my mother will now
have a little rest about her, and that her relations will
either come and take care of her themselves, or
authorise Fordyce to do it. Mamma has been telling
me all the conversation, if it may be called so. She says
sometimes the most affecting things imaginable, and
sometimes is so droll that my mother tells me, shocked
'as she is, she can hardly forbear laughing. She sometimes laughs herself, and sometimes cries bitterly. I
have received a letter from Miss Damer with a few
lines added at the end by Lady Emily expressive of
great resignation as well as great anguish, but I
perceive they did not think all hopes gone. We had
a later account last night, for this letter had been
carried to Luton. The Duchess of Bedford was here
this morning, and told my mother that Lady H. Vernon[1]
imagined from things the Princess had dropped that
she meant to take Lady Emily entirely under her care,
but that it was a secret. I am extremely glad to hear
it ; it is the best protection she can have, and I hope in
God she will accept of it. Mrs. Boughton came here
while my mother was out and asked for me. She made
me sick with her formal wise way of talking upon this
melancholy subject and talking about Lord Lincoln,
Mr. Dunbar, or anybody, in short, just with the same
concern as about her particular friend. I remember
poor Anne Pitt's saying (at Luton) upon some event
or other, ' I wonder when one shall hear of anything
pleasant happening to anybody,' and I am sure one

---

[1] Lady H. Vernon was one of Princess Emily's ladies of the bedchamber, sister
of Lord Strafford, and mother of Lady Grosvenor.

has still more reason to say so now. Lady Murray
Elliot is dying, I am told; the Duke of Queensbury [1]
and Lord Lincoln dead.   We called to inquire after the
Pelhams, for my mother and I took a drive about the
streets.   We have heard nothing about Anne Pitt
since the morning; I hope she is quieter.   My mother
is in better spirits, and went out to-night to Madame
de Welderen's.   I believe she talks of going to the
play to-morrow.   I can't endure it, no more than
Court, which she says we must be at on the Accession.
The Duchess of Portland comes to town again on
Monday for a day, and they are to meet.   Lady
Jerningham [2] is here.   I rejoice that my mother has
a few acquaintances in London, and as much that I
have not, for if I had she would make me see them,
and I am in a very bad humour for playing at visiting.
I am quite afraid this volume of a letter has tired
your patience out.   Pray forgive it, but it relieves me
to tell you everything.   God bless you and bring you
safe and soon to yours,   L. S.

I forgot to say that I saw Middleton yesterday
morning, in high spirits and charmed with your family.
She told me that Lord Carlow was a very pretty
old gentleman.   Once more forgive the length of
this letter, for, considering it is all upon unpleasant
subjects, I cannot help blaming myself for being so
unreasonable.

[1] Charles, third Duke, husband of
the famous Kitty Hyde.
[2] Frances, daughter of the eleventh
Viscount Dillon, and wife of Sir
William Jerningham, the father of
Lord Stafford.

London, Wednesday, 28th October 1778.

I SHALL begin with the best news I can tell you, that we have heard again from Charles by the ships that brought over Lord Howe and Governor Johnstone. My father received a letter last night dated the 22nd of September. He seems well, expresses hopes of being able to return, and says that the regiments are named that go to the West Indies, and his is not of the number.

Now, my dear, a thousand and ten thousand thanks for your letter, but I am very angry with myself for having given you a fruitless uneasiness about the foolish story of Charles being taken; I never can help writing upon the subject most in my head, and I always think you will hear such reports from other hands. Twelve regiments are certainly going out of the kingdom, probably to America. Peace is not at all talked of.

I am sure you will be glad to hear something more of what filled my last letter. I cannot say much either for my father or mother's spirits; she is very well in health, but he complains of a constant sickness in his stomach, that no food or drink agrees with him, and that he cannot sleep, at least this is what I hear from Lady Betty Mackenzie, for my mother has not mentioned it. I do not know how much of his complaint may be imaginary, but he certainly does not eat a quarter of what he did last year. Lady Betty tells me that Mr. Mackenzie says it is all owing to this business and the abuse in the newspapers, which no persuasion can keep him from reading, and since my brother's letter was published, they print the most impertinent, spiteful things every day, which he pretends not to mind, but yet puts himself in such agitation when he speaks of them that it is easy to see the effect they have upon him.

They brought poor Lady Lothian to London on Monday. I saw Lady Emily yesterday; she was extremely agitated at first, but, upon the whole, composed, and much better than I expected. I spent this evening there, and saw Lady Louisa[1] and the Marquis of Lothian. He seemed excessively shocked and affected, for he had just seen his mother for the first time. My mother now does not go to Anne Pitt every day, and stays but a little while, so her spirits are not so much overwhelmed as they were. She spends some of her evenings at Madame de Welderen's, and last night we went to the play, but were both heartily tired of it. It was the *Maid of the Mill*, and Mr. and Mrs. Mattocks squalled intolerably. I forget which morning we went to Kensington; Stuart walks wonderfully better, and with but one stick. He looked very pretty, though rather pale. He quite left off crying, but hung down his head, and would not speak. My mother was very kind to him, and we carried him back to his lodging in the coach. It seems his maid and the people of the house agree very ill. Mrs. Middleton has been here since. I could not find out whether he knew me or not, for he sat between us quite quiet, and only answered 'yes' or 'no' in a soft little

---

[1] Lady Lothian's other daughter, wife of Lord George Lennox.

voice, and smiled now and then.   I asked him what I should say for him to you, but he would not answer.

I quite agree with you about James[1] and Mrs. Stuart, but I suspect she intends to be sick and bring him to London in spite of all his resolutions, for she seemed to be in a very sour temper while she stayed in London, though you may be sure that she *talked* wisdom and prudence enough.   I fancy by her way that the *school* scheme was originally hers, for she said (to me) what could she do with a couple of girls among all the men if they stayed in barracks, and that they would be ruined for want of education.   Now, I declare I do not see that the want of music and dancing, which are the only parts of *education*, as she calls it, that they might not have at home, would ruin them, do you ?

Friday.

I have been with Lady Emily these last two nights, and her mother was a great deal better yesterday ; so much so, that she knew all her children, and gave sensible answers when they spoke to her, but asked no questions herself, so could not be called in her senses. We went to Court in the morning (the Accession has not been kept), and had a most tiresome long Drawing-room, for it was very full for the time of year.   The

---

[1] James, Lord Bute's second son, married Margaret, daughter of Sir David Cunningham, Bart. As already mentioned (p. 13), he succeeded to his mother's Yorkshire property, and assumed the additional surname of Wortley. On the death of his uncle, Mr. Stuart Mackenzie (whose large landed estate he inherited), he also added the surname of Mackenzie. His son was created Lord Wharncliffe. Of his daughters, Mary, the eldest, married in 1813 William Dundas, M.P. for Edinburgh ; and the youngest, Louisa, became in 1801 the wife of the Earl of Beverley.

Duchess of Argyll[1] was in waiting, which they reckoned an *event*, as there has been a great *fracas* between her and the Queen, and she resigned; but now it is all made up. Mrs. Dashwood[2] and Lady Weymouth[3] were there, who are just come to town. Mrs. Walsingham gave me a melancholy account of poor Mrs. Dunbar.[4]

I am charmed with your description of Mr. Conolly's house and your account of your great Duke and Duchess and their family. I have often heard Lady Jane talk of ' Lady Blaney's[5] letters' to her daughter in imitation of Madame de Sévigné's.

Ramsay, the painter, was here yesterday morning, and inquired very much about Mrs. Pitt from Lady Stanhope, who, I hope, means to take care of her, or at least make the other relations do it. Lady Mahon, you know, is her niece, so may take the authority of doing anything; and as Lady Stanhope is reckoned a very worldly woman, she cannot be in better hands. It seems Lord Stanhope is cousin-german to the Pitts, besides the alliance.[6] It will be quite a relief to my

[1] Elizabeth Gunning, who married the Duke of Argyle, then Lord Lorne, in 1759, being then Dowager-Duchess of Hamilton. She died 20th December 1790.

[2] Mrs. Catherine Dashwood, one of the late Queen's women of the bedchamber. Lady Louisa says of her, in a letter to Miss Clinton, 6th December 1829, " Mrs. Dashwood, the late Queen's first bedchamber woman, and what will strike you more, ' Hammond's *Delia.*'

" ' What joy to wind along the cool retreat,
     To stop and gaze on Delia as I go.' "

See Hammond's *Elegy*, xiii.

[3] Thomas, Lord Weymouth, afterwards created Marquis of Bath, married in 1759 Elizabeth, eldest daughter of the second Duke of Portland.

[4] Probably Maria, daughter of the Rev. W. Hamilton, County Monaghan, Ireland, and wife of Colonel Dunbar, who succeeded in 1781 to his father's baronetcy.

[5] Probably Mary, daughter and heir of Sir Alexander Cairnes, Bart., and widow of Cadwallader, seventh Baron Blayney. She married, secondly, Col. Charles Murray, and had two daughters.

[6] See note on page 63.

mother, who has, in a manner, had her to answer for ever since she came to England.

Here is your second letter just come, which is an unexpected pleasure. Charles did not sail in the *Lioness;* and it was lucky he did not, for her passage was a month longer than that of the packet; I believe I told you so in a former letter. I do not like to hear of riots near you; your White Boys are such terrible people. I hope Mr. Dawson is not bringing them about his ears. You will see above what I heard from Middleton about your relations. As for pressing my mother to go to plays, to tell you the truth I have been so much out of spirits myself that I could not do it. Now the news from Charles and finding Lady Emily better than I expected have revived me a little, and I will try. However, Madame de Welderen has a constant party, and Lady Jerningham is in town, so are Lady Betty and Mr. Mackenzie just now, but are going back. I fear my father will not go the excursion he talked of at night.

Wednesday, 11th November 1778.

YOUR letter made me quite happy last night, for not having heard from you for near a fortnight (not since last Friday se'nnight), I really began to be anxious and uneasy; but I fancy the packet has been delayed by contrary winds, as mamma received a letter dated three days later at the same time. I don't know how to thank you enough for all the kind things you say, and am particularly pleased to find you talk of your coming as so near, though I begin to be very much afraid that money matters will make you uncomfortable, and am very sorry Mr. Dawson has such an unpleasant piece of work upon his hands ; but I will make haste to tell you all about Mrs. Pitt and Lady Lothian. The former is as bad as possible, but, thank Heaven, her relations have at last (by Ramsay's means, I believe) taken care of her; that is to say, given Fordyce authority to do it, and he has placed a proper nurse about her, which frightened her so much that for two or three days the fear of seeing the woman (for she was only to be called in if necessary) made her quite quiet and manageable, but now she is as bad as ever, and they have sent to my mother to desire she would not come, which I am glad of. She has not gone to her above two or three times a week lately, so that now it is less upon her mind. As for poor Lady Lothian, she is so bad to-day that I expect to hear it is over every hour ; and indeed it is much better that it should be so than to go on as it has done for near five weeks, every amendment followed by a worse relapse. As for poor Lady Emily, it is very true what you say, that God gives people strength in proportion to their afflic- tion, for I could not have expected to see her so com- posed. I have been there every evening but two since I wrote to you, and have supped with her since Lady Louisa went home. On Saturday and Sunday se'nnight Lady Lothian's life was not expected, upon which Lord Lothian and Lady Louisa thought they ought to have a consultation, and proposed Dr. Warren to Pringle. He seemed displeased, but could not refuse ; so they sent for Warren, who has attended her con-

stantly ever since, and shown so much care and feeling
that they are quite charmed with him, while Sir John,
on the contrary, who has been her physician and friend
these thirty years, is so rough and so unconcerned that
if you saw and heard him, you would swear there was
no sick person in the house ; for as soon as he comes
into it, he sits down and begins talking on news or
politics, or anything he can think of, and hardly asks
or answers one question about her, till Warren comes
and hurries him up to her room.   It has been a comfort
to Lady Emily to have the latter, because his accounts
are always clear and intelligible, and because, you know,
it is always a satisfaction to have every possible assistance ; but he could do nothing, the case being from the
first out of the power of physicians ; yet for some days
last week she amended so surprisingly that he gave
them hopes. On Wednesday she knew everybody about
her perfectly, answered questions sensibly, and asked
how she came to be in her own house, and what had
been the matter with her.   Upon this Lady Louisa
went away, and on Thursday she was still better, and
held some sort of conversation with the Marquis.   But
on Friday she grew worse, and on Monday they thought
her quite dying ; a fresh blister revived her a little that
night and yesterday, but to-day she is worse than ever,
and has the thrush, which, you know, is reckoned one of
the worst and last symptoms.   Lord and Lady Lothian
are attentive to Lady Emily, and the Princess very
uncommonly kind and friendly to her.   She has offered
her her Lady of the Bedchamber's place (don't mention
this till you hear of it from some other quarter, for she

would not let her make any answer till the time came),
and will take her entirely under her protection ; but she
means to live by herself, that is to say, in a house of
her own.   Lord George has pressed her very much to
live with them, but she sees the inconveniences that
would bring her into, and I don't fancy her brother has
made her any offer of that kind.   Mamma is in better
spirits than when I wrote last, though not very good
ones.   She spends her evenings between Madame de
Welderen's and Mrs. Dashwood, Lady Jerningham,
etc., and she goes out constantly in the morning.   My
brothers Mountstuart and Frederick are in town—
William gone into Norfolk., I suppose you must have
got the news of Dominica's being taken before now.   I
would not write on purpose to tell it to you, for I think
ill news are always heard soon enough, and it is very
disagreeable to think what a chance Grenada has of
sharing the same fate ; yet I hope it is impossible she
[Lady Jane Macartney] should be in danger of any
kind, and if it should happen so, they would probably
come home the sooner ; but it might distress their
circumstances very much.   They tell me Grenada and
Dominique are at a great distance, however.

The island of Dominica alluded to by Lady Louisa
Stuart occupies an important position in the portion of
the West Indian group called the Windward Islands, lying
between the French possessions of Martinique and
Guadaloupe, and not far from the Barbadoes, Trinidad, and
Grenada, of which latter island Sir George Macartney was
then Governor. He had been accompanied there by his
wife, Lady Jane (Lord Bute's second daughter), and this fact

naturally added much to the anxiety of her family, who had been startled by the intelligence of the landing, on the 7th of September, of the Marquis de Bouillè, the French Governor of Martinique, on the island of Dominica, with 2000 men. Lt.-Governor Stuart, who had only a handful of 100 men with which to defend the little capital of Roseau and the entire island, was obliged to capitulate, and obtained very generous terms from the French general, who spared the town and its inhabitants, and left the island with a garrison of 1500 men. The unfortunate thing was, that Admiral Barrington had been waiting for two months at Barbadoes for orders to take his fleet to Dominica, but, whether from mischance or negligence, never received them till too late to repair the mischief. The loss of this dependency was aggravated by large sums having lately been spent on its fortifications and the dispatch of numerous and valuable artillery. The attention of the Government had been repeatedly called during the past session to the smallness of the garrison, but the answer invariably given was that every confidence could be placed in the friendly disposition of the neighbouring islands. When, however, France joined America in the war against England, it was seen how invalid this excuse had been ; but it was then too late for Great Britain to do anything to ensure the defence of the island.

THE SAME from the SAME

Evening.

I HAVE just had a letter from Lady Mary [Lowther], who seems very much shocked about this news. I beg, my love, you will not let it frighten you, for after all it is not certain that Grenada will be attacked, and the alarm will probably soon reach them, and give them time to

put their affairs in order. They say they have no
defence, so then, you know, they must surrender, and
there can be no fighting. Lady Mary says she is
extremely well, and hopes to come up very soon, as he
is in a good humour. I am quite sorry I did not know
of Miss Herbert's being in town. I should have re-
joiced extremely to see her, but I concluded she was at
Bath, or with Lady Pembroke, and when we first came
to town there was such a hurry of unpleasant things
that I did not think of sending to inquire. I have seen
nobody but those mentioned. We have been twice
at the play *tête-à-tête—The Way of the World* and
The Merry Wives of Windsor. I never saw so few
people I knew, especially men. Mrs. Charles Stuart
writes very low-spirited letters, and gives a dreadful
account of Lady Vere, who is still alive, and in misery.
I am exceedingly glad to hear I shall find you very fat,
for you were far from it when you left us. You will
find me grown so too, though I am quite sure it is not
with laughing. I dreamt of you all last night, but you
were out of spirits, and we were not comfortable at all.
Sure I may hope for you in about a fortnight. I would
not have had a line of your letter burnt for the world,
and I like your honest country gentlewoman extremely.
But I am so obliged to you for wishing yourself here
for our sakes. I do try all I can to entertain my
mother, but the worst is that from late events half the
subjects we used to talk of are grown painful.

Monday, 16th November 1778.

I AM just returned from supping at Lord Lothian's, and immediately sit down to spend a comfortable hour in talking to you, and heartily thanking you for your letter, which I received this evening, and could have wished longer, but it is so kind and so entertaining that I will make no complaints. You are impatient, I daresay, to know more of what has been the subject of my former letters, therefore I begin by telling you that with respect to poor Lady Lothian the scene is closed. She died between eleven and twelve yesterday morning, very easily, and to all appearance without pain, which, thank God, they have no reason to suppose she has ever felt during the whole course of her illness, and that is the only comfort. I have been with Lady Emily every night, and for these four or five last, expecting the event to happen every moment, and thinking it quite certain whenever I left the house that all would be over before morning, and that I should never go into it again. Think what a feeling this must give one! I never was more shocked in my life. On Saturday, to my great surprise, I found Lady Louisa there again, and was extremely glad to see her, as it was terrible for that poor girl to be alone at such a moment; and she came, as it happened, just in time. Lord Lothian removed them both to his house (what was Lord Lucan's), where they stay till they leave town. Lady Louisa wrote me a note, but we were at church, and as we got into the coach, Jonathan, according to his constant custom, put his head abruptly in at the window with 'Lady Lothian is dead, Madam,' in a manner that quite made us start, and was more unpleasant than you can conceive. In the evening Lady Emily sent me word she would see me, so I went, and found her exceedingly low and quite oppressed; Lord Lothian too seemed very much affected, and Lady Louisa was lying on a couch. I did not see Lady Emily alone, but went again to-night, as did my mother, whom it agitated very much. The will had been opened in the morning, and the contents pleased me very much; nothing can be more reasonable, just, and kind to all her children. She has left Lady Emily the Post Office pension of five hundred a year, and four thousand pounds of Lord Holdernesse's legacy, and made her sole executrix, which, you know, gives her plate, furniture, and everything undisposed of.[1] She has left Lady Louisa a legacy of a thousand pounds, and, on condition that Lord Lothian will stand to his father's will by giving Lady Emily the annuity of £400, or the sum of £8000 (which is but £4000 more than she was entitled to by their marriage settlement), she has entirely released him from all her own claims upon him, of arrears, etc., which, as he has paid her very little, amounts to a very considerable sum. When I saw Lady Emily alone, she told me that this clause affected him so much that he was quite overcome; said he had not the least expectation of being named in the will; that he thought his mother had acted in the most generous manner, and that the

[1] Lady Lothian had inherited a legacy of £20,000 from her father, Robert, Earl of Holdernesse.

disposition was fully as advantageous to him as to her (Lady Emily); and indeed I believe it does not please him better than it does her, for she was in an agony for fear he should not be mentioned sufficiently, and any coolness should arise between them. She is highly satisfied both with him and his wife. Lady Louisa is also perfectly contented with her part. I thought Lady Emily better, though her eyes were quite sunk in her head with crying. She said she had been so happy four or five years that she could not expect it to last, but many people did not enjoy so much happiness in all their lives, therefore she should endeavour to bear the total change of scene as calmly as she could, that she had met with the utmost kindness from all her family and friends, and that she should always look upon the Princess in particular as a parent. She is exceedingly grateful to my mother. It is lucky that she has a good deal of business at present, as it keeps her from giving way to her affliction, and as soon as it is over she goes to Sussex with her sister for a month or five weeks, till Princess Emily wants her, in short. We had a long conversation, and then Lady Lothian [1] pressed me so much to stay supper that I could not refuse, though I felt very awkward. I shall not do it again, but will see Lady Emily every day till she goes. I am afraid I quite tire you out with all these particulars. I never consider that they do not interest you so much as they do me. My mother is but low. I can easily imagine her feelings at the loss of a fifty years' friend, and cannot wonder

[1] Elizabeth, daughter of Chichester Fortescue, Esq., wife of the fifth Marquess.

when she begins reckoning up how many of her old companions are gone. For my part, I assure you, I do as you desire, and endeavour to divert her, but it is not much in my power, as I see nobody but the family above-mentioned; however, I have just got a letter from Lady Mary, who tells me she sets out on such a day, and will be here about the 24th; this is the pleasantest news I have heard this great while.

Tuesday.

My *doubts* about Miss Herbert are pretty much the same as hers about me, but I should have been very glad to see her if I had known she was in town. I have not heard from Mrs. C. Stuart lately, so suppose everything continues the same. The other Mrs. Stuart [Mrs. James Stuart] is at Lymington, I hear, with the regiment, and my mother tells me a little piece of scandal goes about, which is likely enough to be true, that Lady Ossory[1] is violently in love with James.

Pray, my love, do not let Miss Cary interfere with me, for these three last letters have been but of two sheets of paper, and I shall hate her in earnest if you do not increase the next. I do wish you was come; you flattered me it would be this month, and Miss Dawson told Middleton that she need not expect you till after Christmas. Middleton is in a great bustle for fear you should not give sufficient warning for your house to be got ready. I am sorry to hear such bad

[1] For account of Lady Ossory see article in *Quarterly Review*, vol. lxxxiii., on *Horace Walpole's Letters*.

accounts of Mr. C.[1] Indeed, we have not seen his son since I wrote last. I cannot go by myself, because we go out constantly every morning, which, you know, I cannot wish to prevent my mother. Poor Mrs. Pitt grows worse and worse. My mother went to her on Sunday, but I hope they will remove her into the country, as Mrs. T. Pitt wants her out of the house very much.

My best love to Mr. Dawson (my husband, you say so gravely!)—Ever think me your   L. STUART.

Friday, 20th November 1778.

IN case you should not get your letters directly (for I suppose there must be some for you), I write, my dear, to tell you we have just heard from Lady Jane. She says hardly anything but that she is well, and has got our packets of May and June. She tells mamma she has some faint hopes of coming back next year, but will not build upon them. Her letters are dated 30th July. My mother tells me she hears they have sent ships to Grenada, and that they are in no fear of the French. We expect Lady Mary on Tuesday. We were at Court yesterday, and I have been at Lord Lothian's every evening since I wrote last, except one, when I stayed at home alone. Last night Lady Emily was in the lowest spirits I have seen her yet— hardly able to speak, for she had had business which forced her to be in her mother's house all day. Lord Milton and Miss Damer were in town from Tuesday to Thursday, and the latter told me news I did

---

[1] Captain Andrew Corbet, husband of Lady Augusta.

not at all like, that you did not intend to come over
till after Christmas. I wish you would not have
flattered me. I am not angry, for I know you do
it out of kindness, but I would always rather know the
worst at once. I said nothing of this to mamma, though
I believe she suspects it, for she is always preaching
to me not to expect you. Adieu, my love, and God
bless you; but I am very sorry to think we shall not
meet such a long while. I have been dressing up my
old screen with cut paper, and put Ch. Cary's shade
of you in the middle; I think I see some likeness now.

My mother is in better spirits rather—my father
still in the country.

Saturday, 21st November 1778.

I WROTE to you yesterday, but will answer the
letter I have just received notwithstanding, as
otherwise I cannot till Monday, and if you do set
out as soon as you say, it may be too late; but I dare
not flatter myself. However, you have partly put Miss
Damer's story out of my head, and I begin to hope
again. I wish your old gentleman knew his own
mind for five days together, but I can't imagine how
your house in London comes to be a crime all of a
sudden; has he but just found out that you have one?
He did not think it too fine, I assure you, for he told
my father it was exceedingly small. You say you
hope you shall not find me in the dumps; I hope not,
for it must be some extraordinary cause that lowers
my spirits if your coming does not raise them to a
very high degree. However, I cannot say I have

any particular reason to complain of them just at present. My mother has been to see Mrs. Pitt to-day, which always affects her; she said she found her very bad, so I asked no explanations and changed the subject. She is pretty cheerful, upon the whole, and I hope she will divert herself by looking for a house for Lady Emily, which she desired she might do. It must be in your neighbourhood, on account of the Princess, who has already appointed her, as I suppose you see in the newspapers. The Queen inquired very graciously after her of us the other day. She goes into the country with her sister to-morrow, and I shall go to take leave of her presently. I found her better last night, and they made me stay supper by force. I was thinking when I came away that if you had been here I might have supped a second time with you, for they supped half an hour after nine, before you have drunk your coffee. Lord and Lady Lothian are extremely civil to me, and, as you may suppose, seeing them every day for a month or more has made me pretty well acquainted with them, and Lady Louisa too; and an odd family they are, but exceedingly entertaining. My friend is much the least so, and, on the other hand, much the best of them, and I am not sure if she has not the best sense, though not so lively. Lady Lothian seems perfectly good and pleasing. I should not think she had much vivacity. She seems to take great care of her children, whom I am sure you would be quite in raptures with if you saw them. There is a namesake of yours[1] about twelve years old

---

[1] Lady Caroline Sydney Kerr, born in 1766.

that I am tempted to steal away. I never saw such beautiful, agreeable creatures, and not the least trouble-some. I must say my good opinion of Lady Emily is increased by what I see of her. I told you the will. She has since found a codicil, made long before it to another will, which is not good in law, but she says she will fulfil it. It leaves legacies and tokens to the amount of about a thousand pounds to Mrs. Ireland, the servants, etc.

I beg you not to think I care less for your letters, for I shall be very well pleased to get one an hour before you come. I could dance for joy like a child when I think of that moment. Your coming will make us comfortable, whether we are so before it or not, so don't think of that.

Friday, 27th November 1778.

MY DEAREST SISTER—I am sure I shall make you very happy with the enclosed letter from Charles. Capt. Hobart[1] is come, and has sent it. He left him well the 24th of October. The Duke of Ancaster is come, and they say several more, but I fancy there is no news. I was in hopes he would have come himself when I heard that several officers were expected in a few days ; however, it will make Mrs. Stuart very happy to hear from him and inquire about him of her nephew. Lord Brownlow[2] is come to town, and says she is better than they expected. We had

---

[1] Probably Mrs. Stuart's brother-in-law, George Hobart, afterwards third Earl of Buckinghamshire, or her nephew Robert, afterwards fourth Earl of Buckinghamshire, then 18 ?

[2] Lord Brownlow Bertie, nephew of Lady Vere, and brother of the Duke of Ancaster mentioned above, and afterwards himself fifth and last Duke of Ancaster.

the account of Lady Vere's death on Monday, but I did not think of writing on purpose to tell it you. She made both her daughters give her a solemn promise not to leave the house till she was buried; and Lady Betty insists upon it that Miss Carter wrote word to Lady Howe that she made them promise always to be in the room by turns, but that is so strange I can hardly believe it. She has left Mrs. Stuart everything but £1000 to Mrs. Hobart, £900 to her children, and a few small legacies. Lord Robert[1] thinks it will be about £15,000 or £16,000, which is no [?] more than the H.'s have taken from her.

God bless you, my love. I am counting every hour till you come, yet rejoice to think you are not upon the sea now, for we have dreadful storms. I am so afraid your next letter will put me off again.—Ever yours,

L. STUART.

Saturday Evening, 28th November 1778.

My DEAREST SISTER — I have just received your letter, and I must own (though I expected it) your coming being again delayed makes me melancholy, for indeed to be with you is all in all to the comfort of my life, and I do feel so much alone in the world that it is all I can do to bear it, though I must say my mother is exceedingly good to me, and treats me with great confidence, but then I wish you here as much for her sake as my own; you have no notion how much we want you. The town is now very full, but I

---

[1] Lord Robert Bertie, son of the first Duke of Ancaster, and a younger brother of Lord Vere Bertie, father of Mrs. Charles Stuart.

confess I would rather be alone than see any one of my acquaintance that is in it ; and in this respect Lady Emily's leaving town was rather a loss to me (though I was glad of it for her sake), for while she staid, as melancholy as the scenes were, I had something of an object that employed my thoughts.   But you will tell me it is my own fault that when I have not our own family and her there should be no resource left me ; and I own it does proceed from my own temper ; but, however, if I had as many friends as you have, and they were all here together, I should still be just as alone and uncomfortable without my dearest and best friend ; and yet I am half afraid of your arrival, for I protest every event or person we have expected any comfort and pleasure from has so constantly produced the contrary that I begin to be superstitious about it, though I don't know in what way to apprehend your being the cause of any uneasiness to us, unless you should fall sick, or quarrel with Mr. Dawson, and I hope in God the first will not happen ; the last, you know, must be as it may.

My mother went to the Duchess of Ancaster last night for the first time, whose spirits were very much raised by the expectation of her son (I hear he came at seven this morning).   She had had a most affectionate letter from him, and heard that his father's death affected him extremely, and that as soon as he got the news of it he sent for Charles, and shut himself up with him for a week.   Charles writes to my father that he has not been well, and talks of setting out to return this month ; but one would not have Mrs. Stuart know

either, so don't mention them when you write to her.
I am just going to write to her, and mamma bids me
say he gives hopes of coming, but names no time. I
hope he has not in his letters to her, as it will only
serve to agitate her. I am sorry he has not been well.
I fear he is subject to that complaint he had so often
when he was here.

My father's spirits are certainly better than they
were before he went into the country, and I don't hear
that he is ill, but he really eats nothing at all ; however,
I hear him talk of going out and taking his walks, so I
hope he will grow better. My mother saw your letter.
My mother and I are both sorry to hear of your hunting,
for a reason you will guess—indeed, I am very sorry
for it ; but, however, you, I hope, are not of a temper to
let yourself be made unhappy by fretting at it, nor Mr.
Dawson either, and certainly nine times out of ten the
children that are so much wished for give more plague
than pleasure to the parents—indeed, there are instances
enough of it at home.

Sunday Evening.

I can't send this till to-morrow, so I may as well
write a little to-night, though, indeed, it will be only
repetitions of what I have said before. It gives me
such comfort to think of you and Mr. Dawson at your
happy fireside, in comparison to the state of the rest
of the family, that I am drawing the picture to myself
every day. Pray, my dear, let us live very much
together when you come, more than we did last winter ;
it is the only pleasant prospect I have. I hope you have
many others.

Tuesday, 8th December 1778.

I FEAR you will always think my letters the messengers of ill news, and am very sorry to make you so often uneasy; but do not be frightened, for I hope in God there is no reason.   My father has been extremely ill of a bilious complaint, which seized him suddenly on Friday last, with excessive pain, a violent shivering fit, and a high fever.   Till yesterday the doctor gave him laudanum, and opium also, two or three times a day, to quiet the pain of the spasms.   He has been here this morning, and says he goes on as well as he can wish, but he cannot expect him to recover fast.   It came very suddenly.   He had complained for a day or two, but not in a way that made one uneasy, and we were out on Friday morning when he was taken ill.   Fordyce has been very attentive, and came four or five times a day.   I hope, my dear, you will not alarm yourself at this account.   I find his illness is in the newspapers, therefore I must send it to you, for fear you should hear it from other hands, or else I should have deferred writing a day or two longer.   I have been afraid the agitation and fatigue should make my mother ill too, for it is amazing what she has to go through—I mean what anxiety and vexation, besides being confined to a sick-room day and night.   At this time you may suppose the news of your delaying your journey another month is still more unwelcome than it would be at another, and it really quite dispirits me, though I must own you are very much in the right to show all attention to Mr. Dawson's family.   I did not tell my mother any more than that you put off your journey a little longer, but she has said all along that she was sure you would not come till after Christmas. I do not say all I feel and think upon this subject, because I am sure it vexes you not to come as much almost as it does us not to have you here; but indeed we are as forlorn (I should say we were even before this illness of my father's came on) as you can imagine, and have no comfort in anybody.

Evening.

My father is much the same; has eaten a little broth, and the doctor seems satisfied; but he is very low, and complains very much of being sore all over, and which must be expected, especially as the fever is very greatly gone off.

CHAPTER III

ALL the letters in this chapter, with the exception of three from their youngest brother William, were written by Lady Caroline to her sister Louisa, and addressed either to Luton or South Audley Street, from which we gather the family were living their usual life, alternating between the two houses. Unluckily, none of Lady Louisa's answers for those years are forthcoming.

The Dawsons were in London in the spring of 1779 staying at their house in Kensington. The following description of a *fête* evidently relates to one given by subscription at the Pantheon, and of which Horace Walpole, writing in a more cynical vein than Miss Herbert, says :—" The company were led into the subterraneous apartment, which was laid with mould, and planted with trees, and crammed with nosegays ; but the fresh earth, and the dead leaves, and the effluvia of breaths made such a stench and moisture that they were suffocated ; and when they remounted, the legs and wings of chickens and remnants of ham poisoned them more." At last, after the singing and dancing were over, he adds: "It being morning, and the candles burnt out, the windows were opened, and the stewed-

danced assembly were such shocking figures, they fled like the ghosts that they looked." [1]

The Miss Herbert alluded to was a sister of Henry Herbert, afterwards created Earl of Carnarvon. She was a great friend of Lady Caroline's, and accompanied them in 1781 to Scotland. She is thus described by Lady Louisa: [2] "An excellent being, one of those original characters that have something answering to the French word *piquant*. She had a great deal of humour, attended with a certain bluntness, for she thought aloud, and whatever was uppermost came forth unpremeditated, the amusing effect of which was perhaps increased by a difficulty of utterance that gave her a peculiar way of speaking. If her warm feelings were roused by affection, compassion, or indignation, she could hardly bring out her words at all. Friendly and generous to excess, though her income was very narrow, no one ever did so much to assist others, even before she became bed-chamber woman to the Queen. She died of dropsy 1799."

LADY LOUISA STUART from LADY CAROLINE DAWSON

[London], Tuesday, 15th June 1779.

MY DEAR LOUISA — I am sat down to tell you I haven't been so happy this great while, and that I am sure will please you. My heart is so light I could dance or jump about the room. I long

---

[1] See *Horace Walpole's Letters*, vol. vii. p. 210.
[2] From Notes by Lady Louisa Stuart to Lady Frances Scott's Irish Journal.

The MS. is now at the Hirsel, a copy having kindly been placed at the editor's disposal by the Earl of Home.

to have you here to partake of my good spirits, as you have shared in my bad ones;[1] . . . and now, by way of amusing you, I must give you some account of the *fête* last night, as I have just received it from Miss Herbert (for I was not there myself). She says they were at first crowded into the gallery, where their only entertainment was looking down upon the supper, which was upon circular tables under the dome, and which had magnificent nosegays for everybody, besides the chairs being adorned with garlands of flowers.

During supper they had catches; when that was over they were desired to walk down to drink coffee in the room below, which they found done up just like a garden, the pillars covered with bark and leaves, and lit up with lamps of paper, so as to make a sort of moonlight; and in one corner was a hermit, in another a wheel of fortune, with a man distributing papers about, in others were some of the best opera singers, dressed up, and singing or playing upon some instrument; in short, a medley of all sorts of things. By the time they were tired of this they returned to the place where they supped, which was cleared, and benches placed in a circle, where, after taking their seats, the dancers came in procession and danced minuets and minuets à quatre, then figure dances, which was the prettiest thing in the world, she says; when these were over the company danced country

[1] Here a piece of the letter has been mislaid which related to a project of Mr. Dawson having a small house on his father's estate to live in. This prospect pleased Lady Caroline, who found it difficult to keep a large household on a small allowance. The idea, however, was not carried out, probably owing to Lord Carlow's death in the ensuing summer, which made their income large enough to manage to continue living at Dawson Court.

dances, and so finished the entertainment. I can't say I regret not being there, for I am sure I should not have had three guineas' worth of amusement. I must now bid you farewell, my dear, as I am going to dine with the Damers and to see Lady Mary at Brompton afterwards, so I don't think I shall have time to add any more to this. God bless you.—Ever your

C. DAWSON.

Pray remember my most affectionate duty to my father and mother.

I have just opened this to tell you of a match that's talked of and causes great expectation of changes in politics, which is Lord Shelbourne and Lady Louisa Fitzpatrick.[1]

The three following letters were written by William, Lord Bute's fifth and youngest son, at that time only twenty-four years old, and just appointed by his father to the living of Luton, then being held for him by the Rev. W. Copleston. He accompanied his brother, Lord Mountstuart, to Italy, where the latter had been appointed Envoy Plenipotentiary to the Court of Turin. William Stuart became later Bishop of St. David's, from whence he was translated in 1800 to the Primacy of Ireland, and made Archbishop of Armagh. He gave a good example as an active resident Bishop, never leaving his diocese except for urgent reasons or to give his vote in the Upper House, and was ardent in trying to reform some of the abuses which had crept into the Irish Church, particularly that of giving the benefices to non-resident clergy.

[1] William, second Earl of Shelburne (afterwards, in 1784, Marquis of Lansdowne), married, as his second wife, July 1779, Louisa, daughter of John Fitzpatrick, Earl of Upper Ossory.

He married in 1796 Sophia, daughter of William Penn of Stoke Poges, and was the last survivor of Lord Bute's sons, dying in 1822 from the effects of swallowing a bottle of embrocation given him by his wife, through an unfortunate mistake of a servant, who had placed some laudanum where the medicine was usually kept.

LADY LOUISA STUART from HER BROTHER WILLIAM

Turin, 12th January 1780.

MY DEAR LOUISA—As nothing can give me more real pleasure than to hear from you, I write to beg a renewal of our correspondence. At this distance from my family it is no wonder that I am extremely anxious to be informed of their welfare. Make not, therefore, that shabby excuse of having nothing to say, but send me word how *you all go on.*

We are settled at Turin, notwithstanding the fatigues and difficulties of a long journey. Lady Mountstuart[1] lays upon her couch, and receives only a few persons who have been selected for her. As she will be scarcely recovered before the end of the winter, all her balls and assemblies are deferred till next year. At Paris, however, she underwent the preparatory ceremonies, and was curled, dressed, and painted in the newest fashion; the last of which is, indeed, so *outré* that, like Lord Fopinton's wig in the play, it covered half her face, and her nose was the only visible white part about her. The girls, too, have

---

[1] Charlotte, eldest daughter and co-heir of the last Viscount Windsor, was the first wife of Lord Mountstuart. She died in 1800, leaving two daughters and seven sons, the youngest of whom (afterwards Lord George Stuart) was born in March of this year.

had their share of pleasure, new gowns, new caps, and *dressed hair*.

My description, though strictly true, has an air of ridicule which I by no means intended, for if I lived much in company, or sought the approbation of the ladies, I would daube my visage with any colour that the polite world concurs to name pretty or genteel.

Almost the only entertainment I derive from Turin is the conversation of the Abbé Denina. He reads me lectures upon the literature of Italy, and has already considerably changed the opinion which I had formed upon that subject. Instead of having, as I always thought, better translations of the classicks than almost any other country, Nardi's *Livy* is the only prose version, remarkable for elegance and fidelity, of which they can boast. As for *Tacitus* by Davanzati, that has acquired such reputation in England, he deems it so extremely obscure as to be totally useless; his words are, 'Niuno e, che siasi aceinto alleggeolo, il quale non abbia avuto bisogno del testo latino per intendere il volgare.' Of the poets he speaks with all the vivacity and rapture of an Italian. I will not, however, tire you by a longer account of his criticisms. Adieu, my dear Louisa ; pray write to me, and believe me to be your most affectionate brother,

W. STUART.

I have written both to my father and mother since I arrived here.

Lyons, 17th April 1780.

MY DEAR LOUISA—I have been in your debt longer than I intended to be, but I had nothing to write which would have interested or amused you. My situation, however, not being likely to mend in that respect, I determined to wait no longer, and to return you thanks for a very obliging letter which I received in February.

I escaped from Turin the day before Lady Mountstuart was to receive two hundred visits, a ceremony the thoughts of which appeared so irksome to her, that, I believe, she would have escaped too, if it had been in her power. It was, indeed, made as easy as possible, for she received gracefully reclined upon a couch, swaddled in a quantity of fine lace, and scarcely nodding her head upon the entrance of company. In a place where every one is eager and happy to talk, a few ouis, nons, and grimaces is sufficient to keep up conversation, but lest these should fatigue her, Monsieur Dutens[1] stood at her right hand to assist with all the powers of loquacious flattery with which he is so profusely gifted. As I had no inclination to act dumbly in this pleasant scene, I ordered my chaise and set out for Lyons, which at this season of the year I prefer to Turin.

I am glad you like the *Revolutions of Italy*—your observation is extremely just; the first volume is certainly more clear and interesting, for while the others only relate the trifling events and negotiations

[1] See *ante*, page 38.

of petty states, whose internal transactions have very little concern with the rest of Europe, the first volume displays a comprehensive view of the decline and fall of the Roman power, which is an era in the annals of mankind too considerable to be regarded with indifference or inattention.

Abbé Denina is now employed in writing the history of Greece, in which he proposes to trace the progress of arts, science, and eloquence, and to give some idea of the situation of that beautiful part of the globe during the first ages of Christianity.   This work, which has never been attempted by any man of talent, is likely to furnish much entertainment in the hands of an author so eminent for all the graces of style.

I think you mentioned Lady C. Dawson's having some intention of passing the winter in London; I wish she may have done so, both for your sake and her own.   You want somebody to pull you from that little warm room, where with your own good-will you would remain continually.   To mix more with the world would inspire cheerfulness, and render books more diverting.   In truth, you have time enough to study and tire yourself at Luton, where you can have little entertainment but from my worthy and lamentable representative Mr. Copleston.

This will appear a strange lecture, but the fact is I had some thoughts of applying the same thing to myself; the plaster will serve us both.

Adieu, my dear Louisa.   Believe me to be yours sincerely and affectionately,   W. STUART.

Direct to me, Aux soins de Mr. Lavergne à Lyons.

Lyons, 12th July 1780.

MY DEAR LOUISA—I return you many thanks for your account of the depredations and violence of the *Protestant* mob.[1] I had, indeed, received some intimation of that singular transaction, as well from my brother as from my friends in England. I am not astonished to hear that my mother was frightened, for I think you have escaped very narrowly a dreadful scene; if the people, with their usual policy, had directed their first attack against the house in South Audley Street much mischief would probably have ensued. This does not appear to have arisen from the frenzy of fanaticism. Under the colour of religious zeal they concealed deeper designs, and while they sacrificed individuals to the jealousy or resentment of particular persons, they conceived the idea of enriching themselves by the plunder of the town. But whatever was the original cause of this unhappy tumult, I trust that it is entirely finished, and that the ministers are sufficiently wise to seize this favourable opportunity to employ the utmost vigour to crush the mutinous and factious spirit of the London populace; for if they neglect to hold out some striking example of severity, it will be no longer safe to live in England.

My letters, I am afraid, will not afford you much entertainment, and, indeed, the pleasure of receiving yours is my principal inducement to write. The war, no less than my situation, prevents me from being

---

[1] The No Popery riots raised by Lord George Gordon. He was tried for high treason in February 1781, but acquitted.

much amused at Lyons, and renders the circle of my acquaintance extremely confined—two or three old men of letters are almost the only persons I see. Judge if such company can enable me to maintain a correspondence that will not prove tiresome. On the approach of winter I shall retire to Switzerland, and perhaps from thence to Italy, and towards the return of spring I hope to accomplish what I have hitherto vainly endeavoured—the burying myself in the church-yard at Luton. I beg you would never pass by my palace there without offering up a secret prayer to see me established in it.

Your account of Caroline corresponds with the idea I had formed of her. She possesses a turn of mind that will carry her smoothly through life, and is blessed with a happy disposition, which inclines her to improve every incident rather than waste time in peevish and unavailing complaints. I am disappointed, however, to understand that it does not suit her convenience to pass the greatest part of the year in England, as I am sure her doing so would contribute no less to my mother's happiness than to yours.

Lord Mountstuart informs me that Charles has got a house in Richmond Park,[1] where he is settled much to his own satisfaction, and that Frederick proposes to walk out the day [?] in the library at Luton.

Adieu, my dear Louisa; write to me soon, and be assured that I am yours affectionately,

W. STUART.

[1] His brother Charles had been appointed Deputy Ranger of Richmond Park, and lived at Richmond Lodge.

During the two years which have elapsed since Lady Caroline's last letter various changes have taken place in her household. The first of these was the loss her husband sustained in the death of his father in August 1779. William Henry Dawson had formerly taken an active part in local politics. He represented the County of Carlow at the accession of George III., and was sometime Governor of Queen's County. He was advanced to the Upper House by the title of Baron Dawson of Dawson Court, and in 1776 created Viscount Carlow. He married Mary, eldest daughter of Joseph Damer of Came in Dorsetshire, and a sister of Lord Milton. Lord Carlow was sixty-seven years old when he died : he was buried in St. George's Chapel in Dublin. His eldest son, John, succeeded to the title and estates, and schemes for putting it in good order were soon started, the new owner showing much practical interest in the farming, planting, and general improvement of his estate. During the next few years a church was built, and, later, foundations for the present family house of Emo were begun on a new site and larger scale than the old Dawson Court. This, however, was interrupted by the Irish rebellion, and left for his successors to finish. The following year the Carlows were again passing the winter at their house in Kensington, and here it was their eldest son was born, in February 1781, and christened John, after his father. In July the little family, accompanied by Miss Herbert, proceeded north on a visit to Dalkeith, near Edinburgh. Their host, Henry, third Duke of Buccleuch, (then thirty-five years of age), was the son of Lord Dalkeith and Caroline, eldest daughter and heiress of John, second Duke of Argyll, who inherited a large part of her father's property, including Adderbury, in Oxfordshire, and Caroline Park, near Edinburgh. Lord Dalkeith died in 1750, leaving five children, of whom only two were living at this date, viz. Henry, who succeeded his grandfather as third Duke ; and

Lady Frances Scott, who married Lord Douglas in 1783. Their mother, who was created Baroness Greenwich in 1755, married, secondly, Charles Townshend, Chancellor of the Exchequer. They had two sons and one daughter, Anne, who married, firstly, Richard Wilson of Tyrone, and, secondly, John Tempest, a Lincolnshire squire.

The Stuarts were related to the Duke of Buccleuch and his sister through their common greatgrandfather, Archibald, first Duke of Argyll. The following sketch will show the connection :—

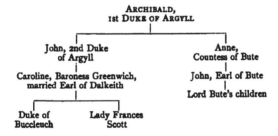

LADY LOUISA STUART from LADY CARLOW

Dalkeith, Saturday, 7th July 1781.

I AM now beginning my old custom of writing to you while my hair is dressing, but the only thing distresses me is that I shall never be able to recollect the particulars of my journey. The first place I saw was Lord Exeter's,[1] which I think the most complete of its kind I ever saw. A noble house, with everything in it the most magnificent style, a charming collection of pictures, besides many other things, and the whole house, large as it is, kept in the most perfect

---

[1] Burghley, near Stamford, built by Queen Elizabeth's famous Lord Treasurer.

order without looking formal. The place is also very pretty, without any great natural beauties, but though it is vastly comfortable, I don't think it the sort of place that would please you, or indeed myself, without a very large family, for there is certainly something very melancholy in a very large house for a few people to live in. I must break off here to thank you for a letter I received yesterday. I am sorry to find you are likely to have Lady M. at Luton, but think you may rely upon her dislike to it hindering her visit from being long, especially if she has taken possession of the house in town, and has coals and candles for nothing.

Did I tell you I forced my way into my brother the night I left you?[1] It was past eleven o'clock, and he was at supper with two or three men, and his servants did not seem to approve of a lady intruding herself upon them. It seems very odd that a year and a half should have made such an alteration in him, but it strikes me that he looks a vast deal older than he did, and the picture that he sent over to my mother, ridiculous as it is, is more like him than I could have thought.

You ask how Lady Frances liked Luton. She has told you herself by this time, for she dispatched a large packet to you upon my arrival here. You are also to have the journal[2] of her ramble, if she can get anybody to copy it, and I have promised to do some,

[1] Lord Mountstuart, our envoy to Sardinia, was then on a flying visit from Turin to London to kiss hands on a fresh appointment by the King.

[2] The journal was probably one in verse of a tour in the English Lakes. The MS. is now at The Hirsel.

but it's very long, and I am not fond of writing. The
first part of it I think charming. It does not go on
quite so well because of the length. You know it is
almost impossible to find different ways of expressing
the same things when they are repeated over and over;
therefore it is a great trial, in which she has succeeded
wonderfully well.

But to go back to my tour. I must tell you, after
Lord Exeter's, the next place we proceeded to was the
Duke of Kingston's,[1] which I admired almost as much,
and the house more; it seems to me the pleasantest
house that can be that either a small or large family
might live comfortably in. The next was the Duke
of Newcastle's,[2] but I don't know why I should describe
places you have probably seen when you was in Yorkshire, and indeed I could not describe them very
accurately, for we were in such a hurry we hardly saw
any of them with comfort, as they all lie close
together, and four is rather too many to see in one
day and get to a good inn to sleep at besides, so
at the Duke of Portland's[3] we only saw the garden
and plantations, and the same I think at the Duke of
Norfolk's,[4] but, as I said before, I regret I did not give
you an account at the time, as I have almost forgot
which was which in the number we saw.

Lord Rockingham's[5] came next, and there we
were offered a good dinner by his servants, but
could not stay long enough to accept of it (though

---

[1] Thoresby, now belonging to Lord
Manvers, but the house has since been
rebuilt. [2] Clumber Park.

[3] Welbeck Abbey.
[4] Worksop.
[5] Wentworth House.

dying with hunger), or to see anything but the offices, which are magnificent, because we had Wharncliff and Lord Strafford's [1] to see that day; but our schemes were frustrated by the postilion not knowing the way, by which means it was near six o'clock when we arrived at the lodge.[2] The good woman stared, and could not tell what to make of us till Miss Herbert introduced me to her, and then she was delighted to show us everything, and when we told her we were starving, she produced all the meat she had in the house, and set herself to cooking with the greatest diligence, regretting that it was not good enough. However, hunger being a good sauce, we were perfectly satisfied with our fare, and after having feasted our stomachs with lamb, and our eyes with the beauties that surrounded us, we proceeded to Wentworth Castle, but to our sorrow did not arrive till it was too late to attempt seeing it that night, and I did not like the thoughts of staying at a very bad inn all night, especially as the child [3] had gone on before all day, and I could not be satisfied without knowing it was safe, so we agreed to give up Lord Strafford's altogether, for the disappointment was only mine, they both having seen it before; so on we went, and between twelve and one had the pleasure of finding the little dear fast asleep in his bed.

The next day we saw Mr. Weddel's,[4] whose place is nothing but a good collection of pictures, and a

[1] Wentworth Castle.   [2] Wharncliffe.

[3] The infant, then six months old, was afterwards John, second Earl of Portarlington.

[4] Mrs. Weddell, née Ramsden, was a great friend of Lady Louisa's, and lived at Newby Hall, near Borough Bridge.

noble one of statues, together with a comfortable house, which makes up for the deficiencies in that. I shall never get on with my letter if I don't hasten to conclude the account of the journey, therefore take it in a few words. Lord Scarborough's two places, in one of which there is a fine abbey in ruins, and the other, called Lumbley Castle,[1] hardly worth seeing; Hackfall,[2] which is charming beyond description, Mr. Lascelles's,[3] which is all made within these few years; and a magnificent house, which, however, we could not see without paying Lady Fleming a visit; and a place called Cocken[4] finished our sights, and was not the least pleasing. I was enchanted with a noble river surrounded by steep rocks well covered with trees.

Dalkeith, Friday Morn.

I have absolutely been a whole week writing this, and, as you see, never have got in a word of our way of life here, which is exceedingly comfortable to everybody but Lord Carlow, and I am afraid he will soon be tired, as the Duke is at camp, so he is the only man excepting Mr. Townshend,[5] and he has been sick most of the time. However, there is a perfect ease reigns here, which you know makes all places pleasant, and particularly so for people that are lazy, as they live in riding habits even on public days, so there's very little time spent on the toilet.

---

[1] Lumley Castle, Durham.

[2] Hackfell Woods and its picturesque glen are about seven miles west from Ripon.

[3] Goldsborough Hall, the residence of Mr. Lascelles, who became Earl of Harewood in 1790.

[4] Cocken Hall, 3½ miles from Dunbar.

[5] Half-brother of the Duke of Buccleuch.

This is an excessive pretty place; I find out new beauties every day, and yet when we first came Miss Herbert and I agreed they had puffed it up most finely when they talked of rocks, etc., for there is not the least appearance of anything pretty at first sight. We have been employed in copying Lady Frances's journal that one might be sent to you, and I assure you we hardly do anything without 'wishing that Louisa was here.' I was saying the other day that you had reason to be flattered, as we thought of you, talked of you, and wished for you. The weather is very cold and unpleasant here, which makes me more inclined to stay at home than go out, so they have set me to painting a copy of a little boy grinning over a bit of bread and butter. He is not pretty, but has a countenance expressive of pleasure; however, I do not think I shall have time to do much to it.

The Duke had at this time the command of all the troops intended for the defence of the east coast of Scotland, including the eight regiments, the South Fencibles, and two of the Sutherland Fencibles. The camp was formed at West Barnes, near Dunbar, in July 1781, and broken up in October.

The Lord Lothian referred to in the following letter was William, fifth Marquis, born 1737. He married Elizabeth, only daughter of Chichester Fortescue of Dromiskin, County Louth. Their eldest son, Lord Ancrum, was in the Midlothian Fencible Cavalry. The family place is Newbottle Abbey. The house which Lady Carlow covets so pleasantly in the next paragraph was probably East Park or Smeaton, and had been bought by the Duchess of

Monmouth in 1708, and was burnt in 1798, while Lord Stopford and his wife (Mary, daughter of the then present Duke) were living there.[1]   The other place, Castlesteads, was bought in 1773, and pulled down the beginning of this century.

THE SAME from the SAME

Saturday Morn.

LADY FRANCES dispatched you four large packets yesterday, which was the reason I deferred sending this till to-day, for I know you like better to receive letters by different post than all at the same time. Yesterday morning we went to Newbottle, where they are expecting Lord Lothian and Lord Ancrum every day.   It is a good, comfortable house, but the place very melancholy, and the more so for having been neglected these two years.   There is a quantity of pictures, and hardly one worth a farthing.

They abound in houses here, for the Duke has three belonging to this place, and one so good a one that I think it a thousand pities that it should be uninhabited ; I would give a great deal for it at Dawson Court.   I joke with the Duchess, and tell her I'll hire it and be her neighbour.   I sent to Miss Mure to offer myself to dine with her mother,[2] but find she is not in town.   We were at a concert at Edinburgh t'other night, a tolerable

[1] See Lady Louisa's letter to the Duchess of Buccleuch, 21st February 1798.

[2] Catherine Graham, a daughter of Lord Easdale, married Baron Mure, who had been Sub-minister for Scotland for Lord Bute when he was in power. She was now a widow, and her house at Abbeyhill, near Holyrood, had long been a favourite resort for Edinburgh society.   Mrs. Mure survived her husband for forty-four years, dying in Castle Street, Edinburgh, in 1820.

good one, but in my life I never felt anything so hot. There seems to be a good many pretty women, but for beaux I never saw such a set of scrub. Miss Herbert asked if I could promise better in Ireland ; I think there's no comparison, in the outside at least.

We are going this morning to see Lord Abercorn's,[1] which they tell me is very pretty. Upon looking over this letter I never saw such a pack of stuff in my life, and to anybody but you I should be quite ashamed to send it, but I know you had rather have it than none. Pray make my duty acceptable to my father and mother, and love to Lady Jane, if she is with you. Adieu, my dear.—Ever your   C. CARLOW.

Dalkeith, 17th July 1781.

Don't think me ungrateful for your second letter because I have taken no notice of it, I haven't had time ; but I am delighted to hear you intend to defy the dulness of Luton.   It's the only way, I assure you.

Wednesday Morn, 18th July 1781.

I SHOULD have begun this on Saturday after I had dispatched my last packet, my dear Louisa, but from that time to this never could find a minute for writing, so I must turn back to that period, though I have almost forgot what we did that day, but I think it was to Lord Abercorn's we went, which is a pretty little spot, very like a villa near London, with this difference that it looks to the sea on one side, a great

---

[1] Duddingston House, near Edinburgh.

mountain on the other, and a ruin of a castle [1] belonging to Sir Alexander Gilmore on another. It's a new-built house, but there is a board put up to desire strangers not to ask to see it; however, he invited us in, by which means we saw the hall and drawing-room, and that satisfied me, for I never saw anything look so uncomfortable—nothing in it, I believe, but six chairs and a table, and these looked as if they had not been stirred for a twelvemonth.

On Sunday we went to the Advocate's, a place called Melville,[2] which has a great deal of wood upon steep banks, with a river in the bottom, so you'll conclude it must be pretty. On Monday we set out for the camp, where we dined and spent the day. It's about twenty miles from hence, close to the sea, and indeed has no other merit, for it's a very small one, and of course looks very shabby to me, who have seen such large ones. We dined in the Duke's tent, and it rained most of the day, so all the pleasure we had was wetting our feet, and then sitting the rest of the evening without shoes; in short, I was tired to death that day.

However, we made up for it yesterday by going to see Roslin Castle, and we found it so delightful that we agreed to dine there, that we might have time to ramble about the rocks, which was quite the thing you would have liked to have done, and I wished for you all the time as we clambered up, without knowing the least where we were going, and

[1] Craigmillar.
[2] Melville Castle, the residence of the Rt. Hon. Henry Dundas, who was Lord Advocate from 1775-1783.

found something new to admire every step; we, after pursuing the path a great way, were obliged to return, as there seemed to be no passage across the river, and by the time we got back everybody was ready for dinner, which was spread out in a very neat garden looking upon the castle, and, to speak for myself, I never enjoyed anything more, as we had the most delightful strawberries and cream that ever was.

You must know that it's a custom for people to make parties to come and eat them here, and therefore their fields, instead of being covered with corn, are filled with strawberries.   After our repast we agreed to walk to a place called Hawthornden, but it proved to be too long a walk, so went in the carriages.   Here we were carried into a rock by an old woman with a candle and lanthorn to see rooms carved out of it, one of which she informed us was the king's bedchamber, but what king she could not tell.   Miss Herbert thought it resembled the den of thieves that Gil Blas lived in, and insisted upon it the old woman was Dame Leonora. After this we went to try to find a way to a place called Mavisbank, belonging to a Mr. and Mrs. Clerk,[1] whom you saw with the Duchess in London; but after climbing and scrambling till we were all tired we were obliged to give it up and return the same way we came, but not till we had admired every part of this romantic place, which put me vastly in mind of Wharncliff Lodge, both as to the view and the house,

---

[1] Robert Clerk of Mavisbank in Midlothian was a great-grandson of John Clerk, first Baron of Pennycuik. He married Margaret, daughter of John Urquhart of Cromarty.

which seemed quite in that style, and is inhabited by
an old Lady Hawthornden[1] and her niece, as old as
herself, and as we went through her yard we heard a
window open and a voice issue forth to invite us to
come in, which was this piece of antiquity, and after
using several arguments without effect she said, 'Wall,
then, it canna be helpt,' and shut down the window
again.   Lord Carlow and Lady Frances scrambled
about so that we were a long time finding them ;
however, we got home by supper time.   I forgot to
mention an old chapel we saw at Roslin Castle, which
was a great curiosity, from there being such a variety
of ornaments, and all so perfect, and it was built about
700 years ago, by the old woman's account.

Thursday.

Yesterday we prosecuted our intention of going
to Mrs. Clerk, whose place is in a charming situation,
but nothing done to it. We walked part of the way
home, which was delightful, but not a little fatiguing,
from the steepness of the hills.

Friday Night.

I never shall get on with this letter, I am convinced,
for I can't get a minute of time to tell you what we
do. Yesterday we were very quiet in comparison, because we only drove about this place in the morning, and
in the evening drank tea under the trees in what they

---

[1] Probably Barbara Mary Drummond, only child of William Drummond of Hawthornden, born in 1722, married firstly Mr. Murray of Glengarnock, and secondly Dr. William Abernethy Drum- mond, Bishop of the Episcopal Church in Scotland. Her only child had died in 1777, aged thirteen. Mrs. Drummond lived till 1789.

call East Park, which is where there is the good house
I told you of that nobody lives in.   After that Lady
Frances drove me to see two neighbouring towns.   Thus
ended that day, and for the present one I am more
tired than if I had gone 100 miles.

I went to Edinburgh to pay visits to my relations;
the first was Lady Elphinston, whom I found at home.
I then went to Lady Glencairn to please Lady Betty
Cunningham; then to Lady Gracie Campbell, who
was not at home, but I was obliged to leave a message
to know when I might come again, and proceeded to
Mrs. Mure, whom I found looking better than ever I
saw her, and Miss Mure just the same, only a little
fatter.   As to Annie, that you have heard them talk of
as a beauty, she's a great strapping thing, the very
picture of her father, so if that can be called a beauty
she is one.   However, I saw one of the youngest, who
does promise to be pretty.   I dined there, and was
tired enough, as all the family sat together, and you
know Mrs. Mure don't let her daughters get much of
the conversation.   I saw by Miss Mure's manner that
she is not cordial with us about our corresponding, so
I said very little upon that subject.   In the evening
they went with me to see Lady Gracie Campbell,
whom I found set out in great order to see me.   I
think she is like my father, and she doesn't whine like
the Ruthvens, but she seems quite broken-hearted for
the loss of her sons; as to him, I never saw such a
detestable creature, and he talked me to death.   Mrs.
Mure said he was drunk, but I fancy he's not more
agreeable when sober; their youngest son seems a

good-looking young man.   After this penance was over I returned to Mrs. Mure's, where Miss Herbert called me, and very glad I am that it is over.

The ladies referred to by the writer were two of her father's sisters: Lady Gracie Stuart, who married Mr. Campbell (Lord Stonefield), a judge in the Scotch Court of Session ; and Lady Anne, who married James, third Lord Ruthven.   Their daughter Anne was married to John, eleventh Baron Elphinstone.

Lady Betty Cunningham was the unmarried daughter of Lady Glencairn, and lived with her in the quaint old edifice of Coates House, which is still standing under the shadow of St. Mary's Cathedral in Edinburgh.   Lady Glencairn was the eldest daughter and heiress of Hugh Macguire of Drumdow in Ayrshire, and had married in 1744 William, thirteenth Earl of Glencairn, who died in 1775.   Her two sons, John and James, succeeded their father as fourteenth and fifteenth Earls of Glencairn, after which the title became extinct.   Besides Lady Betty (who lived on in the old house after her mother's death till her own in 1804) there was another daughter, Harriet, who married Sir Alexander Don of Newton Don in Roxburgh.   They had one son, Alexander, who succeeded to the Barony of Ochiltry in Ayrshire on the death of his grandmother in 1801, and two daughters, whose tragical deaths by drowning while bathing in the river Eden in the year 1795 will be found referred to in letters of that date.

THE SAME from the SAME

Saturday.

I AM staying quietly to-day, for I really am quite tired of going from one place to another, and wish

myself at home most heartily. We once thought of
going to Portpatrick by Ayr, but find it will be a
great way about, so have now fixed upon going the
straight road, though it is ugly, and we mean to spend
one day with the Galloways,[1] as they are close to the
road, and when we get over the water we are to stay
another at Colonel Burton's, because it is a beautiful
place, and we have determined to remain here till
Wednesday.

Sunday Morn.

We are going to hear Doctor Blair preach at Edinburgh, and afterwards proceed to Hopetoun House,
which is twenty miles from hence. It will be a fatiguing
day, as we mean to return at night, but it would have
been a shame to have been so near without going to
see a house one has heard so much of. I almost repent
changing the day of our going from hence from Monday
to Wednesday, but as the races begin the first of those
days, I thought it would appear cross, and as if we
despised them, to go just when they began. The
reason I repent is, they will insist upon my going to
the ball, which is on Tuesday, and I don't like having
my things to pack up that night, which must be the
case, as we go early in the morning. Did I tell you
Lord Herbert is arrived, and is to be quartered in
this town? which delights them all here very much,
particularly Lady Frances, who, I think, is a little
in love with him. Lady Pembroke wanted to have
come with him, and is very melancholy at Lord Pem-

---

[1] Galloway House, the seat of the Earl of Galloway, in Wigtonshire.

broke's[1] refusal. It is very ill-natured, as it could have made very little difference to him where she was.

Evening.

We set out for Edinburgh this morn, at half after nine, to hear this Doctor Blair, who disappointed me very much, as I think he has a very unpleasant delivery ; therefore I had much rather read one of his sermons than hear him preach one. Afterwards we bent our course to Hopetoun House, and saw Lord Rosebery's[2] in the way to it, which is a most desirable place. The only fault I found with it was the house being too near the sea, and in a bad day it must be miserable ; however, it is charming, from having quantities of wood quite into the sea, and I really give the nasty little wretch some credit for planting so much. I believe I must defer the account of Hopetoun House till my next letter, for we are going to the play, and I have only time to give you loves in general from everybody here, and so God bless you. Adieu.

James, third Earl of Hopetoun, had married in 1766 a daughter of the sixth Earl of Northesk. The son so anxiously wished for never arrived, and Anne, the eldest of the five daughters, became the heiress to the great estates to which he succeeded in 1792, on the death of his great-uncle, the last Marquis of Annandale. He added,

---

[1] Henry, tenth Earl of Pembroke, married a daughter of Charles Spencer, third Duke of Marlborough. Their son, Lord Herbert, succeeded as eleventh Earl, and married first, in 1787, his cousin, a daughter of Topham Beau-clerk, and secondly, in 1808, Catharine, only daughter of Count Woronzov.

[2] Barnbogle Castle.

on this occasion, the family name of Johnstone to his own, but never assumed the two Earldoms of Annandale and Hartfell, to which he had succeeded. His daughter Anne married her cousin, Admiral Sir William Johnstone Hope.

The Tenducci alluded to was a celebrated tenor, and much the rage in London at that time. Smollett, in *Humphry Clinker*, speaks of his 'warbling so divinely, I thought myself in paradise.' [1]

The meeting at Hopetoun House between Mr. Douglas and Lady Frances Scott, who subsequently became his second wife, is of interest here. He was the only surviving son of Sir John Stewart of Grandtully and his second wife, Lady Jane Douglas, and was returned heir of line on the death of his grand-uncle, Archibald, Duke of Douglas. The Duke of Hamilton, however, disputed the claim on the ground of his birth being supposititious, and the Scotch court gave the decision in the Duke's favour. On appeal to the House of Lords this decision was reversed in 1769, and thus the famous Douglas cause (which is said to have almost caused a civil war in Scotland) was lost and won by Mr. Stewart. He assumed the name of Douglas on the Duke's death. He married in 1771 Lady Lucy Graham, daughter of the second Duke of Montrose, and a great friend of Lady Frances Scott, to whom her early death, in 1780, had been a great shock. It may be imagined that in the ensuing two years Mr. Douglas and Lady Frances must have often met, till they agreed in 1783 to console each other for their mutual loss. He was created Lord Douglas in 1790, and lived till 1827, when he was succeeded by his eldest son, Archibald, who when only six years old had followed his mother's bier to its last resting-place.

[1] See *Horace Walpole's Letters*, vol. iv. p. 294.

THE SAME from the SAME

Portpatrick, Friday, 27th July 1781.

I MEANT to have begun this before I left Dalkeith, but found it impossible to find a minute of time to do so, as you shall hear, for I will begin where I left off, which was at Hopetoun House, if I recollect right. I should tell you we first went to hear Doctor Blair preach, and he did not answer my expectations; we then proceeded to Hopetoun House after seeing Lord Rosebery's, which lies in the way, and is beautiful; the other is a most magnificent-looking house, but seems very uncomfortable within, the situation charming, but the plantations in straight lines, and the gardens in the style of Kensington Gardens; however, the cut hedges being taken away would make an amazing improvement, and that is easily done.

I can't say I thought Lady Hopetoun seemed very glad to see us. You know she's an odd woman, and it seems they are very much out of humour at the late Lord leaving everything away from his eldest son that he possibly could, so that they have that great house to keep up upon £4000 a year, and, having no son, they cannot provide for their younger children. This is a little hard. However, he is heir to another great estate, and they still may have sons, for she lay in but three months ago. You never saw such monsters in your life as her two eldest daughters are grown. From being pretty, genteel little things, they are the coarsest, vulgar-looking things you ever saw. The eldest is but fourteen, and has a waist and neck that would vie with Miss Hotham. I fancy they are brought up in an odd way too, for there's Tenducci living with them, and there always is some fiddler or singer. We were very much discomposed at our first coming, and repented very much the going when she told us Mr. Douglas was there, as none of us had ever seen him since poor Lady Lucy's death. We were all ready to die when he came into the room, and Lady Frances did not recover herself the whole time we stayed, and I felt more flurried than I have been for some time. He seems to have recovered his grief, though, to do him justice, not his spirits, for we have seen him two or three times since. Lady Frances tells me he made his eldest son attend her funeral with him, and the room and everything hung with black, that it might make an impression upon his mind and not forget his mother.

We did not get home till near twelve o'clock, and heartily tired, so we agreed to be quiet the next day, and Tuesday we began early in the morning, as the races are about eight miles from Dalkeith, upon the sea sands, so they are obliged to run according to the tide (but I forget to tell you we went to the play at Edinburgh on Monday night). The races proved very dull. However, it was a very uncommon sight to see the shore crowded with people, and millions of carriages and servants upon the sands. You must know everybody piques themselves upon having a number of attendants and smart liveries upon these occasions. I was very well entertained, though there was no sport, with the cheerfulness of the sight ; there was one poor

horse killed in the running, but I was lucky enough
not to see it.

After this we proceeded to Edinburgh, where we
went to some shops in quest of fine things for
Miss Herbert to make a show at the ball, and she
hit upon an expedient (which you would not guess
if I gave you 100 years) to do it at a small expense, which was making Lady Frances buy them,
and she gave her so much to wear them that night,
and this produced a charming agreement drawn up by
Lady Frances which I will enclose you some of these
days, but there's too much of it to copy at present.
Our shopping being over, we went to the Advocate's
house, which the Duchess had borrowed, and were
entertained by his sister, whom I mentioned being at
Dalkeith when we first came.   We then dressed, and
proceeded to the ball, which is in a shocking bad room,
but put me a little in mind of Bath, from the style of
the people and feeling myself among strangers.   The
Mures were there, and Miss Katie sat by me the whole
evening, which, I believe, hindered her from getting a
partner, for her sisters danced.   By the way, I must tell
you she looks much better when she is dressed, and
her third sister is rather a good-looking girl.   She
charged me to beg you to write to her, which I
promised, as also the renewal of my correspondence
with her.   I am afraid they must all make up their
minds to be old maids, for I see no beau of any kind,
excepting Lord Maitland,[1] and Lady Wallace[2] has

[1] James, afterwards eighth Earl of Lauderdale.   He had just passed as Advocate at the Scotch Bar.   [2] Sister of Jane, Duchess of Gordon.

seized him. The Duke and Duchess of Hamilton were there. She came up to me and invited us to Hamilton. Lord Eglinton[1] also made a great sputtering to prevail upon us to go by Glasgow and visit him, but we declined, and after staying till we were all dying with heat, we returned to Dalkeith, which we reached about twelve, and were to set out at six the next morning.

I own I would have given the world to have stayed another day to rest, but would not ask Lord Carlow, as he had been very good to stay so long, especially as it was so little entertainment to him and a continual expense to us, for whatever they may say of the Duke's extravagance in his way of living, I see none, for they have but four horses to use, and those job, so that wherever we went we were obliged to have horses, and only dining at the camp cost us above four guineas; and as to his table, there is no more dinner than my mother has at Luton when there is none but her own family, even on the public days, so it is very odd how he can have got himself into such distress, unless it is by the Ayr Bank.[2]

But to return to my story. Off we went at six o'clock on Wednesday (Lady Frances made me come to her bedside to give her a parting kiss), and got

---

[1] Archibald, eleventh Earl. He married twice, but only had two daughters, the eldest of whom, Lady Mary Montgomerie, married her kinsman, Archibald Montgomerie, whose father succeeded as twelfth Earl of Eglinton. He was then a widower of three years' standing.

[2] In addition to the sums paid by him as mentioned in Mr. Home's note to *Lady Mary Coke's Journal*, vol. iv. pp. 92, 93, he subscribed £7500 on 23rd November 1778 in aid of the shareholders.

to Dumfries in good time, and found tolerable inns; but far different was our fate yesterday, as we could get nothing to eat hardly, and no horses, with very long stages and hilly, bad roads. The poor child, I suppose, was not well, as he cried all day, which did not add to the pleasantness of the journey, and I could not let him go in the chaise, as there are so many boxes, and the wheels not good, besides that it could not keep up. We went on in this tiresome way to a place called Glenluce, about eleven, where we had the pleasure of hearing there was no supper, no beds, no horses. This put us in despair. However, at last they got some horses, and we got some stinking goat cheese, bad bread, bad porter, and then proceeded, and arrived at Stranraer about two in the morning, without the least chance of getting the maids for some time. I made the nurse make the child's bed upon some chairs, and we were preparing to go to bed without nightcaps, when they arrived about three o'clock in the morning.

You may imagine how tired we all were, and cross into the bargain, especially as we were obliged to get up and set out for this place before eight o'clock this morning, and, now we are here, the wind is against us. However, we are likely to have a little better fare than we had yesterday, and the beds seem tolerably clean. I believe I mentioned to you our intention of stopping at Lord Galloway's, but finding he lay fifteen miles out of the road, I begged to be excused, for I am sure the pleasure of their company would not have made up for travelling thirty miles of these roads, in addition to our journey.

The only advantage gained by our misfortunes is your getting this letter, if it can be reckoned one to receive a catalogue of complaints and grumblings. However, I shall not dispatch it till I get to the other side. Adieu for the present. I have wrote till I am tired.

Sunday, 12 o'clock.

Here we are still, and just going to sail with a contrary wind, which is too provoking, after taking so long a journey for a short passage ; I am quite in despair.

Monday Morn.

I have only just time to tell you we did not get in here [Donaghadee ?] till twelve last night, after a most tedious passage, and being sick all the time, and here we came to the most stinking, dirty place I ever beheld, famished with cold and hunger, and did not get to bed till after two. However, the child is well, and so are we all now, but I fancy we shall not be catched going the short way again.

The 'shocking bad room' mentioned in the preceding letter may have been in the High Street, where the fashionable Edinburgh balls were generally given until 1784, but from the ladies dressing at Henry Dundas's house in George Square, it was more likely the Assembly Room in Buccleuch Place. These balls still retained a great deal of the solemnity so amusingly described by Oliver Goldsmith some thirty years earlier. "When a stranger," he wrote, "enters the dancing hall, he sees one end of the room taken up by the ladies, who sit dismally in a group by themselves ; in the other end stand their pensive partners that are to be, but no more intercourse between the sexes than there is between two countries at war. The ladies indeed may ogle and the gentlemen sigh, but an embargo is laid on any closer commerce. At length, to interrupt hostilities, the lady directress, or intendant, or what you will, pitches upon a lady and gentleman to walk a minuet, which they perform with a formality that approaches to despondency. After five or six couples have thus walked the gauntlet, all stand up to country dances, each gentleman furnished with a partner from the aforesaid lady directress: so they dance much, say nothing, and thus concludes our assembly." [1]

[1] See Prior's *Life of Goldsmith*, vol. i. p. 141.

CHAPTER IV

OUR travellers have now arrived at their journey's end, prepared to settle down at Dawson Court, and bringing with them the little son and heir who had been born in England. They were both intensely fond of their country home, where they had a thousand interests to prevent their ever feeling it dull, but we can imagine that to Miss Herbert, who lived a busy social life in London, varied by visits to country houses, where she met the same set of friends, the family life in a quiet place, with only the local gentry for neighbours, may have seemed a strange and not very lively experience.

LADY LOUISA STUART from LADY CARLOW

Portarlington, 7th August.

MY DEAR LOUISA—You must be contented with a common shabby letter this time, for I have so many to write, and I have been so lazy that they are all to be done at the last moment. We arrived here the night before last.

[Written by Miss Herbert]. (" While Lady Carlow is gone out of the room I take the opportunity

to desire you will not believe one word she says
about me, for she maybe will say that I don't like
the place, etc., etc.   I do really think it ——
and —— ; we are very comfortable, at last, at our
journey's end ; and we were received by the natives
with bonfires, dancing and howling before us, with
garlands, etc.   I thought it all for me, but it was for
the young hero, as in this country the custom is to
howl people in and out of the world.   Here comes
Lady Carlow, so adieu.")

[Lady Carlow continues.]   Isn't she very affront-
ing with her strokes, as if she couldn't find a
word to say about the place ?   She is afraid of my
telling you I think she is tired and repents ; and
I am sure it looks very suspicious when she forbids
you to mind what I say, but I haven't time to say
much about her at present.   I wrote my mother
word how provoking our passage was, and the inns,
etc., so I shall defer saying anything to you about it
till my next.   I am quite disappointed at not finding
letters here from all my friends, and I only found one
from you, which contained reproaches I did not deserve.
I hope you have done me justice by this time.   I am
quite in a fright about Mrs. Legge, as her silence is
very unusual.   I must conclude this now to write to
her, but will begin my journal very soon.   Adieu.
My duty as usual.

Tuesday Night, 28th August 1781.

HERE I am just beginning when it's almost time to
send my letter away; if I don't make up for this

idleness you will have reason to reproach me, but, as I told you before, I have not got into the way of journal-writing yet, nor cannot for the life of me. However, I am determined to make Miss Herbert enliven this for me by adding some of her wit. [By Miss Herbert.] ('She won't, indeed ; so good-night.')

Wednesday.

You see what she has wrote, but I shall make her do something before I seal this up. I am writing now to pass away the time, for they all went out but me this morning, and it's now almost five o'clock, without any tidings of them, and here am I almost famished, and mean to forget my hunger by talking to you ; and in the first place I have a letter to thank you for. Indeed, poor Lady Jane [Macartney] is very much to be pitied. I have just been writing to her, but as I am totally at a loss how to comfort her, I have not attempted it, but tried to draw off her thoughts from melancholy subjects by talking of my own affairs and nonsense. Don't you think that a better way than to dwell upon disagreeable things? I am glad she was not with you when she got the account of poor Mrs. Jackson's death.

I had a letter from Lady Mary [Lowther] t'other day ; she seems quite happy and contented, and indeed I think she has reason to be so, for, to be sure, she has now got the art of managing him and getting her own way in everything. She talks a vast deal of her house, which she says is charmingly comfortable.

Friday Evening, 31st August 1781.

[By Miss Herbert.] ("A very entertaining journal, indeed, of four days! You see how we employ our time, etc., etc.! Lady Carlow insists on my finishing her letter while she roasts herself over a great fire; but, my dear Lady Louisa, I have eat half a Grasier for dinner and drunk so much black cherry whisky that I must beg to be excused as I am asleep. I wish Miss Cary would not make such a great noise; she will wake me.")

Friday Night.

[Continued by Lady Carlow.] Did you ever see how she has served me instead of sending you something entertaining. Pray scold her, as you will me, for having waited so long for this curious epistle. You must know it was my intention to have dispatched it on Thursday, but I overslept myself, and when I waked I found the post was gone; but I promise you I will be more punctual for the future, and more entertaining too, if I can, though I don't know what has occasioned a fit of stupidity to come over me for some time without having anything the matter with me, so don't fancy that.

We still have Mr. Palmer and Mr. Dietz, whom, to tell the truth, I am almost tired of; at least the latter, as he is apt to drink too much, and then grows so familiar and so much at his ease that we are obliged to keep him at a great distance, and the chief use I make of him is to take a part in catches of an evening, which, with the help of Miss Cary, we perform tolerably, and sweet things they are.

I often wish we could be transported to the drawing-room at Luton to entertain my mother a little, for I never think of all the money she spent in my accomplishments, and how little advantage she has had from it, without regret. We have hardly done anything since we have come here but receive and return visits, and yesterday we began with our dinners, for, you must know, our cook has at last arrived, and seems to promise well both in his appearance and his cookery, being a clean, good-humoured-looking man, and the things we have seen of his dressing have been very well done; so now follows a train of dinners that will try my patience to the utmost. Miss H. may say what she will, but I rather think she likes them. By the way, I have never told you the people here seem charmed with her affability and good humour; she and Charlotte Cary are as intimate as if they had been acquainted all their lives, and quarrel and romp together all day long. The latter thinks Miss H. what she really is—excessively droll and clever.

The Coote family were our company yesterday, and the Dean would insist upon it to me that one of my brothers was in the East Indies, and was chosen one of the council.[1] I did not know how to believe it, and disputed it with him, but he asserted it so positively that he had it from a person who knew, and that it was a son of Lord Bute's, that I begin to be staggered. Now, do tell me if you think it is likely that Frederick[2] is gone there. I

[1] Dean Coote's family at Shanes Castle were related to Sir Eyre Coote, who had just defeated Hyder Ali at Porto Novo.

[2] Frederick Stuart, the writer's brother. He died in 1802.

shall be delighted if his distresses have brought him to think seriously of engaging in any way that may make his fortune. The newspapers say that Hider Ally is certainly quite beat off, and also that the French have withdrawn from thence, so I begin to have hopes still that Lord Macartney[1] may do well, and I also hope poor Lady Jane is more at ease.

I assure you it is a great compliment to you my writing at present, for we haven't a pen in the house, and I am ready to fling this into the fire, I am in such a passion with it. We expect Mr. Fisher, a painter, here on Monday, which I think will induce me to begin the little boy's picture, for he will clean my brushes and lay my palette, which is what makes me lazy about beginning a picture.

I can't conclude my letter without telling you how well he looks and is; he is grown amazingly fat and strong, and is the best-humoured little thing I ever saw, which last perfection I hope he will retain. I have begun a bed with my stamps, which I think will be beautiful; it is bunches of roses fastened together by a brown ribbon, quite in a different way from Mrs. Stuart's, and I think full as pretty.

Miss Herbert does nothing but grumble at Irish weather, and indeed she has reason. I never saw anything so bad; we have had a storm of wind and rain to-day, that I really have been expecting this infirm house to give way, and dreamt of it all night, my fears were so strong; and as to our goods and

---

[1] Lord Macartney was at this time Governor of Fort St. George, Madras.

chattels that were to come by sea, we had an account to-day that it's a month since they sailed from London, and no tidings of them at Dublin, so they are probably taken, or gone to the bottom; however, I shall not let this be an affliction, for it is only forgetting I ever had them, and it comes to the same thing. The only provoking part of it is that everything that is *lost* here is *said* to be coming in one of those boxes, so I don't know what my loss is.

I have no pleasure in the place this summer, for, as nothing has been done in our absence, it is all in the greatest disorder — not a walk in the garden free from weeds, no water in the river, and the weather so bad that, in short, I comfort myself, as Miss Herbert says, with a good fire; not but the sunshine tempted me to get up this morning at seven o'clock, and I walked out from eight till ten, but was almost blown to pieces, and have been so stupefied all day that I don't think I shall repeat it, at least till the weather improves. I am in pain for the poor people's corn, for most of the richer people have got in their harvest, but the poor creatures will suffer very much. I think I have now scribbled enough for one time, but don't ask me to write oftener than once a week, for you see the difficulty I have to make one out as often as I do. Pray remember my affectionate duty to my mother, and my father if he is with you, and love to the rest. Pray send me word what all the branches of the family are about. God bless you, my dear.—Ever your   C. C.

It may not be out of place here to call the reader's attention to the real talent for painting which the writer had, and how much good work of hers is still extant among her various descendants. She had profited much, it is said, from watching Sir Joshua Reynolds when working for her father's gallery at Luton, and certainly, if so, had managed to catch not a little of his charm of colouring and graceful composition. She was also very clever at all sorts of handiwork, and various little desks and tables painted on satin wood remain as witnesses of her good taste and dexterous workmanship. We may mention here that the sketch on the cover of this book was taken from one of these little tables. The flowers in the original are painted in their natural colours on white painted wood.

[Written by Miss Herbert.] ("Questions to be answered by the return of post :—

Did Lady Duncannon ever lay in, and of what and when ?

When does Lady Althorp lay in? who is Nanette to marry ?

What's become of Miss Molesworth ?

What's Lady Betty Compton about ? Is Lady Weymouth brought to bed ?

Is Miss Thynne married ?

Is Lady Fanny Finche's match off ?

Has Madam Kutzlaben produced ?

How does Lady Amelia Kerr do ? and when is Lady Louisa Stuart to be married ?

We wish very much to hear all the gossip of

London, and in return you shall hear of everybody
that is married or dies in Dublin.

Is Miss Sackville married yet to Mr. Herbert?

Who else is going to be married, and is anybody
dead?")

Wednesday Night, October.

I FEAR you will find this very stupid, and fall short
of the quantity, for I have but just now taken up my
pen to finish, and feel as if I could not possibly put
three words together, especially as the post brought
me nothing to comment upon. We are now in a
manner a female party, for I reckon Lord Carlow
nothing, as he is so taken up out of doors that we see
very little of him, and Charlotte Cary is here at
present.

I am sorry to hear London is so empty. I hope
there will be some good plays for your entertainment, for I suppose the theatres are the only places
that are open. By this time you have received a
parcel of nonsense containing questions from Miss
Herbert, who is dying to know a little more of the
gossipry of the world in general, and complains nobody
tells her any, so do take compassion on her; indeed,
I fear she will heartily repent of her determination to
stay the winter with me, especially if we don't go to
town till after Xmas, though at the same time she says
the time goes so quick, she's quite astonished to think
of its being four months since she left London. She
now says nothing shall make her stay in Ireland
longer than the first of April. I tell her I am sure
she has made an appointment with somebody in

London, for I told her perhaps we might be thinking
of England in May or June, and it would be much
better for her pocket to take the chance of going with
us, but no, she would not stay a day after the 1st of
April for any inducement whatever; don't this look
like something extraordinary? By the way, I do not
think she would dislike proposals from the *Mopstick*,
let her say what she will, because she is always talking
of who he will marry, and she has just had a letter
from her friend Miss Cerjat [?], abroad, mentioning Miss
Mills being there, and quite recovered, so Miss
Herbert will have it that she will come back and be
my Lady Loughborough.[1]

By the way, did I tell you Lord Wentworth's[2]
family is broke up by the death of his *Lady*,
and Lord Carlow has been writing to recommend
matrimony? I am frightened out of my wits that
Lady Anne will now gain her point, only that he wants
money. Do you know what she is about? I heard
of her not long ago in a large party at Lord
Palmerston's, whom I suppose she was besieging with
all her might.

Supper bell rings, so I haven't much more time to
write. We have just had an offer of a house, but I
suppose it will be too small by the description, and I
don't care. Did I tell you we are now entirely without
footmen, as the only one we had, which was John, that
you may remember in London, took it into his

[1] Lord Loughborough, eldest son of the first Earl of Rosslyn, married in 1790 Henrietta, eldest daughter of Hon. Edward Bouverie.

[2] Thomas, second Viscount, uncle of Lady Byron, married the widow of Lord Ligonier in 1788.

head to hire himself to Mr. Eden the night before we left Dublin, and we were obliged to come away without? Penncan also intends to leave us, so we have got another man by way of butler, who has a good character, but I think is rather too old. He puts me in mind of old George. Lord Carlow don't mean to have any *valet-de-chambre* but a footman, which I am very glad of, as if he dresses hair well enough, he will be of much more use than an upper servant. I always regret Michael, for I have never had a footman I liked since, and he now is Li Damer's[1] *valet-de-chambre*, though still in livery, and he likes him as well as I did. Pray send me some more franks, for I find those you sent me are all gone, and I really grudge making my mother pay 3s. 6d. for such a letter as this. Mrs. C. Stuart made me pay it not long ago, which I think was very stupid, when she might have directed it to Lord Carlow. My duty as usual. Miss H. desires her love. Adieu.—Ever your   C. C.

Wednesday Night.

I had almost forgot that to-morrow was the day for dispatching this, and I fear you will be displeased at the shortness of it, for I haven't time now to add much more. I was rather disappointed to-day, when Lord Carlow brought me in two packets directed in your hand, to find nothing addressed to me in them; however, your verses to Miss Herbert made amends, for I admire them mightily, so does she, and she desires

---

[1] Hon. Lionel Damer, third son of first Lord Milton, see *ante*, p. 79.

me to return a thousand thanks for them; I assure
you they are particularly just in the first part, for she
hardly ever fails to recline upon the sofa and take a
nap after dinner, which I abuse her for, as I am sure
nothing can be more unwholesome; and I really believe
the grapes are sour about my Lord C., and she
proposes following him now in her turn to England, as
he followed her to Ireland. [By Miss Herbert.]
("She desires I will tell you that Lady Staples[1] is
brought to bed of a son or daughter (very ugly)—
she has forgot which,—and Mrs. French has got a
son, but, poor soul, she is very ill; Mrs. Parnell has
not miscarried, as it was thought she would; Lady
Carlisle lyes in about Xmas; it is thought Mrs.
Beresford is with child, and numbers besides. I
have had a very good nurse recommended to me.
We have been to-day to drink Lady Staples's caudle
—not very good. Miss H. desires I will tell you
that she has just had the pleasure of seeing the
Lyon's Den, which is near here, and she wishes him
confined in it, for your sake. Mr. John's exactly eight
months old this day.")

Abbeyleix, Friday Morning, 26th October.

I gave her my letter to write something in,
and you see what she has made of the pen; and it's
all to pass for mine, too! She says she has wrote all
the news she has heard since she came into this part
of the country, and she hopes it will entertain you.
I should make you apologies for not sending this on

---

[1] Lady Staples's first child who lived was born in 1794. See *ante*, p. 60.

the usual day, which I intended when I began this sheet, and then changed my mind upon finding the post going directly, thinking you would be better pleased to wait a day or two longer than have such a short letter ; besides, I thought there was a chance of the same post going out a different day from hence, but I am sorry to find it is not so ; however, I'll make up for it some way or other.

We left Dawson Court yesterday, but did not arrive here without accidents, for the coachman contrived to run against a car, and broke the pole and several things about it. Luckily, it was not above a mile from hence, and at first we proposed to walk, but they found they could lead the horses with tolerable safety, and so we proceeded in the pace of a funeral till we came to a little rising ground, and then were obliged to get out and walk, and surprised the family here by making our appearance on foot. We found but few people here in comparison to what there generally is ; however, the company consists of old Lady Knapton,[1] who is a great favourite of mine, Lord Westmeath, and Lady Catherine Nugent, and a Colonel and Mrs. Sherlock, who are by far the most agreeable of my neighbours, and therefore I am not sorry to meet her. All the people hereabouts are lying in, as Miss Herbert tells you, so that I have had a great deal of conversation, which will be of some use to me. Lady Knapton was very eager to recommend a nurse to me whom she says she has known about five-and-twenty years, therefore I

---

[1] Granddaughter of Lord Abercorn, and mother of Lord De Vesci.

desired her to engage her for me; so that point is settled.

Lady Knapton also wants to recommend a wet nurse, but I am too partial to the one I have to drop the scheme of making her suckle the next, especially as my mother approves of it, so I shall do my endeavour to get a very good nursery-maid to take John from her. I now almost repent not inoculating him, as he has got no teeth yet, and no more appearance of any than he had at three months old. We are to go and drink caudle with Mrs. French to-morrow, and go home on Sunday. I am now tired of this scribble scrawl, and daresay you are so. Adieu. I was a fool to forget to bring a frank, and I am sure this is not worth what it will cost. Pray remember my affectionate duty as usual.—Ever your   C. CARLOW.

[By Miss Herbert.] ("Miss Herbert begs me to tell you she expects her other angel, Lord Herbert, to do the next foolish thing. Pray have you heard from Lady Frances lately? We think we have struck her dumb with our witty letters. The last was an excessive good drunken one, wrote under the waterfall, as yours was, and all the cleverness of Dalkeith inhabitants are not able to answer it.

Tallow candles, by Jove! Ha, ha, ha, ha! He, he, he, ha! A discovery we have made.")

Wednesday Evening, 31st October 1781.

I AM very late beginning this time, but really I have had nothing to say, but thanks for your last, which I received when I came home, and I beg you will not think a journal tires me because there is nothing particular in it, for it is an amusement to me to know what you are doing every day, if it was ever so trifling.

I am sorry poor Lady Jane is so tormented with those Irish people, especially as I think they are very likely to leave her no rest whilst they remain in London, as they are doing exactly what I suppose they would be delighted to have her do with them here, for it is the Irish way to make no difference between friends and strangers, and they are just as fond of you, and as delighted to have you the first minute they are acquainted, as we should be with an old friend. Now, for example, when I was in Dublin I received a long message from a lady I hardly know to speak to, saying how sorry she was we did not make use of her house instead of going to Mr. Damer's, and begged if we wanted to be in town again any time till after Xmas that we would go there, as she had a family of servants, and beds always ready aired; and I really believe I shall accept her offer, which I should never think of doing in London unless it was an intimate friend, but I am sure she had rather we did than not, and so we need have no scruples. I believe I told you we returned from Abbeyleix on Sunday. We left Lord Carlow behind us at Frenche's; he did not come home till Monday night. Miss Herbert was much pleased with that part of the country, and, I am sure, is surprised to find Ireland so like England.

The little boy in my absence cut a tooth, and a second appears very plain, so I hope he will get them all easily, as he has begun so well.

You are much in the right about my box of things, which I shall be obliged to you to send me, as it will take a good long while to come.   If Mrs. Parker will have it opened you will find it is not full, therefore Miss Herbert wants you to get her a fashionable dressed cap, and anything that is wore on the neck this year. She also begs for some blue flowers, and I shall also be obliged to you for a cap and tippet ; you know what I reckon genteel without being violent.   I wish you and Lady Jane would put your heads together about this important business ; we want them to be different, because they will be more for patterns than anything else.   Miss H. desires hers may have as little blond as possible, out of regard to her pocket, and I beg you will have some attention to mine also.   I should think it likely the box would contain these if they are well packed, and I shall be obliged to Mrs. Parker to pack the linen well, as I am sure Robe did not know anything of the matter ; and then will you be so good to direct the box for Lord C., to the care of Mr. Hart, at the White Lion, Chester?

Some of the servants will find out where the stage sets out from in London.   If the box won't hold the caps, I believe you must get them packed alone, for I don't think Miss H. will be satisfied unless she can set off her beauty to the best advantage to captivate the Dublin beaux.

By the way, there is a report come to Portarlington that some captain[1] fell in love with Miss D. at Bath, and has followed her to Ireland. I suppose it has risen from the old affair, and I hope his being come here is an addition to the story. Miss Herbert has a great deal of news about lyings-in which she wanted me to tell you of, but I tell her she may add it herself. We have been airing in the post-chaise to-day, like two old dowagers, which I hate of all things, but am afraid of not having exercise enough, as I am very soon fatigued with walking. This letter drags sadly, for I really have nothing to say, so you must not be angry.

Miss Thynne's[2] match is just such a one as I thought they would make for her. I suppose her being married will be an advantage to her sisters, who have been kept back on her account. I daresay the Duchess of Portland is highly pleased with it. I had a letter two posts ago from Lady Frances, who gives a melancholy account of the family at Dalkeith, whom she represents as invalids as well as herself. She talks of Lord[3] and Lady William being there, and the latter in a producing way, and he the most attentive and tender of husbands. Lady Frances says the Duchess [of Buccleuch] is likely to stay late at Dalkeith, which I am sorry for, on your account, though she says in that case there will be more chance of her coming here; however, I had rather pay you all a visit, if it could be so contrived, and I won't despair.

[1] This refers to Miss Dawson's admirer, Major Metzner, whom she married in 1785.

[2] Louisa, eldest daughter of Viscount Weymouth (afterwards created Marquis of Bath) and Lady Elizabeth Cavendish. She married in 1781 Heneage, fourth Earl of Aylesford.

[3] Lord William Gordon, who was intimate there.

Now I cannot write a word more if I was to be hanged, so let Miss Herbert fill the rest of the paper with her nonsense ; and so adieu. Remember me as usual. I hope I shall be in a brighter humour when I begin again.—Your   C. CARLOW.

Saturday, 3rd November.

[By Miss Herbert.] ("She has not a word to say for herself. The best news in the country is that Mrs. Harry Cary's pregnancy is declared and Mrs. Robert Cary's time is out, and it is not yet known whether Mrs. Deveux is with child or no. Mrs. Chetwood was brought to bed just six months after she was married. The Duchess of Leinster has got a dead son and heir. Lady William Gordon is, I hear, with child, and Lord William very anxious about her. So good-night. I am as stupid as Lady Carlow, so shall go and stretch myself by the flaming turf and dream of my destiny, etc., etc.

Apropos—I still recommend to you my dear Mr. Wyndham,[1] though he has been a little silly or so, for Lord Egremont has given him Lord Thomont's place at Short Grove,[2] a very pretty place and good house ; so don't refuse him, or I will say in my turn that the grapes are sour.")

Dublin, Friday Morn, 16th November 1781.

I WROTE you a little bit of a scrawl yesterday, just after I had received your uncomfortable letter, and

[1] Lord Egremont's brother.
[2] Shotgrove, in Essex, belonged to Lord Thomond, another brother, who
died in 1774. See *Lady Mary Coke*, vol. iv. p. 451.

it was only just to tell you I had never failed writing at the usual time, and if the post won't take my letters I can't help it.

Saturday Morn.

We were at the Castle last night, after a wonderful piece of work to get ourselves ready, especially Miss Herbert, whose gown was not finished till the minute before we went, and very ridiculous she was in her great hoop, dancing minuets about the room. I don't think I ever saw her in one before, she goes so seldom to Court. It was a very full drawing-room, and I did not dislike it, for I was lucky enough to get a seat, and there were Mrs. Eden and Lady Anne Leveson, and several people I knew, which made me feel a little at home.

You must know it's quite a delightful thing to us English people to have so many faces one knows about Lord Carlisle,[1] and then there are continually people coming from England to see him. We were at a very good opera the other night, and knew almost everybody there, and I was quite charmed with Mrs. Daly[2] at the play. She acted Miss Hardy in the *Belle's Stratagem* and the opera singer in the *Son-in-Law*, which she did most admirably, notwithstanding her being ready to lye in.

I haven't told you we have at last got a house here, and a sad dirty one it is, but we are obliged to put up with it, for there was no lodgings of any kind to be got. I am out of all patience with the

[1] The Earl of Carlisle was Lord-Lieutenant at this date.

[2] Wife of Richard Daly, the proprietor of the theatre.

slovenliness and dirt of the people in Ireland, and I have just been hiring a housemaid who is an English woman, in hopes of getting my house kept clean. I have also heard of a good nursery-maid, whom I intend to inquire after for to take John from his nurse.

I am very anxious to hear from you again, to know that you are free from anxiety, for I have just re-collected that after losing two of my letters, the one you will receive was sealed with black wax. However, when I did it I wrote upon the part which you must see the moment you open it, that it was only occasioned by having no other.

Wednesday Night, 21st November.

I regretted that, by being in a great hurry and confusion, I could not send this on Monday, which, of course, delayed its going till to-day, as there is no packet sails of a Tuesday; but I am not sorry now, as I received your letter to tell me you were satisfied nothing was the matter, and that makes me in a much better humour to conclude this, though you must not grumble if it isn't so long as usual, for I do not mean to confine myself to a certain quantity nor a certain day any more, that you may have no more alarms, so I shall write a little as often as I can.

We are sitting at home quietly for the first time since we came to town, and it's by mere accident, having been engaged to the opera, and then a supper and a ball at Mrs. Clement's, which last being put off on account of the old Mrs. Clement's illness, we agreed also to defer the Opera and recruit ourselves a little after the ball at the Castle last night, and an assembly and supper at Mrs. Perry's the night before, especially as we have another at Mrs. Cunningham's to-morrow. Don't you think these are violent doings? Miss Herbert rejoices in the idea of growing thin by the time she returns to London, which indeed I think is most likely. She is just now in the act of writing to you in the cover for this.

The Castle last night was really very pleasant, being full enough, and yet not crowded. There was but five minuets, and two of them very good ones, by Lady Anne Leveson[1] and Mrs. Eden, so that part was not fatiguing, and the country dances went on with great spirit as soon as Lord and Lady Carlisle set down to cards. The Master of the Ceremony wanted to confer the honour of playing with the Lord-Lieutenant on me, but I declined, as his game is cribbage, which I said I did not know how to play, upon which he entreated me to learn.

I like Lord and Lady Carlisle's manner very much, for it's without any airs, and they just talk to you as they would in London, only he seems not quite at his ease, which makes people here think him proud; in short, I perceive they are not popular in general, and I fancy will be less so in future, as they had a private ball the other night, which gave great offence to all those that were not invited. Mr. Storer[2] did the company the honour of dancing last night, and, I think, made a very bad figure amongst the pretty young men belonging to

[1] Married, 1784 (Vernon Harcourt), Archbishop of York.

[2] Mr. Storer did not like crowds.

See Lady Minto's account of his behaviour at the Elector of Cologne's levee.

the Castle.   I am quite in love with one of them, which
is Lord Strathaven ; [1] he is the prettiest creature I ever
saw, and dances charmingly.   You have no notion how
much at home Miss Herbert is here ; she certainly
knows everybody, and I am quite astonished to see her
flirting and chattering away to everybody, just as if she
had lived here all her life.   I hear the post bell, so must
conclude.   Remember my duty to my father and
mother, and love to Lady Jane, to whom I mean to
write as soon as I have time.—Ever your

C. CARLOW.

Dawson Court, Sunday Morn,
16th December 1781.

AT last here's a fine day, which comforts me a little
for Lord Carlow's absence, for he was obliged to
go to Dublin to-day.

My chief amusement since I came from town has
been making myself a white polonaise, in which I have
succeeded to a miracle, and repent having given one
to a famous mantua-maker in Dublin, who spoilt it
entirely for me.

I am sorry the opera proved so dull to you, but I hope
Lord George Gordon [2] will not continue to persecute you
with his acquaintance.   However, if he ever asks you to
dance I should always have an engagement.

I see by the newspapers Miss Thynne is married.   I
wonder if she will be a gay bride this winter, or if she
will be kept still like a child between her own family and

---

[1] Afterwards Earl of Aboyne, and eventually Marquis of Huntly.
[2] The hero of the Gordon Riots, which had taken place in 1780.   Lord George was acquitted of high treason in February 1781.

her husband's? You must know I have taken rather a fancy to Lady Anne Leveson.   She always desired to stay with me at the Castle, so I had an opportunity of knowing more of her than I ever did in London, and I think she seems a pleasant, good-natured girl, but very quiet and reserved.   It seems she and her brother return to London against the Birthday, and I daresay she'll not be sorry, for she is suffered to go nowhere but where Lady Carlisle goes, and that is very little, for she is so near lying in that she cannot appear at the Castle much longer, I suppose.   They have given out a match for her here, but I daresay there's no truth in it, only he is almost the only man worth having, a Mr. Fitzgibbon, a nasty man with an estate of five or six thousand a year.

Monday Morn.

[By Miss Herbert.] ("Miss Herbert says old Mother Cole[1] is a nasty old soul, and a nasty old soul was she, so she begs if you ever work, you will buy your needles of her, or a top-knot, etc.; the nasty old thing is £60 in debt, and writes to desire she will pay it.   Pray ask Lord Herbert if Lady Pembroke is dead, and desire he will put her in mind of his cousin Georgy, as she has forgot her entirely. Pray do you know if Mr. St. John is come home, and if he marries Miss Collins of Winchester?

We chattered so fast to Dalkeith, and we thought they did not understand our wit, so now we are dumb, but I expect Lady Frances in Dublin in February, and she is to return with me in April to London, and I can

---

[1] Mrs. Cole, a dressmaker in London.

show her two such cascades in Wales near Snowdon. Tell her all this when you write.")

Miss Herbert has filled all the rest of that sheet out of charity to me, who am so stupid. You tell me I should send you longer letters if I talked more about the child, and yet I don't know that I have anything to say of him but his having got another tooth, and that I believe he will run about in another month or two, for he is amazingly strong, and so fond of being upon his legs that he crys when he is taken up. I should like vastly to see Mrs. C. Stuart's boys, and to hear the eldest chatter. Does he seem sensible? Pray is there another coming? I can't help owning she has some reason to complain of me as a correspondent, but I do not write to anybody but you, and in my own family I reckon it the same thing who it is to, provided they hear of me, and I always conclude you tell them I am well. By the way, perhaps you will be shocked at our Irish manners when I tell you I am writing over a jug of whiskey punch, which Miss Herbert and I enjoy very comfortably, and she bids me say she drinks long life to you. She takes very kindly, I assure you, to these sort of things, and proposes to take a hogshead of whiskey to England for her own drinking, and will treat you with some at supper if you are not engaged the 1st of April. She has already sent a Xmas box of Irish curiosities to Lady Porchester, containing snuff, whiskey, black bog, and several other good things.

Monday Morning, 24th December 1781.

AT last Lord Carlow has come back, which I thought he never would do, and I have been quite uncomfortable without him, notwithstanding Miss Herbert, for there has been such storms that I expected to have the house blown down every night, and, in short, she is not satisfied without some little diversion, which it was impossible for me to give her, and so she sits the whole day wishing the time over, as I used to do at Luton, and yet will not allow she is tired; but I am sure it looks very like it, and it makes me wish I had not pressed her to stay longer than her first intentions, which were to have returned to England in February, or else I wish I was to lye in sooner, for I can't bear her to think herself obliged to stay, when she is certainly envying everybody in London. Lord Carlow has asked her friend Mr. Skiffington to come to entertain her, and he and his brother we expect the end of the week, and her favourite Mr. Cunningham is also to be here before we go to town.

Lord C. tells me the boxes are arrived, and he got them safe out of the custom-house, but as they are to remain in Dublin till we go, we cannot yet give our opinions of your purchases; but I daresay they are better than anything we could get here, and as to the price, everything is dear, and if one don't pay dear one must go without, so I daresay we shall be very well satisfied.

I was delighted to get Lady Jane's letter, and hope she is now perfectly easy about Lord Macartney,

though she has not heard from himself, as there seems
to be no doubt of the truth of any part of the news, and
it will certainly be a very advantageous beginning to
his Government. I suppose he will have an opportunity of putting a good many thousands in his pocket.
After wishing him to make his fortune, one can't help
being a little selfish ; therefore, I hope he will put Mr.
Popham in a good way.

By your letter you do not seem to have much
more diversion than we have here, so I am glad you
have got Lady Emily.

Miss Herbert begs you will ask her how her friend
Lady Jarrard does, and that she will give her compliments when she sees her. She also insists upon my
telling you that she has grown such a vast favourite
with the little boy that I am jealous, and I believe it's
true ; but the fact is I can't at present play with him
half as much as he likes. She threatens to carry him
to England, and if I could bear to part with him, I
should like you to see him.

She wishes you a Merry Xmas and Happy
New Year, and hopes you'll captivate her Mr. Wyndham, though she allows Mrs. Legge's Mr. Wyndham,
whom she knows a little, may be more entertaining
in conversation, but hers is everything that's good,
etc., etc.

You must know she has sat over me, and dictated
every word of the last page. I must say a little more
about the boy, or else I shall not be satisfied. He has
now got four teeth, and could trot about alone if one
would let him, and has such spirits that I do not at all

repent letting him suck so long, for I am sure he is not the least heavy, though as fat as butter. Did I tell you I have hired a nursery-maid, and expect her every day, as I think the longer she is here the better before the other brat comes, that he may be so used to her that he won't mind having the nurse taken from him? We have been reading the *Count de Narbonne*,[1] and I own I think very little of it. I don't know if you'll agree with me. I think it might have been much more interesting, and indeed the language is nothing extraordinary.

We expect Miss Dawson and Mr. William, so we shall have a Merry Xmas. However, we are to have a fine ball by subscription at Portarlington, and if I did not think it foolish to throw away so much money to entertain a parcel of impertinent people, I believe I should give one, but they don't deserve it.

I wish you would make excuses to my mother for me, as I fear I shall not get her purse done time enough to send it by New Year's Day, but I will as soon as possible. I fear it will be a very ugly one, as I have no pretty twists, and there are no choice of those things in Dublin. I have been trying to work an apron in the tambour, which I mean to send Lady Jane, if it's ever finished, but it goes on very slow. Miss Herbert, who is always cobbling aprons, finished one the other day which she was mighty proud of. When the nurse brought the child into her room, she said it was to beg her not to be angry with the maids, who had amongst them burnt a dozen great

---

[1] A tragedy by Robert Jephson, published in 1781.

holes in this fine apron.   She took some time to consider whether she should laugh or cry, as one or the
other was absolutely necessary on the occasion, and at
last thought it rather more philosophic to fix upon the
former, so down she came to me laughing so im-
moderately that I was impatient to hear the joke, upon
which she produced her apron, and I could not but
allow it was a good one; this is our way of treating
misfortunes, like Heraclitus.

[By Miss Herbert.] ('Huzza! Huzza! Mr.
William Dawson is just arrived.')

Isn't she very saucy?   Now I shall bid you adieu,
for we are come to an end of our jokes.   Perhaps you'll
not find out any in it.   However, you must take it for
better, for worse, and you see I am in good spirits, so
I hope will be contented.   My affectionate duty to my
father and mother as usual, and now God bless you, my
love.—Ever your   C. CARLOW.

Pray remember me to Mrs. Parker.   How does
she do?

I am glad my letters got safe to you that were
enclosed to that nasty old soul, Mrs. Cole.

Thursday Morn, 27th December 1781.

I AM quite revived this morning by the appearance
of a little sun, and with having slept well, for I
really have been quite uncomfortable for some time
past from the violence of the storms.   The night before
last I believe there was not a soul could shut their
eyes, and I thought of nothing but the house coming
down every instant.   I hope there has not been much

mischief done, though I suppose it must have drove back the fleet. Miss Herbert is so impatient for the New Year, as she thinks we have no chance of any good in this, and to be sure in regard to public affairs it has been a most unfortunate one.

The post brought me no letters yesterday, but I always get a great deal of gossiping from hers. What a shocking thing Miss Cripps going out of her senses is! I think all the people who have wanted to marry her may hug themselves upon not succeeding. Mr. Herbert writes her word from Bath that Lady Maria Bayntun is gone off with some captain. It appears to me the strangest thing that ever was her finding anybody that would intrigue with her. I should think her husband cannot be very sorry to have such a nasty thing taken off his hands. What a pretty pair of daughters that poor Lady Coventry [1] produced! I shall take care how I wish for one. Pray what are the Lucans doing this winter? You never tell me if they are upon any scheme. I suppose they are, by being quiet. I hear young Bingham was the finest man that ever was at Brighthelmstone this summer, and by way of being very expensive and extravagant, I wonder how they like that? I daresay they expect to get Miss Child for him, if they think the connection good enough for him.

---

[1] Daughter of Maria Gunning, first wife of the sixth Earl. The eldest daughter, Mary Alicia, married Sir Andrew Bayntun, Bart., and died in 1784. The other daughter was a Mrs. Foley, and married secondly a Mr. Wright.

In Lady Louisa's *MS. Notes* she says of this lady : " The only daughter of Mr. Child, the banker, looked upon as the greatest heiress in England. Lord Herbert had made her proposals, and was most warmly received and recommended by her father, but Lord Westmoreland, whom he had positively refused, contrived to correspond with her by clandestine means, and prevailed upon her to elope with him, an act which Mr. Child never forgave. He entailed all his fortune on her second son, or, if she had but one, upon her eldest daughter, who (Lady Jersey) now enjoys it ; tying it up by every method he could devise, so that Lord Westmoreland should reap no benefit by his marriage. It proved an unhappy one to her, though she was both handsome and amiable enough to have engaged a husband's affection." It was said that Mr. Child pursued the runaways, and that Lord Westmoreland, through the back window of his chaise, pistolled a leading horse, and so escaped.

THE SAME from the SAME

Friday Morn.

WE have had another storm to-night, which is not yet abated, and you must not wonder if I appear out of spirits, for nothing worries me so much as a high wind, besides that it hinders my sleeping. I agree with Miss Herbert's wish, for there is nothing but disagreeable things to expect while '81 continues. I suppose the taking of Barbadoes has put most people out of spirits, for it paves the way for the rest of the West India islands to follow. I wish the post to-day would bring us something comfortable. Miss Herbert is keeping her bed upon pretence of a toothache, but I really believe it is only from being so tired of all this dismal weather. Isn't she unlucky? for I never remember such a season since I came to Ireland. I was uneasy last night about the boy. His teeth hurt him so much he could not help groaning and crying, and nothing would divert him. He seems better to-day, though he had a very bad night, but he does not grind his teeth and work his mouth about so much. I can hardly find a place to sit in to-day, being turned out of the drawing-room by smoke, and here's a whirlwind in the library. All our brilliant Xmas set are almost collected. Miss Dawson we expect to-day, little Damer came yesterday, and William Dawson and Mr. Gandon,[1] the architect, have been here some time.

Monday Night.

I am going to take leave of you and the old year at the same time, and I hope the new one will prove happy to us all. You must not grumble if this is short, because I must write my compliments upon this occasion to my mother, besides which I have nothing in the world to say except that the weather has continued bad, therefore we have been confined to the house, and I have done not one thing but netting, though I haven't got my mother's purse finished, which was what I wished. Some of our party are broken up already, Mr. Dawson and Mr. Gandon being gone. I cannot say I regret them very much. I haven't yet thanked you for your letter. You see you need never be under apprehensions about me, for you always get my letters sooner or later, and the delay is not my fault.

[1] James Gandon, the architect of "The Four Courts," Dublin, etc.

I am delighted to find that you really feel cheerful and in good spirits this winter, for you know nothing can give me greater pleasure, whether I am present or not, as I partake of it even at this distance. I got a letter by the same post from Lady Jane, and by its coming so soon after her last, I imagined she had heard from Lord Macartney, and was rather disappointed at not finding it so; however, I hope the time is not very distant. I shall get you to wish her everything she can desire in the new year, as I think it's hardly worth while to write to her on purpose when she has had so many of my scrawls lately.

I suppose the intelligence you send to Miss Herbert, or at least part of it, relates to what I mention in the former part of this letter, so you will see that her correspondents take care to inform her of scandal sooner than you do. She will have the pen to say some impertinent thing or other, which I refuse to do. [By Miss Herbert.] ("She hopes Lady Macartney won't write to her, as she said she would, as she much fears she shall be affronted, for what does people think she stays all this time in Ireland for but to take care and nurse me, and not to eat potatoes and drink whiskey. She will be off the moment she is affronted, and she is very, very touchy. A merry Xmas party, we all wish you a Happy New Year. If Lady Carlow has not told you the Xmas party, I will. A Methodist parson, a painter, a builder. Two fine beaus were expected, but never arrived, alas!")

Did you ever see such a saucy creature? And she has had the impudence to write the beginning of her paragraph in my name, too! However, I hope you perceive the difference of her scrawl from my fine hand, besides the style.

I am so impatient for the new year that I find it impossible to add any more as I must go to bed, so God bless you.—Ever your   C. CARLOW.

CHAPTER V

DURING the visit of Lord and Lady Carlow to Dalkeith the preceding summer the Duke of Buccleuch and his sister had promised to pay them a return visit in Dublin, where the Duke was anxious to see his old friend and schoolfellow, Lord Carlisle, who was now Lord-Lieutenant. This project was duly carried out, and gave rise to Lady Frances Scott writing a charming series of letters from Ireland, for which Lady Louisa Stuart added the *Notes* mentioned before.

LADY LOUISA STUART from LADY CARLOW

Thursday. Night, 10th January 1782.

AFTER waiting very near a fortnight I was at last regaled with a long letter written between you and Lady Jane which came by last night's post ; both Miss Herbert and I were delighted with it, as you must have been in good spirits when it was wrote, and we only regretted that we were not with you that evening laughing in person at all the strange, vulgar manners of your cousins, the simplicity of Mary Last,[1] and the significant looks and words of Lady Mary, which I perfectly comprehended by the strokes you put, being

[1] Lady Jane Macartney's maid.

so well used to her way.   As to the Leslies, I can't
help being out of patience with them, and more so with
Lord Macartney for saddling his poor wife with such
trumpery people, which I am sure they must be, for
there is none even of my Portarlington neighbours
that are half as vulgar as you describe them, and I call
Miss Herbert to witness if she has ever heard any of
them make use of such vulgar language excepting a
physician who dined here one day, and diverted her
with saying 'at all at all.'   I have not mentioned a
word of this to Miss Dawson, that there may be no
fear of its getting back to them, but she disclaims any
further acquaintance with them than what arose from
being at school with her, and she always says he is the
greatest fool that ever was, and is violently henpecked.
I shall be delighted to hear that they are tired of
London, or rather that their money will hold out no
longer, for I fancy that will happen first.   Your description of Mary Last is very good, but I don't think
I should (if I was Lady Jane) suffer her to be dosed
by Atkinson when a little more scrubbing and washing
is a more effectual remedy.   I should set her to all
the hard work in the house, for I suppose it is not
having enough to do that has put all these whims into
her head, but pray don't let her take that nasty old
Johnson [1] again—anything is better than her.   My
foolish Robe would do better than that—not that I
mean to recommend her.   We approve very much of
the society of good housewives.   I will subscribe old
Mrs. Beck and Robe, and Miss Herbert her nasty old

[1] Lady Macartney's old maid, whom she sent back from the West Indies.

Mother Cole with pleasure. Miss Dawson begs to add Mrs. Crow. If gentlemen are admitted, we beg old Edward may be one of the party. [By Miss Herbert.] ("Our little boy is the handsomest, jollyest little fellow possible, so good-humoured, it would do you good to see him; there ain't such another in the Queen's County! Oh no! though I say it that should not say it.

We are sorry to hear, for your sake, that the Duchess and Lady Frances are not to be in town this winter, so says Lady Pembroke, who has wrote at last to Georgy. Lady Aldborough is arrived, and very troublesome. She insists on her going to Belan to be eat up with fleas. We don't know how to get out of the scrape.")

Friday Night.

[Lady Carlow continues.] We were all rejoicing yesterday at the sight of a little frost, but it's all gone again, and we have exchanged it for a violent storm, as usual; however, it's a little abated to-night, so I hope to sleep in peace, but we had no letters.

Monday Night, 14th January 1782.

HERE are we still, poor, miserable creatures, without pacquets, the winds are so perverse. We always reckon it very unfortunate when it hinders the Sunday letters from coming, as we have no post again till Wednesday, so you see our patience is tried as well as yours sometimes. We are beginning to think of Dublin again, for the weather is so disagreeable, there is nothing to induce us to prolong our stay here, and though I don't expect to be confined till March, yet I have several things that I could wish settled, such as seeing the man who is to attend me, and having a little conversation with the nurse, also buying several articles of linen for the child, as this one has taken care to wear out a great many that might have done for another.   I think I need make no excuses for the encomiums upon the little boy in the former sheet, as you will see by the hand whose production it is, though it's wrote in my name.   I am wishing every day I could show him to you, he improves so much.   I am sure you would like him better than the generality of your nephews.   By the way, do you know anything of poor little Corbett this Xmas? I regret that he has the mortification of staying at school in the holidays, though he generally behaves so ill to Lady Jane that I don't like to ask her to have him home.   I wish when you see him you would make him write me a letter in his own words, and you could enclose it to me.

We have got rid of all our Xmas party at present, and I am in hopes the rest we expected have found better entertainment elsewhere, for I had much rather be without their company.   I intend to be more comfortable than I have been when I next come to this place, for, by the persuasions of Miss Herbert, I am going to do up a small room above stairs for my sanctum sanctorum, in which I intend to have everything to myself, and retire to it to paint, read, or write, let who will be in the house. In the first place I had it painted, part of which I was obliged to do myself, and I have got a very pretty white spotted paper with a glazed ground for four-

pence a yard (so it won't ruin me), and a festoon of
roses in orange colour and green to go round the top,
with a border of some of Adam's patterns to go down
the seams.   Miss H. is all impatience to see me
settled in it, but I don't know if I shall be able to get
it done before we go, the people are so slow and
indolent.

Dublin, Saturday Night, 16th March 1782.

I AM only going to write you a few lines, my dear
Louisa, as I have very little time, and (as you say)
nothing to tell you that you will care for. I have
been out every night this week, so ought to have been
amused, but I cannot say a crowd of strangers does
amuse me, as it does Lady Frances; you can't imagine
how she keeps it up! She has dinners, suppers, and
two or three assemblies for every day, so that I see
very little more of her than if I met her in public in
London, and sometimes when I am to carry her home,
and propose going at twelve, which I think sufficiently
late, she thinks too early. She has now got a violent
cold with all her raking, and has entirely lost her voice,
but that makes no difference; in short, you never saw
her in such spirits, and I really believe it is from the
novelty of being made so much of, after spending so
much of her life where she has been neglected and
mortified. This is not to be wondered at, for flattery
and attention certainly have great charms, and she has
it to a degree we have no notion of showing to anybody in England, let them be foreigners of ever so
high a rank. Miss Herbert and she are delightful
about their engagements, as they compare notes every

morning at breakfast, and Lady Frances crows over the former, who does envy balls a little, for you must know she is a great dancer here. I tell her I shall report what a young miss she is grown in Ireland, for she has commenced wearing feathers and gauze sleeves. I assure you we have plenty of engagements for next week ; on Monday a dinner at Mrs. Gardiner's, and on Tuesday she and Lady Frances go with the Dowager Duchess of Leinster to dine at Castletown, at Mr. Conolly's, and return in the evening for a ball at Mrs. O'Neil's, but, alas! it's only Lady Frances that has that happiness. We are obliged to be contented with an assembly at Lady Ely's ; then on Wednesday we have another ball at Mrs. Trench's, which I don't think I shall grace with my presence, as it is a great way off, and it being a small house, I don't think it fair to take up room when I am of no use. On Thursday we have two balls, and on Friday two concerts, so I think we shall do pretty well.

The Carlows, as will have been perceived, were now arrived in Dublin, and settled in a house in Merrion Street, which they had taken for the winter. Miss Herbert was still with them, and also Lady Frances Scott. It may be interesting to add here another quotation from Lady Louisa's notes, *àpropos* of the visit to Castletown mentioned above : " The Dowager Duchess of Leinster and Lady Louisa Conolly were sisters of the Duke of Richmond. The former had been the most celebrated beauty of her time, the Venus of Horace Walpole's poem—

> " ' Ten Queens of beauty sure I see,
> Yet sure the true is Emily.'

She married, secondly, Mr. Ogilvie, the tutor of her younger sons. Lady Louisa had no beauty, but a countenance expressing such benevolence and goodness, that she won your heart at first sight. The then Duke of Leinster's wife had been a Miss St. George."

The Carlows' eldest daughter and second child was born in Dublin on 21st March 1782, and was christened Caroline Elizabeth. She afterwards married Sir Henry Parnell, created first Lord Congleton. Miss Herbert reports the great event to Lady Louisa as follows :—

LADY LOUISA STUART from MISS HERBERT

Friday Evening.

DEAR LADY LOUISA—Lady Frances would not let me write yesterday, as *she* chose to have the pleasure of notifying the happy event to you. Nothing could be better than Lady Carlow was—only half an hour in labour. She awoke at six in the morning, and sent for my maid to comb the powder out of her hair, and had hardly time to put on her night-cap before she was delivered; and I was in luck and heard none of the bustle till my maid came and told me at 7 o'clock, and I would not believe her. She is perfectly well to-day, and had a good night, and seems in fine spirits. We keep her very quiet, and the little girl is quite well, has sucked, and likes it very much. The nurses assure me that it's very like Lady Carlow and has blue eyes. I don't think it so pretty as my little dear John was when he was born. He already looks better for being weaned, and got a little collour, and is at this moment in violent spirits. He is delighted to kiss his little sister. You may depend on hearing every day how Lady Carlow goes on, and we nurse her as well as ever you could do. Last night Lord Carlow, Lady Frances, and I went to a very agreeable ball at Lord Ely's. I did everything that was to be done, danced, played cards, and supt, left Lady Frances there at half-past three o'clock; maybe she breakfasted there, for it's a custom here to end with a breakfast. Lord and Lady Carlisle danced one dance—not together. Lady Carlisle danced with the greatest man that would dance, which was Lord Antrim, as the Dukes of Buccleuch and Leinster did not dance. We outdo you in dissipation all to nothing, and Lady Frances talks of London as retirement. Lady Frances injoys it all very much. I tire of continual crowds of uninteresting faces.

We talk of England about the end of April, after Lady Carlow's month's up. She desires her love to you, and has received your last letter this morning, and begs you'll write on.—Yours most affectionately,

G. H.

——

The following letter is from Miss Herbert, describing a ball at the Castle. Lady Ann Leveson, who did hostess on this occasion, was the third daughter of the second Earl Gower, and a sister of Lady Carlisle. She married in 1784 the Rev. and Hon. E. Vernon-Harcourt, Archbishop of York, and lived till 1832.

LADY LOUISA STUART from MISS HERBERT

Dublin, 11th April 1782.

WE were most graciously received at the Castle on Friday. It was very full, and a great many

Lady Mary Humes.   Last night was the ball, opened
by Lady Ann Levison.   Miss H. did not dance.   We
lose the great Mr. Storer[1] to-morrow.   Alas! nothing
can be so gay as Dublin is—the Castle twice a week,
the opera twice a week, with plays, assemblies, and
suppers to fill up the time.   Every assembly ends
with a supper.   We were engaged to the opera and
after to somebody's to supper and a ball this evening,
which was put off, so we cut the opera and sent our
maids to the play, and I have the honour of writing to
you, which I hope will arrive safely in less than a
month, but don't grumble if it should not.   Lady
Carlow is quite well and in spirits, and seems to like
Dublin now better than ever she did.   Lord C. is
gone to the opera; it's very dear, 11s. 4½d., and only
two acts, but that's quite enough for me.   Everything
is dear.   I hope to have a very smart cap and blue
flowers.   Will you be so good as to ask how Lady
Charlotte Herbert does, as I heard she had not been
well, and I have not heard from Lady Pembroke this
age?   You will think this stupid, but we are even with
you, and sometimes, not always, think yours stupid.
Mrs. Chapman has not wrote to me lately.   I don't
know that I know anybody as she has wrote to, not
one of the Lady Mary Humes; indeed, the beaus
admired me very much, and I flirted with a great many
last night.   How can I help it ?

Dublin, 11th, 1782.

N.B.—Miss H. begs to inform Lady Louisa, for
the sake of her character, that she has one poor little

[1] See *ante*, p. 31.

brown tale (*sic.*) in her cap which Lady Carlow laughs at—she owns something like sleeves, but not hanging sleeves. Lady Frances is now gone to the opera, and then to an assembly at Lady De Vesci's to a supper. I had the advantage the other day of Lady Frances, and had a private puppet show of my own, and nobody else invited. She likes Ireland so well, and Ireland likes her, that she is in no hurry to leave it, and won't talk on that subject, so don't expect us this age. I never can come, I am afraid, as the bankers broke with my Irish Tontine, so old Mother Cole and I meet in jail.

Lady Carlow won't let me write any longer, so adieu.

Miss Herbert accompanied Lady Frances Scott to England the end of April, and we have no more tidings of Lady Carlow till we find her staying with her parents at Luton in the following July.

———

LADY CARLOW from LADY LOUISA STUART

Monday Night [1782 ?]

YOUR letter has given me a great deal of unexpected pleasure, for I gave up all hopes of hearing from you, and I am quite happy to think you could remember me in the midst of all your amusements and hurries. I do indeed wish myself with you, yet believe me sincere when I say it is really more for the sake of being with *you*, than of seeing the sea and the shipping, though I should like that extremely too. Do you know that the

Duchess [of Buccleuch] and Lady Frances [Scott] are upon the same expedition? They set out on Friday, after going in mask to Lady Derby's the night before, and they were to lie at a house of Mr. Leyte's, two or three miles from Portsmouth. This is what my mother tells me, and she says too that Lady Mary Coke is fire and fury against them, as she had proposed belonging to the party, but they seemed to give up all thoughts of it, and so went off suddenly, and left her in the lurch. I hope you have met with them by this time. We went to the R. A. Exhibition, where I think I saw no one picture I liked, and to two or three shops. This is all I have to relate, so you see we are dismal enough, and indeed I feel so little myself, and you are not within reach, that I hate the thoughts of the summer more than ever. This is a delightful, fine warm night: I see you walking on the sea-shore, the ships tossing, and the moon (but I fear there is none) glittering on the water. Pray bring yourself safe back, and meet with no accidents either by sea or land.

CHAPTER VI

THE letters in the present chapter from Lady Bute reveal a charming character, but are quite wanting in the epistolary talent so conspicuous both in her mother, Lady Mary Wortley Montagu, and in her own daughters. Lady Louisa had gone north on a series of visits which gave rise to graphic descriptions of the places and persons with whom she came in contact. The Duchess of Buccleuch so often mentioned in these letters was the daughter and heiress of the last Duke of Montagu, and though looked on with considerable awe by most of her own family, won a large share of the admiration and affection of her friends, and seems to have merited the cognomen given to her by Lady Ailesbury of " Pure Gold."

In the preceding May, Lady Frances Scott, the Duke's sister, had married Mr. Douglas[1] as his second wife, and Lady Louisa was much interested in seeing the family places of Bothwell and Douglas, the former of which she often revisited.

[1] See *ante*, p. 140.

MARY, COUNTESS OF BUTE.

MARY, COUNTESS OF BUTE.

LADY LOUISA STUART from LADY BUTE

Luton Park, 11th July 1783.

I AM better than my word, my dear Louisa, for as I think it long since I saw you, I judge you may be also a little impatient to know how we do. I have pity'd you extreamly for travelling in such sultry weather. I was almost overcome with the heat in coming here yesterday, and even this place is so hot I have not been able to go out of the house; the evening was closer and hotter than the day, last night, with thunder and lightning, from which we have reaped no benefit, it being full as hot to-day. I really hope you have travelled in the night, and slept in the day.

Lady Carlow is to come here on Monday, and when she goes, Lady Macartney takes her place. James and Mrs. Stuart are to come soon after. William is in good health and drank tea with us yesterday. We find the trees blighted, the flowers decayed, and this place not at all in beauty. I am, according to custom, wishing for rain, but for nothing more at present than to hear you are got safe and well to the end of your journey and are spending your time agreeably. I am sure you would not do so here, tho' I confess you bear solitude better than most people. Your dear father sends his blessing, to which I will at present only add the fondest wishes of your affectionate mother and faithful friend,   M. W. BUTE.

Comp'ts in abundance to all you are with.

Luton Park, 15th July 1783.

AS I was better than I promised, my dear Louisa, in writing on Friday, I go on sending letters oftener than you had any reason to expect, my lazyness considered.   Lady Carlow came here yesterday in perfect health, and does not complain of heat half so much as I do, notwithstanding her situation.   The Abbé Grant[1] and Mr. Dalton are also here, but do not add greatly to our amusement, tho' they try who shall tell us the longest storys of Rome, the Pope, the Cardinals, and the travellers they have met abroad.   William is here every day and seems very well.   The weather is compleatly disagreeable, being very hot with a high north-easterly wind and fog that blights everything, and makes the evenings quite unpleasant; I have therefore hardly stirred out of the house.   I long to hear from you, my dear child, and assure you I expect accounts of everything you see and hear; you shall have my remarks on your travels in answer.   At present I really want a subject, and shall add no more to this epistle but that I am ever, my dear child, your most affectionate mother,   M. W. BUTE.

Your dear father is well and sends his blessing.

[1] The Abbé (Peter) Grant, an old friend of the Bute family, as already mentioned, had just returned from Rome, where he had lived and been well known to every English visitor for nearly fifty years.   He intended to spend his few remaining years in his native country, but finding the climate too severe he went back to Italy in 1784.   His brother was head of the college at Douay.   See Lady Mary Wortley Montagu's *Letters*, vol. ii. p. 238, and Sir W. Fraser's *The Grants*, where several interesting letters from the genial old man are printed.

Luton Park, 20th July 1783.

MY DEAR DAUGHTER—I am much obliged to you for your two letters, and am very glad to find your journey was less unpleasant than I imagined the great heat would have rendered it. Tho' you seem to think you shall be too much hurry'd at Edinburgh, I daresay you will be amused with the new scene and all the gaiety the races will occasion. I told you in my last that Lady Carlow was here in perfect health. I don't know whether I mentioned Abbé Grant and Mr. Dalton; the first is very entertaining from the variety of anecdotes he has to tell of all the English, Scotch, and Irish that have visited Rome for these forty years; the latter is so tiresome that we are out of all patience with him. Your dear father is well, as is William[1] also, who generally comes every other day and gave an excellent sermon this morning. As to myself I was quite overcome with the heat the first day I came here, and the day after had some blood taken away which immediately relieved me, and I have been perfectly well ever since, but not so stout as Lady Carlow, who, big as she is, can walk much more than I can. We had yesterday Mrs. Walsingham[2] and her daughter at dinner, who, as you may suppose, commended the pictures, etc., in the most proper and elegant terms, but all her comp'ts did not compensate the fatigue of walking about with her and shewing the tombs!

I should guess that Lady Ruthven[3] would leave

---

[1] He held the living of Luton at this time.
[2] See *ante*, p. 68.
[3] Lord Bute's sister, Anne, had married Lord Ruthven, who died in July 1783.

Edinburgh immediately; if she refuses, then I beg you would shew all the attention in your power. My dear child need not regret the leaving me on account of the solitude of this place; I shall seldom be alone, and I am glad you have an opportunity of seeing the sights of the world and a greater variety of company, as I think it of great advantage to young people; the mind is enlarged and divested of the prejudices that are commonly contracted by living in a small circle. I flatter myself your health and spirits will also be improved, and of course you will be every day more comfortable.

Lady Macartney comes to-morrow, and I believe Lady Carlow goes home the next day. I shall have the less regret at parting with her, as I think she grows too big to be anywhere but in her own house. Adieu, my dear Louisa. Your father's blessing with the best wishes of your affectionate mother,   M. W. BUTE.

Pray continue the account of your life and conversation, as it amuses me extreamly.

Luton Park, 25th July.

MY DEAR LOUISA—I yesterday received your entertaining letter of the 19th, and can easily conceive that the hurry at Edinburgh was more fatiguing than your journey. However, I daresay you was amused, altho' bewildered with the variety. We have had the same weather you describe till Sunday, when a most tremendous storm of thunder, lightning, and rain cleared the air, and it has since been extreamly pleasant (by the way I now recollect I told you this before, having wrote on Sunday or Monday). Lady Macartney leaves here in good health and in tolerable spirits. Lady Carlow went on Tuesday morn. Lady M. Coke came that day and staid till this morning. Abbé Grant and she have had all the conversation to themselves; she has set him right in many particulars relating to Italy, which he submitted to with great patience and politeness. I have now told all the news of this place, except the most material, that of your dear father being perfectly well.

You are certainly right to accept of Lord Stonefield's[1] civility, tho', as I suppose none of the inhabitants of Dalkeith chooses to be of your party, you will be at a loss to have any company, except you take my old friend Mrs. Mure and her daughter. I can imagine Mrs. Mure to be what you describe, a true gossip in her own circle. However, you can want no information relating to Edinburgh, its scandal, fashions, or partys, that she cannot supply.

It is indeed provoking that the fog should obstruct the sight of so many fine views as there really is about Edinburgh: when you see the hills you will find they resemble those of Derbyshire we see at Wharncliffe. I shall send you no account of marriages, etc., as I know Lady Greenwich is a constant correspondent, and I daresay omits no news of that sort, but one I will mention, which is Lord Denbigh's[2]

[1] See *ante*, p. 137.
[2] Sixth Earl. His second wife was the widow of Sir Charles Halford, Bart., and daughter of Mr. Farnham of Quorndon.

getting a rich widow to marry him; he is certainly a better judge of the sex than I am, having always said he should sell the title of Countess for a good price, whereas I thought it not possible than anything above a beggar to accept of it with all the incumbrances belonging to it. I admire the Duchess of Hamilton's behaviour, and hope they will really visit Lady Frances and Mr. Douglas when they are settled at Bothwell, putting an end to all animositys.[1] I don't know when Lady Macartney goes, but suppose it will be about the time that James and Mrs. Stuart come, which I understood is to be the first of August; you may therefore make yourself easy with regard to my being alone, and I tell you again and for the last time I shall mention the subject, that I am much better pleased with your being amused for a time than to have you here; not that I am impatient to be rid of you altogether, both your company and correspondence being a very great pleasure to your affectionate mother,

M. W. BUTE.

Your father's blessing.

Luton Park, 31st July 1783.

MY DEAR DAUGHTER—I was very stupid to forget sending you in my last directions for planting the old roots of trees, which is nothing more than cutting off the branches to about the height of three feet and taking up the root as entire as possible (hazle, maple, ash, thorns or sallows will all do), and

---

[1] Caused by the great law-suit already noted. See *ante*, p. 140.

planting them in holes dug for them, covering in the earth upon the roots either in spring or autumn. As this will not arrive till you have left Dalkeith it may serve for part of a letter to the Duchess.

And now, my dear, I thank you for your letter of the 24th, which entertained Lady Macartney and I extreamly, and the more I think, by your manner of writing you are not at all tired of the company or the place you are in. Bothwell Castle will be a new scene, and I suppose bring you acquainted with many more strangers. I take for granted you will soon be visited by the Duke and Duchess of Buccleuch, which will add greatly to your pleasure. I wish the Duke and Duchess of Hamilton may visit Lady Frances, as it will give you an opportunity of seeing their place.

I daresay Lord Stonefield's civilitys distract you, but am very glad you accepted them. Your account of Lord Breadalbane agrees with Abbé Grant's, who commends him very much : by the by, he is still here, and I can assure you entertains us very much. I don't believe Lady Macartney has laughed so much this twelvemonth as she has done since she came here at his ridiculous storys and jokes. She stays with me till Monday. James and his wife are to come to-morrow, if not prevented for a day or two by their attendance on Lord Eglinton's wedding. Lady Carlow went to Tunbridge for a day or two to Mrs. Legge, but returns to Hampton this day. Lady M. Lowther is to come here when the Stuarts go away ; you therefore see I am not likely to be much alone, but really, my dear Louisa, there would be no punishment if I was, the weather is so fine. I am much abroad, and your dear father is, I think, better than I have seen him for many years. I daresay, my dear child, you are glad to hear from me often, but as you know me to be a very lazy correspondent, you must only blame my idleness if I happen to be longer than usual without writing, rememb'ring that I am always your most affectionate mother,   M. W. BUTE.

Your dear father's blessing with Lady M.'s comp'ts and love.

Pray say all that is proper to Lady F. etc.

———

The castle of Bothwell was, from its grandeur, position, and strength, one of the most important of Scottish fortresses, and of its ruins enough remains to testify to its ancient reputation.

The keep, a cylindrical tower 90 feet in height, and 65 feet in diameter, suggests in its dimensions, and to some extent in its architecture, the celebrated Keep of Coucy, from which its design is thought to have been derived.

It was founded in the thirteenth century by a Lord of Moray, and was afterwards acquired by Archibald Douglas, Earl of Angus, in exchange for Hermitage and other property, and it has descended, with other possessions of the House of Douglas, to the Earl of Home, their heir of line.

Besides a large fragment of the keep and a curtain wall of unusual height and thickness, it contains traces of a baronial hall and a chapel, both in dimensions and decoration such as might be expected in the chief seat of the house of Angus. It is, however, a mere ruin, and has long been deserted for a modern house, built at no great distance, and in all respects a contrast to the castle.

LADY BUTE from LADY LOUISA STUART

Bothwell Castle, 5th August 1783.[1]

VERY little or rather nothing worth mentioning has passed, my dear mother, since I concluded my last. The retirement in which we live, the silence of the place, and perhaps the situation (upon a ridge), almost reminds me of your cottage in Yorkshire, though the view there is more extensive, and in all respects but one much fairer and the mansion something less. This house consists of a body and two wings; the first (very old and tottering) contains only, besides servants' and children's rooms, three spare bedrooms and one dressing-closet, which as the state apartment falls to my share; in one of the last are the offices; and in the other (built by the Duke or Duchess of Douglas) a large dining-room and a moderate sized drawing-room below stairs, and above, an apartment for themselves. This is the sum total, so you will not wonder that Mr. D. should be impatient to build. His design, I find, is to leave the wings standing, which, of course, will contract and to some degree embarrass his plan, but considerably lessen the expense of his undertaking, and when completed will be more a comfortable living house than by any means a fine one. The place is rough and ill kept, but perhaps loses none of its beauty by that circumstance; it looks immediately down a steep bank upon the fine windings of the river Clyde, overhung on each side by

[1] Lady Louisa's letters during the Scotch visit are not accessible previous to this date.

hills covered with wood, and (at a stone's throw from
the house) by the beautiful remains of the old castle,
which appears most noble when seen first from the
opposite shore, standing upon a high woody bank,
and half encompassed by the river. It has been a
great pile of building, parts apparently more ancient
than the rest, and it is easy to distinguish the chapel
and the great hall, now containing a little grove of trees,
that threaten to weigh down a vault that supports them,
and hasten the fall of the edifice. In one large and
very high tower there remains entire a steep winding
staircase, which leads you to the very top, and up it
you may be sure I have scrambled. I was repaid by
a lovely prospect of the river, and a fine rich enclosed
country, many miles in extent, the steeples of Glasgow
very visible, and I suppose many other objects in clear
weather. Directly fronting Bothwell stands Blantyre
Castle, another but a much smaller ruin, rising from
amongst wood, and looking infinitely higher than it
is, because built upon a perpendicular rock of its own
red colour, which is not to be distinguished from it.
You may imagine what the effect of such ornaments
must be, bordering such a river. Blantyre is called a
castle, but said to have been a priory, and according to
custom, the country people believe in a subterraneous
passage between it and the other under the bed of the
Clyde. We have taken several rambles under Mr.
Douglas's direction, to the great detriment of our
shoes and petticoats, for the climate of this country
you know is wet, and the soil a stiff clay, which can
never be otherwise ; nor does the country produce

gravels or anything fit to make walks except the river sand. We ferry over in a boat, but can do no more, as it is seldom free from stones for a hundred yards together; if it were, it would be delightful to row down it. There are marks of the height to which it has risen at different times, some very surprising, and whenever this happens I need not say it tears down its banks and destroys the paths made by its side— one reason why they are in a rough condition. The woods are all upon declivities, and beautiful to the eye, and the plantations healthy and thriving, but we have not many good single trees. The best are oaks. No Duke H[amilton] has yet appeared at these gates, nor is there any sign that he will—I fancy his Grace is wiser when drunk than when sober, as he promised it to the Ad. ! [Admiral?] at a great dinner in the race week, when they were very *notorious*, as Mrs. Mure says. Probably the Ad.'s persuasions prevailed upon him at the time, and his pride has risen since to prevent them from taking effect.

Wednesday the 6th.

Our solitude is interrupted to-day by Lady E. Home [1] and Miss Clementina Elphinstone,[2] who come from Hamilton full of all its gaieties and pleasures, and in love with both Duke and Duchess, but especially the latter. They have had a very large company at their races (all lodged in the house), abundance of beaux, and dancing every night. The

---

[1] Lady Eleanor, daughter of the ninth Earl of Home, afterwards wife of Colonel Thomas Dundas. What an ideal marriage this was may be read in Mrs. Dundas's *Memoirs of Dundas of Fingask*, privately printed in 1891.

[2] Daughter of tenth Lord Elphinstone, afterwards Lady Perth.

Duke and Mr. Baird rid their own horses. The Duke won the match, etc. etc. etc. The only person *déplacé* was Lord Morton, who indeed, by all accounts, appears to be an insupportable animal; they describe him as herding altogether with the women, not out of gallantry, but as if he had been a woman himself, for the pleasure of showing . . .

[Here the letter breaks off.]

LADY LOUISA STUART from LADY BUTE

Luton Park, 11th August 1783.

I THANK you, my dear Louisa, for your entertaining letter from Bothwell Castle. I daresay I should join in the opinion you give of Hopetoun House and Craigie Hall. I have always heard the former described as one of those magnificent places, made by dint of expense for the admiration of strangers, and very little calculated for the comfort of the inhabitants.

I can easily imagine the first days spent at Bothwell Castle must have dampt the spirits of all the party,[1] but hope a short time will accustom you to the present state of affairs, and banish the retrospective thoughts that are of no avail. However, for the sake of the children, I wish the impression may never be worn out either in the husband or wife, and that any new-comers may only hold their proper place in the family. Mr. and Mrs. Stuart and Mr. Martin are here. Lady Mary Lowther is expected in a day or two, who, I suppose, will stay till Lord and Lady

---

[1] This alludes to the death of Lady Lucy, the first wife of Mr. Douglas, and the great friend of Lady Frances and Lady Louisa.

Mountstuart come, that is till about the last week of this month. Lady Macartney has offered to come back, but I shall not allow it, till Lord Carlow's return from Ireland. As our fine weather has continued the time passes on very well, your dear father being really better both in health and spirits than I have seen him for many years. We had very hot weather the Saturday you mention, but it has since been moderate, not so much fog, and now and then a shower of rain, but not enough to stop the harvest, which is going on successfully and promises a great crop. The fruit is also good, tho' not in such plenty as I have seen it, but enough to satisfy me, which you know a little will not do.

I am very glad you wrote to Lady Ruthven, as she seems to take it kindly. Lady Betty's letter to me is full of her great affliction, which to say the truth I do not entirely credit. People in general love a melancholy story and to have their particular misfortunes painted in the strongest colours.

Your letters are so well written and your descriptions so lively, I hope you will continue to treat me with them. I can return you no amusement, tho' I flatter myself my letters are welcome, even when they tell you nothing, but that I am well and ever your most affectionate mother,   M. W. BUTE.

Your father's blessing and my comp'ts as usual.

Luton Park, 21st August 1783.

I HAVE to thank you for yours of the 7th and 14th, my dear Louisa. I am delighted with your description of Bothwell, and fancy with you it may resemble Wharn-cliffe, but hope you are in many respects more comfortable than that place is at present. The Duchess [of Buccleuch ?] must be a very agreeable addition to your society, tho' Miss Elphinstone and Lady Eleanor were not, yet the Scots songs must have been a great resource when conversation flagged. I am surprised not to hear you mention going out in a carriage, which I imagine would be good for Lady Frances at present. Pray tell her tho' I do not approve of hurry or fatigue, yet gentle exercise is necessary for her health, and that too much indulgence is as hurtfull in her situation as too little, having always observed the people who move about a good deal (without fatigue) are much better than those who lye upon a couch half the day. I wonder as Glasgow is so near, you have not been to see it.

I have been delighted with the Bishop of Chester's[1] sermons ; there are few so good. I don't know whether I do not prefer them to Blair's, as they are more simple and seem less study'd.

I suppose, as you do, the Duke of Hamilton's pride has got the better of his good intentions of civility to his neighbours ; it seems a matter of small moment to the Duke, and only puts his Grace more in the wrong.

Mr. and Mrs. Stuart went from here last Saturday, when Lady Mary came and is to stay a week longer ; you know conversation never languishes where she is, and as she is now more upon her guard than usual, we go on extreamly well. The weather is now very hot again (after being very cold the beginning of last week)

[1] Dr. Porteous.

with the detestable fog, which is as bad here as you describe it, and no rain or dew, which is good for getting in a very pleantifull harvest, but the grass is burnt and the leaves growing yellow for want of moisture; therefore I am, according to custom, wishing for rain.

I have not very lately heard from Hampton; Lady Macartney has been employed attending Mrs. Hoare's[1] wedding, which was happily concluded on Monday.

James and Mrs. Stuart say they were in the secret of Lord Eglinton's wedding,[2] that her friends were against it, but he believes the lady was dying for love, and he took her partly out of compassion. I am glad you are to go to Loch Lomond, having always had a curiosity to see it, from the accounts I have had. If you are lucky in weather I daresay it will be a very amusing expedition. Your dear father continues in perfect health and good spirits, desiring me to join his blessing to that of your most affectionate mother,

M. W. BUTE.

Always remember my compliments.

Luton Park, 29th August 1783.

I HAVE received my dear daughter's letter of the 22nd, and am sorry to find this extraordinary weather seems to prevent your enjoying the beautys you are surrounded with. I had imagined Glasgow would have appeared to more advantage in your eyes, but find

---

[1] Richard Colt Hoare, eldest son of Rich. Hoare, Esq., of Barn Elms, married Hester Lyttelton, eldest daughter of Lord Westcott of Hasley Park, Worcestershire, on 18th August 1783.

[2] Archibald, eleventh Earl, married, as his second wife, Frances, daughter of Sir W. Twisden, 9th August 1783.

you saw little of the environs or the boats of the Clyde ; the meteor you mention was certainly very remarkable, and 'tis wonderful we did not see it, having never shut the shutters of the windows during the hot weather, and we were all in the drawing-room at the time it was visible in this neighbourhood.   Lady Macartney writes me word she saw it on Ham Common, which she happened to pass that night from Mrs. Hoare's wedding and entertainment.   She and Lady Carlow are both well, and now expect Lord Carlow in a few days. Lord and Lady Mountstuart came here on Monday last, Mr. Martin a day after, and James is expected today.   Lady M. Lowther was so good to remain here, which adds greatly to the society, especially as I have been confined above stairs since last Sunday.   You will be much surprised, my dear Louisa, when I tell you why.   A regular fit of the gout, a distemper you have so often heard me say I thought I could never have reason to apprehend, but it has pleased Providence to punish my presumption and afflict me with this distemper (perhaps in its great mercy and has prevented something worse).   I found my right foot swelled and red on Sunday morning when I awaked, and was lame all that and the next day ; on Monday night the pain increased so considerably I had no sleep, my foot intolerably sore and inflamed, since which I have had less pain, but great heat and uneasiness (though not sufficient to hinder my sleeping at night) ; and here I am lying on a couch, my foot wrapped in flannel, and wheeled from one room to another, unable to set my foot to the ground, perfectly well in every other respect, and very thankful (since it pleases God I should have the gout) that I have it so favourably. When I shall be able to get downstairs I don't know, but I believe we shall remove to London very soon after, as I shall wish to know what precautions I ought to take to prevent very frequent returns. The company assembles in my dressing-room for tea and spend the evening with me very cheerfully, therefore as nobody here is uneasy about me, I beg you will not be so, my dear Louisa. Old age must be attended with infirmity, and they all tell me this will rather prolong than shorten my life. I don't know whether I should have given you this detail, but thought it possible you might hear I was ill, and would be less alarmed if you knew the whole truth ; this long story has filled my paper, and only leaves me room to tell you I send a letter from Mrs. Charles, whom we have had a very good account of. Adieu, my dear child. I hope you will have good weather for your races, and Loch Lomond ; and the reflection that you are passing your time pleasantly is the greatest satisfaction to your affectionate mother,

M. W. BUTE.

Your dear father is well and sends his blessing.

Luton Park, 31st August 1783.

I REFLECTED, my dear Louisa, that my last letter might give you some impatience to hear from me again, and therefore take the first post day to tell you that I am much mended. I have got a large shoe on, and put my foot to the ground (though I can't yet walk with ease) ; all pain is I hope over, and so much for a hand-

some first fit of the gout (to use Dr. Fordice's term).
Our company are still here with the addition of James ;
they seem all very cheerful and jolly ; Lady Mary has
been so good to prolong her stay, which is of infinite
use to the society ; you know she is an admirable help
to conversation, and indeed, with great good humour,
endeavours to please everybody.   By a letter from
Lady Macartney I find Lord Carlow was expected at
Hampton last night, which leaves her at liberty to
come here, but I believe I shall not let her have the
trouble of an unnecessary journey, to stay only a few
days, as I think we shall certainly remove in a week
to London, for though I am really and truly in perfect
health at present, I shall wish to have a consultation
how to avoid serious and frequent returns of the gout,
if it can be done without injuring my constitution in
other respects.   Adieu, my dearest daughter.   Let me
hear you are well and passing your time with comfort
and pleasure, which will ever be the greatest satisfaction
to your most affectionate mother,   M. W. Bute.

   Your dear father continues in charming health and
sends his blessing.
                   ————

   The castle of Douglas, the head of the barony of Douglas
Dale, was also for many centuries the chief seat of the great
Scottish family.   It stood upon a mound on the margin of
the Water of Douglas, from which were supplied its moat
and an extensive morass, which added much to the strength
of the fortress.   As a work in masonry it is first mentioned towards the close of the thirteenth century, but the mound probably is part of a much earlier structure.   It was a sharp

thorn in the side of the monks of Melrose, whose pilgrims and visitors to their shrine were thence much molested. The fire of 1307, connected with the famous 'Douglas Larder,' probably left the walls standing. It was then occupied for some years by its English invaders, and restored by them, but finally recovered by the Douglases, of whom the first Earl of Douglas and Mar died here in 1384. But the rising splendour of the House of Douglas probably outgrew the narrow limits of their castle, and they were then only as occasional visitors. It partook of the vicissitudes of the family, and was levelled, more or less partially, by James II. in 1455, though only to reappear with Tantallon as the grant of James the Fourth to George of Douglas in 1488. With the accession of James the Sixth to the English Crown it ceased to have any military value, but was kept up by the family, and in 1700 spoken of as one of the great Scottish Houses, and the seat of the Marquis of Douglas. In 1758-60 it was partially destroyed by fire, and the Duke of Douglas began a larger and more ambitious edifice on the same site from the designs of Adam. This, though continued by his successor, still remains incomplete, but is now one of the seats of the Earl of Home, who represents, as heir of line, the House of Douglas.

The Church of St. Bride, at no great distance from the castle, contains the Douglas monuments, long neglected, but now well cared for.

LADY BUTE from LADY LOUISA STUART

Douglas Castle, 29th August 1783.

WE had as unfavourable a day for the first view of this place as 'tis possible to conceive, alternately thick fog and drizzling rain, but excepting some beautiful country about Hamilton, there was not much to see upon the road (by the way the distance is but two-and-twenty miles), and the scenery here consists of only one high purple hill above another. The house stands in a small valley surrounded by these moors, and is pretty well sheltered by trees. You know I can endure a black mountain with more patience than most people, so upon the whole I do not think the situation so disagreeable as it was described to be, but you must read this with allowances for my particular taste. The house itself is a great piece of a great building which, were it finished, could make a noble appearance. If you will not laugh at me for pretending to draw a plan, I will try to give an idea of it

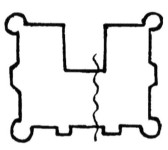

thus. This part only is finished, and contains certainly room enough to lodge a considerable family, but there would be no possibility of completing it to the eye without executing the original plan or one as large. It is built in the Gothick style, of a fine white stone, and the rooms are both good and convenient, but neither painted nor papered, and of course scarcely at all furnished. You may suppose the grounds are not in any sort of keeping, but Mr. Douglas is making very great plantations. We find ourselves in so different a climate that we are well contented to spend our evenings over an excellent fire: the weather indeed has been much cooler ever since I wrote to you last, and a great deal of rain has fallen; yet we are seldom

thoroughly rid of a fog. However, we were lucky
enough to have a fine day (as days go) to see the Falls
of Clyde at Bonnington, with which I was delighted
beyond conception : I shall not attempt to describe a
scene so much above my pen, the finest I have seen
since I came to Scotland (indeed ever in my life),
uniting rock, wood, and water in the utmost perfection

30th.

I had no time to say more of the Falls of Clyde,
being summoned to breakfast, immediately after which
we took flight, the races [1] being at twelve and the
course ten miles off. We had company in the house,
two gentlemen of Angus, a Captain Milne and a Mr.
Graham of Fintry,[2] who (the last I mean) is one of the
most polished and gentlemanlike men I have seen in
Scotland, and besides them Mr. Douglas the younger [3]
(the Duchess's heir, a genteel-looking youth of eighteen)
and Mr. MacConochy, the agent, factor, or whatever
the word is, an old family piece of furniture, rather
than break whose heart we consented to dine at the
ordinary, which he assured us was expected by all the
ladies, and could not be avoided without giving offence.
But when it came to the point behold there was not
a female but ourselves, for not expecting any such
condescension, the few ladies who were upon the course
had taken themselves away, and left us to our great
joy, freed from half of the day's burthen ; the other
half were dining with about a dozen squires of no very

[1] At Lanark.

[2] Robert Graham of Fintry, the
patron of Burns, to whom the poet
inscribed more than one of his

poems. He married a Miss Mylne.

[3] Mr. Campbell Douglas of Rose
Hall, a place left to his father by the
Duchess of Douglas.

charming appearance, but we made short work of it, and escaped long before the horses were ready to carry us away, leaving the good company to get drunk unrestrained. Mr. Douglas, you must know, was steward of the meeting, therefore toast-master at dinner, and we expected to see little more of him or his friends that night ; however, they returned before nine o'clock in a very decent condition, after being elected Burgesses and putting on their hats with much ceremony. The strangers are now gone as well as poor Mr. M'Conochy, who was provoked beyond measure by yesterday's desertion, swore he would have no more to do with races, wished the town at the D——, cursed the Provost for a stupid old blockhead, and used a stronger expression of good-will to the ladies who had proved his promises vain. We flatter ourselves they have all gone to this day's dinner in their best array, for we have had a very comfortable *tête-à-tête*, but the two Mr. Douglases are not come home to tell us the news.

This morning's diversion was near proving very unpleasant ; one of the horses threw his rider (which was a frightful thing to see, but fortunately the jockey escaped unhurt), then raced round the course alone, and coming up first, ran in among the crowd, and trampled down a woman before he was stopped. Lady Frances was going so fast into hystericks, that I never felt much more terrified in my life. I sent the servant for Mr. Douglas, who came up immediately, and assured us that nobody had been the least hurt, and that the woman was quite safe, of which in a little while repeated accounts convinced us, and she got the better of her fright; as you will see, for she is scribbling to you at this moment.

The servant has just told me very bad news of the post; it goes out to-night, but he says my letter will reach England as soon, if it is sent from Bothwell on Tuesday : this really vexes me, for I fear that being ten days without hearing from me will either give you uneasiness or make you think me very careless and inattentive, but I have some hopes that you will sa (*sic*) what I told you of our intended excursions, and guess some part of the true reason. If I had had a notion that the post here was so irregular and went out so seldom, I would have writen a few lines before I came, though with even so small a fund of materials. I am a little disturbed that among the letters just come from Bothwell there is none for me, which obliges me to wait for our return, for we shall have no more sent to us. Adieu for to-night.

LADY LOUISA STUART from LADY BUTE

Luton Park, 7th September 1783.

I WAS in hopes of hearing from you to-day, my dear child, but suppose your expeditions have deranged your correspondence, and know that if you went into the Highlands 'tis not so easy to write from thence. I think my last letter must have made you easy about me, but, however, think you will be glad to have the good account confirmed and know that I am perfectly well and that your dear father is so likewise. We settle in town on Tuesday, partly from my wishing to consider with the doctor how I may safely prevent a gouty habit, and partly from the weather having been rainy and stormy for this last week, which always makes your father impatient to leave the country. Lady Mary[1] went home yesterday. She has been so reasonable, good-humoured, and agreeable, you can't imagine how sorry we were to part with her, and how much I lament her unlucky fate in not having been matched to a tolerable creature. Lady Macartney is to meet me in town, where she would have gone upon business if I had not been there, having no regret at leaving Lady Carlow for a few days (as Lord Carlow is arrived). I hope in my heart I shall send you the best account of her.

Lord and Lady Mountstuart and James are still here, and do not move till we do. Adieu, my dearest Louisa. You shall hear again when I am settled in town.—Ever your most affectionate mother,   M. W. Bute.

Lady Bute from Lady Louisa Stuart

Bothwell, 1st September 1783 [a fragment].

Now, I talk of sermons, I assure you I have heard none here so bad or so ill delivered as our friend Mr. Coppleston's, unless from the Dalkeith minister, who yet is thought a sensible man. We were at Douglas Kirk yesterday. The parish is large and the congregation wonderfully numerous, the church a new building just opened. In the old one[2] I heard there were several curious monuments which I wished to see, but nobody

---

[1] Lady Mary Lowther, whose husband was not 'a tolerable creature.'

[2] The old church of St. Bride, where Lady Lucy, Mr. Douglas's first wife, was buried.

proposing to go there, it struck me that there was a reason which would make it a melancholy visit to us all, therefore I let the subject drop. I always think it a pity when the family seat is not the family residence, and I bemoaned the deserted condition of Douglas, but I confess the two places will bear no comparison for beauty. Adieu, my dearest mother. I have almost wrote myself asleep, and need not wish to lengthen my letter. My duty to my father, and love to Lady Mary, William, etc., and to yourself everything affectionate from your most dutiful and grateful,   L. STUART.

This place is many degrees warmer (than Castle Douglas), but we have all voted for a fire. Count Douglas[1] is with us, *alias* the Cornet, *alias* the Colonel, *alias* big Archy, *alias* young Archy, for he goes by all these names in the family according as he is mentioned by the father or the sons.

Bothwell Castle, 14th September 1783.

LADY HARRIET,[2] Sir Alexander, and Lady Betty [Cunningham] arrived on Thursday, and the same day, unexpectedly, Mr. Shaw Stewart, and a Mr. Macdowal, who seems to have formed himself upon the pattern of Shakespeare's Malvolio and conned state without book.[3] I did not think the house could possibly have held so many people, and it is with much contrivance and inconvenience, but they drank their bottles and did not care. My old acquaintance Lady Harriet has lost a good

---

[1] Mr. Douglas's eldest son, Archibald, was Colonel of the Forfarshire Yeomanry.

[2] Daughter of William, thirteenth Earl of Glencairn, wife of Sir Alexander Don of Newton Don. See *ante*, p. 137.

[3] 'That cons state without book.' —*Twelfth Night*, Act ii. Sc. 3.

many of her charms since I saw her—her outward
charm I mean; she has grown extremely large and
coarse, and looks by no means young, but her pleasing
countenance remains, and her mind does not seem the
worse for wear. Sir A., too, has become fat and clumsy;
his appearance is rather squire-like, yet there is something better within, if I am to believe Lady Harriet's
friends, who tell me he has parts, good-nature, and a
turn to a many little agreeable accomplishments, provided a glass of generous wine, as they call it, does not
come too often in his way. Lady Harriet surprises
me by saying she has been here with the Duchess of
Douglas [1] (who lived here till she died), and I am not
a little entertained with some anecdotes she told me
this morning of the Douglas cause. The Duchess, she
said, after warming herself with a cup or two after
supper, began one night to talk very freely of her own
life and adventures, among other things relating her
marriage with the Duke, their parting reconciliation,
but when she came to the great point, she declared she
always favoured Mr. Douglas; but what gave her first
a desire of supporting him to the utmost was a visit
she made to the Duchess of Argyle, whom she found
lolling in her usual nonchalante manner upon a settee,
and beating the Devil's tattoo with one leg over the
other. Down she set herself opposite, and for some
time tried to enter into conversation, till at last, tired
with the other's careless, contemptuous manner and
impertinent answers. 'I looked her,' said she, 'in the
face and thought to myself! Ay! play awa' with that

[1] Margaret Douglas of Mains married the Duke in 1758, and died 1774.

bonny fit! Play awaw and show your leg, and what a
bonny ankle ye ha! Gif my Duke were alive it micht
cast dust in his e'en, but troth! I am a woman like
yoursell, and I'll gar ye rue your wagging your fute at
me!' So much for old stories.

The oddest new one in these parts of the world is
a whimsical action of Lord Marchmont, who has sent
down his will to be registered (and of course made
public) in the office at Edinburgh, for no visible
reason but to enjoy the vexation he means it should
cause in his lifetime. He leaves his fortune first to
his eldest daughter and her heirs, and then to Lady
Dy Scott and the children the hon. woman (who you
know is old and almost dying) may have by any
husband she shall marry after Mr. Scott's death,
disinheriting all her present family, both sons and
daughters, to the uttermost. Then goes on to entail
it upon every relation he has, and at last ends with a
proviso that if any person to whom, in course of time,
that entail may convey it happens to be of the name
of Scott, they shall be without and for ever incapable
of inheriting any part of his estate. They say it has
had its full effect upon Lady Dy, and shocked her so
cruelly that it is thought she will never recover it.—
Your most dutiful and affectionate   L. S.

Bothwell Castle, 21st September 1783.

I AM interrupted by my maid, who calls me to dress
and tells me ill news—the arrival of a very tiresome,
stupid gentleman—a Mr. Stewart (son to Sir John
Stewart, Mr. D.'s elder brother by the father's side)—

Lady Frances's *dutiful nephew*, which name he got among us for being ready to hand her about the Edinburgh Assembly in every corner where she could possibly put herself. He has a sister to whom the children are made to write, and who, I find, had some share in managing them since their mother's death, but her I have not seen. They say the chief Baron[1] is a shrewd, sensible old gentleman, very eminent in his profession, but his conversation was very like the thing called prosing, and he fondled Peggy his wife, and Peggy his daughter—nay, and other peoples' wives and daughters too—as if they had been babies of two years old, and this in *word* and *deed*. The elder of the Peggies seemed extremely insipid, which Lady Frances tells me is her character, the girl not being above fifteen or sixteen was dumb as a young lady should be. There are two or three families who propose themselves the honour of waiting upon our hosts at the same time with the Dons. I described the house to you when I first came to it. It has not increased since, and it may be diminished before these last arrive (for to-night's hurricane may blow part of it down), therefore you will guess how we can lodge them and their wives in companies. There is, indeed, one more room, strictly speaking, than I reckoned, belonging of right to Mr. Mackonochie, and as he was absent, the Captain was stuffed into it the other night to make room for his betters; but even including that, we can but number three—however, what is impossible

---

[1] Chief Baron of the Scotch Exchequer, a court abolished in the present reign. The office at this time was held by Sir James Montgomery of Macbeth-hill.

is impossible, so they must not come, and I shall be half glad that it so happens, though the Lord and Lady Binning, who are two of the candidates, cannot be called disagreeable visitors. I hear she is wonderfully improved. If I remember right I described the owner of the above-mentioned curious name in the letter I wrote you from Douglas. I have at last learned how to spell it, which I found no easy matter. He was much employed in *the* cause, and spent some years in Paris on that service—did business for the late Duke of Queensberry, is a trustee of his will, in short, a necessary person in the family. He told a story the other day that will hardly tell again, much less succeed on paper, but from knowing the ways of the people I was diverted with it, and so perhaps may you. The Duchess (of Q.), honest woman! took it into her head to carry him with her to Wilton,[1] where she introduced him, etc. But as soon as the first bows and how d'ye-s were past he overheard Lord Pembroke whispering her to ask *what was that gentleman's name.* 'I told you,' she said, 'Mackonochie.' 'God save us, Mac-a-hon-kock-a-kock-a- pray, Madam, how may it be spelt?' 'Why,' said she, 'let me see—I'll tell you this moment, M-a-c-k-o-p-q-r—' and so went on with all the letters of the alphabet, counting them on her fingers, which I can see her doing.

LADY LOUISA STUART from LADY BUTE

London, 11th September 1783.

I WRITE a line, my dear daughter, to tell you I have just received your letter wrote from Douglas,

[1] Probably from her place *Amesbury*, which would be within a drive of Wilton.

along with Lady Frances's, when I had despaired of ever getting it (yours of the 4th having come on Tuesday, which made me imagine you had sent an account of the races). It has arrived in a very tattered condition, tye'd with a bit of packthread, and wrote upon, 'worn out in the mail'; where the mail carry'd it I can't guess, but pray tell Lady Frances that I suppose they opened it, and finding her letter so entertaining, they kept it back in order to take a copy, and that perhaps she will see it in the newspaper in a day or two. However, they were very good to let me have it at last. I shall say nothing more to her till another post, but proceed to tell you I am quite well and settled here, where there is nobody at present but Lady Macartney, who has been in town ever since I came, and spent every day with me. I have been at Hampton this morning and had the happiness of finding Lady Carlow and her little ones in perfect health; she is as well and merry as if nothing had happened.[1] I'm sure, my dear Louisa, this letter with so good an account of myself and her must give you great pleasure; I have therefore no occasion to add more, but to join your dear father's blessing with that of your most affectionate mother, M. W. BUTE.

London, 19th September 1783.

I HAVE another letter to acknowledge, my dear child (since the torn packet), and am much pleased and obliged by the amusing description you send me. I

[1] The birth of a second daughter, christened Louisa, had lately taken place at Hampton. She married, in 1829, the Rev. Walter Davenport-Bromley of Baginton.

am sorry the weather is so perverse, but hope it will not spoil your enjoyment of the views at Loch Lomond; these beauties are well bestowed on those who can enjoy them and compare the difference and poverty of artificial landscapes with the sublime and magnificent scenery of Nature; but after they are sufficiently admired we must descend from the clouds, and confess that a convenient, well-furnish'd apartment warmed by a vulgar coal fire (though not capable of inspiring such lofty ideas) is no small comfort, therefore I wish Lady Frances had more of them at Bothwell that she might not be obliged to refuse the friendly visits of her acquaintances, as I think when one has company in the house 'tis better to have three or four than one pair at a time.　I don't wonder you regret a little the desertion of Douglas Castle, but both are family seats, in which case most people would choose the most beautiful and convenient to reside in, everybody not having your partiality for a black or purple hill.　I am sorry to hear Lady E. Macleod[1] is going to produce, as (if I am not much mistaken) she is likely to find difficultys enough to encounter without the embarras of children.　Lady Frances is in a different situation, and I daresay will not show partialities, though I defy her not to feel them; there is so much of instinct in a mother's affection to her infant (implanted in our natures for the wisest and best reasons) it must get the better of all resolutions.

I have nothing to say of myself but that I am quite

---

[1] Lady Emily Kerr had married, on 26th December 1782, Captain (afterwards General Sir John) Macleod.　See *ante*, p. 13.

well. Lady Mary or Lady Macartney have spent every day with me since I came to London. I have some straggling acquaintances in town, as Mrs. Boughton, Lady F. Medows,[1] and shall shortly have my party at Lady Egremont's, who is coming in a few days. As a proof of my being well I design going to the play on Tuesday and the christening at St. James's[2] on Thursday. Sir W. Fordice is out of town, which has prevented my seeing him, but I really imagine he can prescribe no other remedy than patience. You say you wish yourself here, my dear Louisa; but I assure you it gives me more satisfaction to have you comfortably amused, and your letters are a real pleasure and amusement to me.

I have been this morning at Hampton, where I found Lady Carlow, her little ones, and Lady Macartney in perfect health, and very comfortable. Lord Carlow is going into Dorsetshire to-morrow for shooting. Indeed Lady Carlow is so well she required no further attendance. Lady Macartney is to come to town on Thursday to attend the christening, which may convince you that, notwithstanding her teezing disappointments, she is in very tolerable spirits. Indeed she has an amazing command of herself. I think I have wrote a very handsome letter; 'tis now time to give you your dear father's blessing with that of your affectionate mother,   M. W. BUTE.

I suppose Lord Stonefield thinks he can never be civil enough, and does not suspect how ungratfull you are.

[1] Lady Frances Medows, daughter of Evelyn, first Duke of Kingston, and mother of the first Lord Manvers.

[2] Princess Amelia, daughter of George III., born 7th August 1783, died 2nd November 1810.

London, 22nd September 1783.

I HAVE yours of the 14th, my dear child, and join with you in lamenting the weather, not only that is likely to hinder your amusement, but for the more important reason of spoiling the harvest, which will be a very serious misfortune to Scotland and the north of England, for in Bedfordshire and all round London the corn has been safely lodged three weeks ago, our rainy weather not beginning till that time; it has pour'd almost ever since we came to London; I am therefore not at all sorry to be here. The doctor says (as everybody else does) that I shall live twenty years the longer for having now and then a fit of the gout, and advises very little change in my diet or manner of living, except an additional glass of wine after dinner, but promises the fits shall neither be long or frequent, in which I hope he will keep his word.

I was much diverted with your story of the Duchess of Douglas, which I daresay was literaly true, and have often heard she would never have countenanced Lady Jane[1] or her son if the Duchess of Argyle had not been intolerably impertinent to her. Lord Marchmount is a brute, and therefore not worth mentioning.

To convince you I am quite well I went to the christening, where there was less company than I've usually seen there; some of the Queen's ladies came on that occasion, but flew out of town the next day. Lady Weymouth call'd on me for a moment, and told

---

[1] This refers to Lady Jane Stewart, the Duke of Douglas's sister, and mother of Lady Frances's husband.

me Lady Aylesford[1] lies in again in February, and that they shall all stay in the country till the birthday.

Lady Egremont by what I hear is not much better, but comes to town in a week or ten days; in the meantime I have parties at Mrs. Blodens,[2] or Lady Mary [Lowther] comes and passes the day with me; I have literaly not been one evening alone, so your ladyship's conscience may be at rest.

Your father and I have been at Hampton this morning in a deluge of rain, but had the pleasure of finding Lady Macartney, Lady Carlow, and her babes in perfect health. And now, my dear Louisa, I conclude with your dear father's blessing and the best wishes of your affectionate mother,   M. W. BUTE.

London, 30th September 1783.

I HAVE yours of the 21st, my dear Louisa, and am glad your journey to Buchanan is to take place. If the weather is as fine as we have had it here for this last week, I think you will be greatly rewarded.

I have nothing to tell you from here but that everybody you care for is well; Lady Carlow is so entirely recovered she is no longer worth inquiring after; I wish Lady Frances would follow her example and have as few complaints in the course of the business she is about, but indeed few people are so fortunate.

I am sorry Lady Harriet Don's situation is such, it is not likely she should often quit her own quiet habitation, though perhaps 'tis more for her own advantage

---

[1] Lady Louisa Thynne, daughter of Marquis of Bath. See *ante*, p. 169.
[2] Probably Bladen.

that she should live peaceably at home, especially with the sort of man you describe her husband, who may be respected among his neighbourhood and would be displaced in the great world, which to a sensible woman is a continual mortification ; but after all, I talk often my own feelings, for I daily see women of much better sense than their husbands who are satisfied with their own share of consideration in the world.

I don't wonder that everybody in Scotland is scandalised at the proceedings of the Duke of Queensberry, but I daresay their censure or approbation is alike indifferent to him, and that the gratification of his own fancy (whatever that may happen to be) is the sole motive of all his actions, even his avarice can have no object but the pleasure of possessing so much money, there being no mortal he wishes to leave it to, nor can he hope for the privilege of carrying it to another world.[1]

I intended finishing this epistle yesterday, but went in the morning to your sisters at Hampton (who are both in perfect health, and took Richmond Park on my way, which brought me home so late, I was tired. I saw Charles's little boy, John,[2] who is much grown and improved, and really has now the appearance of health ; little Charles[3] is sent to a clergyman at Hammersmith (a Mr. Taylor, related to Mrs. Stuart), where he will certainly be better taken care of. I'm sure you will be glad to hear that the accounts of Mrs. Stuart's health

---

[1] Of course there was *one* mortal, Mlle. Fagniani, Lady Hertford.

[2] Born 1782, afterwards Captain R.N.

His son was General Stuart of Hobarne.

[3] Charles Stuart, eldest son, afterwards Lord Stuart de Rothesay.

have been much more comfortable for some time ; I find they intend passing their winter at Venice and returning early in the spring. I fancy you will not be sorry to go to Dalkeith, where you may pass some time with the Duchess before Lady Betty summons you. I'm afraid your journey back will not be so pleasant. However, I flatter myself, Abbé Grant's being of the party will make it more tolerable. Adieu, my dear Louisa.—Ever your most affectionate mother,

M. W. Bute.

Your dear father's blessing.

London, 3rd October 1783.

HAVING two letters to thank you for, my dear Louisa, I take up my pen to tell you how much I am delighted with that of the 24th ; you give a charming description of Loch Lomond, and I rejoice with you that you have viewed such delightful scenes.

I can't compliment Lady Frances so far as to say I am sorry to hear the time approaches when I may expect to see my dear child again, but I own I am grieved the parting with you is so painful to her. Pray tell her I am convinced Mme. de Sévigné is in the right when she says it is much better to have disagreeable visitors whose departure is matter of joy. However, I will join with you in wishing you could be in both places at once, or that you could transport your person from one to the other as quickly as your thoughts.

How could you be so ungratefull to poor Mr. Smith to rip up an old story in dispraise of his beloved hero. I wonder after such blasphemy he would show the letter, or the George, or anything belonging to a

Graham.   I have been this morning to breakfast with
Mr. and Mrs. Pitt[1] at Petersham ; Mr. Pitt is as fond of
Loch Lomond as yourself, and will join with you in
praise of the Highlands, tho' I doubt whether he is as
partial to Highlanders.   I shall make this short, my
dear daughter, as I shall write again the beginning of
next week, directing my letter to Dalkeath, where, I
suppose, you will be found the end of it.   Everybody is
well, and your dear father bids me add his blessing to
that of your most affectionate mother,

M. W. BUTE.

In a letter dated from Bothwell at this time, from Lady
Louisa Stuart to the Duchess of Buccleuch, occurs the following passage relating to her expedition to Loch Lomond with
Lady Frances Douglas : " We, and I in particular, were so well
received and *fêted* by the old gentleman who manages his
Grace of Montrose's affairs that I thought I was likely to
have remained in the neighbourhood, but, alas! all my
conquests prove married men, and, indeed, I got into such a
scrape by producing an old ballad rather disgraceful to *Sir
John ye Grame*, whose broadsword I had the honour of
handling, and who lived, an't please your Grace, in the year
twelve hundred and something, that I am not sure if I
should now stand any chance, were the main obstacle
removed.   But I swallowed my words again as well as I
could, and upon the whole we parted friends."

―――――

THE SAME from the SAME

London, 7th October 1783.

ACCORDING to my promise, I write once more,
my dear Louisa, hoping we shall soon have no more

[1] Probably of Boconnoc, the Rivers family.

occasion for pen and ink to express our thoughts. I fear it will be a sad change for you, for I know of no mortal in town that you will be desirous of seeing. I fancy your two sisters will stay at Hampton till December without Lady Carlow goes to Ireland (a point that seems not yet to be decided), but I rather guess the irresolution will end in her staying on this side the water.

I went on Saturday to see Mr. Kemble act Hamlet. I hear it is the fashion to puff him as much as his sister, but I own (tho' he is better than any actor we have except Henderson) I think there is great room for improvement. His figure is very well, his face rather handsome, with a good deal of expression, but he takes rather too much pains and overdoes his part. I should guess he will be better in serious comedy.

The Duke and Duchess of Cumberland are going abroad for a twelvemonth, which will occasion a considerable blank in the divertion, but I suppose the Prince of Wales's entertainments are to make up for this loss; he is building an immense room at Carlton House for the purpose of balls, etc., which I hear is to be decorated and furnished in the highest taste and magnificence, but upon recollection I might have spared myself the trouble of telling you this, as you will see the Duke of Montagu at Dalkeith, who must be much more *au fait* of all these proceedings.[1]

We had on Saturday night another extraordinary meteor appeared in London, which I was so unlucky not to see; but the people gathered together in the

[1] He was Master of the Horse, 1780-1790.

streets with great amazement, thinking the end of the
world was come; we had had very remarkable hot
weather for some days preceding.   Pray let me know
if this phenomena was seen in your neighbourhood.
The heat and fogs of this year have certainly been
extraordinary, and I suppose these wonderful appearances are in some way connected with it, though I
am not learned enough to account for them.

By a letter your father has received from Mr.
Mackenzie I find you are not to put out for England
till the 18th or 19th, which I'm glad of, as I imagine
you will be glad to prolong your stay at Dalkeith
and put off the parting from Lady Frances for some
days.

I have been this morning at Hampton, and found
all well there.   Your name was given to the infant[1]
yesterday.   I wish she may be as agreeable to Lady
Carlow as you are, my dear Louisa, to your most
affectionate mother,   M. W. BUTE.

Your dear father's blessing.

———

Encouraged by the revolt of the American colonies, who
had resented restrictions on their trade and the imposition
of taxes by the mother country, Ireland determined also to
assert herself, feeling that since France had allied herself
with America, Ireland had become a most important factor
in the game.   In the year 1778 she procured a partial
relaxation of the restrictions upon Irish trade, and in the
following year further restrictions were removed.   About this
time (1779) the country, drained of its usual army, had

---

[1] The Carlows' second daughter, afterwards Lady Louisa Bromley.

recourse to raising corps of volunteers; and in Ireland these men, numbering some 42,000, and under no civil or military control, demanded with one voice the liberation of their native Legislature from the control of the British Parliament.   These views were given eloquent expression to by Mr. Grattan in the Irish House of Commons.   At this juncture the British Government thought fit to sever the Annual Mutiny Act in Ireland from the one in England, and to substitute a *permanent* Mutiny Act in Ireland, thus denying the power of their Parliament to object to a standing army. The volunteers, headed by the Earl of Charlemont, made loud demonstrations against this injustice, and a large convention was held by them at Dungannon, in Ulster, in February 1782. In the same month Mr. Grattan and Mr. Flood asserted the right of the Irish Parliament to reject this measure, and moved an address to the King asserting these principles, which was, however, rejected.   Lord Rockingham's Liberal Administration being then formed, Lord Carlisle was recalled, and the Duke of Portland appointed Lord-Lieutenant.   Mr. Eden, Lord Carlisle's secretary, hastened over to England and presented the claims of Ireland in an enthusiastic speech to the House of Commons; the King sent a message recommending the state of Ireland to the consideration of the House, and the Duke of Portland presented a similar message to the Irish Parliament; this was followed by an address from the latter, usually called the Irish Declaration of Independence.   The British Parliament then, with great wisdom and liberality, acceded to their claims, gave Ireland authority to make her own laws, and repealed the Perpetual Mutiny Act (April 1782).   The volunteers, not contented with having secured national independence, now confronted their native Parliament with cries for Parliamentary Reform, and an able speech by Mr. Flood, who was their organ in the House of Commons, proposing a motion to that effect, was rejected in November 1783. The Dublin Parliament was indeed at this time governed by her native Legislature, but was none the less factious, turbulent, exclusive, and corrupt. The elective franchise was wholly denied to five-sixths of the people on account of their belonging to the Catholic religion, and two-thirds of the House of Commons was attached to the Government by offices, pensions, and promises. The House of Lords was composed of prelates and nobles of the Protestant faith, and nearly all in alliance with the Castle.[1] Notwithstanding, however, a large amount of justice in their demands, the *manner* of carrying on the revolt added as usual to the disturbance of the country, and many of the more peaceably disposed of her countrymen resented, as did Lord Carlow, the state of revolt and disaffection into which the unhappy island was drawn.

***

LADY CARLOW from LORD CARLOW

Dublin, 31st October 1783.

MY DEAREST CAR—After I landed at Dublin I stayed one day to refresh myself, and proceeded to the country. Beck, expecting you, had furnished the Hall as a greenhouse with your geraniums, which are all in great beauty, and make a pretty effect. I immediately took a view of the river, which I found, in a manner, finished ; so much so, that this week finishes the work, and the water will be let in on Monday.

I remained only Monday and Tuesday in the country, during which time I set my farmer to work, and gave my directions about the church, etc., and returned here on Wednesday. The first thing I heard

[1] See Sir T. Erskine May's *Constitutional History of England*, vol. ii. chap. xvi.

when I came to town was the altercation in the House
of Commons the preceding evening between Mr. Flood
and Mr. Grattan, which for invective and personal
abuse on both sides exceeded everything that was ever
heard in any assembly. Mr. Grattan appears to have
provoked Mr. Flood to this language, and in the
course of the contest abused Flood in a personal
manner, pointing out the defects of his person and constitution of body in a manner very unbecoming of a
man of education and talents. I enclose to you a
short account of it, in a newspaper in which you will
see the strength of their expressions in abuse. But
there is not, I am told, a quarter of it inserted.
They were ordered into custody, but escaped out of
the House, and spent yesterday, concealed, settling
their affairs. They went out this morning to fight,
but were taken into custody on the ground. It cannot,
however, stop the personal determinal of the dispute,
as Flood, I suppose, will never put up with the abuse
he received. Grattan, I understand, is Prime Minister
here, from which I suppose we shall be torn to pieces
for want of a Government, as he will probably be too
much biassed by the people to take any decisive
measures to restore this country to peace.

In respect to the demands of the volunteers, I do
not believe they will in themselves cause any disturbance against Parliament, who will, I believe, assert their
own constitutional authority; but they have thrown out
such views to the Papists that they begin now to claim
a share in the Legislature, and this country (as I have
said everywhere for these two years past) will in a few

years become a very unhappy scene without a stand can be made and a final stop put to their demands. I shall hesitate in prosecuting my building schemes till I see a little further into our situation and prospects.

I have got very good lodging, No. 105 in Grafton Street, where you will direct to me ; my sister [1] and Miss Trevyllian have a very neat house near me. I gave your locket, for which she returns you many thanks.

There are very few ladies in town, so that the Castle ball will be very ill attended for some time. I got my whist yesterday evening at Mrs. Jones's ; only Mrs. Cunningham and Lady Kingsborough, Mrs. Luttrell and Mrs. More, and half a dozen men—a very comfortable party. I have missed your letter, which was sent to the country after me.—Your ever affectionate

CARLOW.

Dawson Court, Saturday,
8th November 1783.

HAVING no very material business to keep me in Dublin, I returned here last Thursday to push on my planting and church building, neither of which are attended to in my absence. The church has been neglected, but now gets on apace, and I believe I shall have the whole body of it fit for roofing before the winter sets in. I shall not, however, put on the root till spring. My planting, of which I have a vast deal to do, goes on very slowly for want of hands. I am at present planting on each side of the cascade, and

[1] Mary Dawson, married to Mervyn Archdall, Esq., of Castle Archdall. See *ante*, p. 25.

making the lower bridge and road to it, all of which I shall have finished in two days, and shall then let in the water, which I am very impatient to see in its improved state, and to try the effect of the cascade.

I think you do very right in going into Dorsetshire, as you may amuse yourself there for a little time, and get fat with their strong beer, and make Miss Damer very happy. I should think you had better take Miss Herbert with you, as it will make your journey more pleasant. I give you joy of Lady Louisa's arrival and her good looks.

Having postponed my journey to Dublin till Sunday, I this day received your letter, which has relieved me from my anxiety, for you say nothing particular of yourself.

Dublin, Tuesday, 29th November 1783.

HAVING nothing particular to say, I have not taken up my pen for some days past. I now do it to keep up my promise to you, rather than from any new matter to communicate. In regard to our political measures one cannot form a proper judgment, nor do I think much light will be given till after Christmas. Our prospect is not pleasing, but yet, from seeing the principal men in rank and property anxious to preserve the present constitution of the country, I should have no doubt of a favourable issue if Government took an able and decided part. But they have no certain plan, shrink from every appearance of danger, and are in part guided by men who have risen on popular ground, and have a double game to play.

Thursday Night.

In regard to public news there is nothing yet worth notice. The Convention is sitting still on our lives and properties.

Though it is not a very pleasant sight, I walk there often in a morning, as it is a good lounge, and the best Coffee House to meet people. Did I ever tell you my Lord Bristol's sentiments? His first principle is—that all religion established by law is only a method of legalising hypocrisy. His first toast—The Irish Harp, new strung; that must and will be heard. He does not honour the Parliament with his presence—attends only the Convention. I breakfasted this morning with the Jarnacs, and dined and spent the evening with the Jones's.

Friday Night.

I this morning received your letter, and as you say nothing particular of your own health or Louisa's,[1] take for granted you are both quite well, and reconciled to your change. I am vexed about poor John's face; pray take some good advice about it in London. Sir R. Jebb, whom I consulted once last winter, seemed to be a sensible man, but I suppose you will have seen somebody about him before you receive this.

Your account of Miss Damer gives me a great deal of concern; it is a disagreeable accident, and she is so delicate that one can't help being alarmed about her when anything's the matter. I hope your next letter will bring a better account. I thought it likely

[1] Louisa was the then youngest daughter, and John the eldest son of Lord Carlow.

that something or other might detain them in town, and I directed a letter to Lord Milton a few days ago to London.

Your account of Louisa's improvement pleases me very much, and particularly that part of it of her resembling you, for I do not think either of the other children do.

I am very glad you have remembered to make a sketch from the room in your brother's lodge, as I am sure you would do them equally well with a little practice. I must make a little tour with you when I return, to see Lady Di's, Lady Pembroke, etc. I fear you have not received all my letters, as I wrote you word that I had spoke twice in the House. No material has since occurred in which I thought worth while to take a part. I intended to leave town to-morrow for a few days, but as I understand that Mr. Flood will to-morrow produce the resolutions of the Convention in the House of Commons, I shall wait to see the event, and shall let you know it to-morrow night.—Your   CARLOW.

Dublin, Friday Night, 5th December 1783.

NOTHING particular has occurred since I wrote to you till this evening, when the Absentee Tax was brought into the House of Commons by a Mr. Molyneux, whom you may remember at Tunbridge. Nobody spoke for it but himself, and when the House divided there appeared for it 22, against it 184. The idea is entirely scouted, and I believe we shall never see it agitated again.

Dawson Court, Monday Night.

I came down here this day to plant some fruit-trees I sent from England, which will make a provision for my walls for some years. A very smart frost has, however, taken place, which is very unlucky, having a great many trees to see planted before I leave this place. The river is full within two inches, and looks extremely well. I expect to see the cascade play in a day or two, and shall give you an account of it in my next. The More's water comes in so well that the watercourse is not able to contain it all. I have taken my walk in a hurry, just before nightfall, so have no more home intelligence at present.

I expect to hear from you on Wednesday, and hope to have something more satisfactory about poor John's face, which makes me very uneasy. I shall be obliged to go to town on Parliamentary business this day s'ennight, shall return here for a week, and sail for England the 28th. Adieu, my love.—Your ever affectionate　　　　　　　　　　　　　　　CARLOW.

Dawson Court, Wednesday Night,
10th December 1783.

I THIS day received my dear Car's letter, which was very acceptable to me, as I found by it you were well, and amused yourself in the society of your friends, of whom I am glad you find so many in town. The delights of Dublin are not so captivating as you fear to make me forget I am a married man, for I do not think there are any existing there without one can employ or interest oneself about public affairs, and it

is altogether the last town I know of that would make
me forget the pleasure and comfort I have at home in
my own family. Here, indeed, my attention is much
taken up, especially as I have had it so seldom in my
power to leave town since I came over. I do not find
half time to attend to and lay out my planting, and
other matters necessary for the comfort of this place.
One thing, however, I have the pleasure of seeing
completed, which answers my expectations completely—
I mean the river and cascade. The river, with its
accompaniments, forms several fine scenes, and the
cascade answers just as well as if I had cut it out of a
mountain river and transplanted it. The supply of
water is quite sufficient, and falls in as natural and
pleasing a way as you could wish, and with the assistance of large weeping willows which I have planted
hanging over it, and arbutus among the rocks, forms a
very picturesque effect.

I am very well pleased to hear that John's heats
are not more troublesome, and as you have a good
opinion of Fordyce, expect he will make both him and
little Car fair and well-liking for me against my
return.

I have concluded my work at the church for this
season; it is within six feet of its intended height. It
will make a very conspicuous object to the new house,
and to the whole province of Leinster. The Warwick-
shire farmer I brought over with me has not the kind
of activity and knowledge of accomptent business to
direct everything just as I might wish, but is a very
sensible, plain man and good farmer. He has, how-

ever, just received a letter from his friends acquainting him that his uncle has left him a farm, well stocked, and as he has an inclination to return on this account, I shall send him off in a few days, as I should be sorry to deprive him of a better settlement than he could meet with me.

I have received my last cargo of books from London, and arranged them in the study, which looks very comfortable with the assistance of an easy chair (like the Duke of Buccleuch's) which Gulliver has made for me. Having found that Beck had a little red leather of the dining-room chairs to spare, I got him to make three more chairs of it with my own cherry-tree wood, which answers very well, and looks better than the mahogany of the former chairs. Your guinea fowl are increasing fast. The great farmers in the county have been much distressed this autumn from there being no demand for beef for exportation, and the best beef in our markets has been disposed of till yesterday at three half-pence the pound. But I had the pleasure of hearing this morning from Higgins that every beast that came yesterday to Mountmellick Fair was bought up at a high price, so I hope we farmers may live again.

Dublin, Monday Night, 15th December 1783.

I CAME here this morning to attend my business in the House relative to the new buildings; Lord Carhampton opposed me, and the consideration of it is put off till Thursday, and from what I see brewing about it, I have some doubts if I shall carry it at present, as objections are made to the expense. This matter will keep me in town till Friday, when I shall return to the country for a week to give my final directions, and then for England.

Tuesday Night.

I sit down to write a few lines, though I have nothing material to say of this day's occurrences. I dined with Trench, whose fair lady was brought to bed of a daughter a few days ago. His father dined with us, and made a long relation of the manner in which his wife died in childbed, to the great comfort of his son. But I daresay there is no fear of Mrs. Trench. She has an old proverb on her side. I do not hear that Lord Landaff is yet married to Lady Catherine Skeffington,[1] but it is to take place immediately. Mr. Bernard, son to the rich Bernard of the county of Cork, is to marry Lord Shannon's daughter, a fine girl, who has just made her first appearance at the Castle. His father gives him £12,000 a year present maintenance.

Thursday Night.

I had the pleasure of your letter yesterday morning, and should have answered it last night but that I expected to have been able to inform you this evening that I had concluded my business in the House of Lords about their new buildings. That matter is, however, not yet concluded, and I must wait a day or two longer in town to settle it. It is very hard on me to be kept from my country business so much for this public one, which gives me more trouble than I ex-

---

[1] Francis Mathew, first Earl of Landaff (Irish), married secondly, 1784, Lady Catherine Skeffington, daughter of Clotworthy, first Earl of Masserene.

pected. I am very glad to find that John is recovering. I hope to find him restored to his good looks. I think you do well to run about and amuse yourself everywhere, and if Miss Damer leaves town, to go down there for the Christmas, as you will be too fashionable not to spend your holidays in the country. If I get over time enough I shall join you, but I doubt it, as I cannot leave Dublin before the 28th.

We have been in a very quiet state since the breaking up of the Volunteer Convention, and nothing material has occurred except some answers of Lord Bristol's to Volunteer addresses, in which he advises them in pretty direct terms to take up arms. Government have as yet taken no notice of his publications, I suppose as they do not immediately come within the description of high treason; but they are certainly of a nature to induce other people to become guilty of it.

Charles Fox has not much reason to brag of my Lord Northington's[1] management here. The fact is, there has been no management or government, and if a number of independent gentlemen had not thought it necessary for their own sakes to support Government, my Lord Northington would have passed a disagreeable winter. The crisis of affairs, not his management, supports him, and of course there is nothing to be called opposition; no such thing exists.

I am not sorry for Mr. Flood's reception, but I am not pleased that Irishmen should be the only persons that rise to abuse their countrymen. Your countrymen

---

[1] Lord Northington was appointed Lord-Lieutenant on 3rd June 1783 by the Coalition Ministry, which existed only from April to December of the same year.

would not do it.   My paper being out, I must conclude.
I shall write one more letter at least before I leave
Ireland.   You need write but one letter, which I beg
may be the day you receive this.—Yours ever affectionately,   CARLOW.

Dublin, Saturday Night,
20th December 1783.

THIS evening, after a troublesome debate of two or
three hours, I got my building business well through
the House in the manner I wished ; I had both Government and Opposition to contend with on account of the
expense of the object.   I had, however, friends enough
to establish the majority against them, and carried my
point.   It will be of great convenience to the Lords,
and contribute very much to the embellishment of the
town.   I must carry up our address on it to my Lord-
Lieutenant on Monday, which will detain me in town
till Tuesday, when I must run to the country for a few
days to settle my country business.   I left Damer
there a week ago, promising to come back to him in
two days, but I daresay he amuses himself very well
between the library and Beck's room.   As I stay in
Dublin till Tuesday, I shall get a ball at General Burgh's
on Monday.   It's confined to fifty of each sex.   I went
this evening to a little theatre in Capel Street that is
opened for English operas under the direction of
Giordani.   Leonie sings there, and a Miss Wheeler,
who has studied at Venice and sings with some taste,
but with a weak voice.   The music is very pretty.

There is a strong rumour here that the opposition
to the Indian business in the House of Lords will dis-

lodge the Ministry, and Lord Mornington went off this morning to the Head on the strength of it, expecting to find a new Ministry when he gets to London. To-morrow's packet will, I suppose, give us some light about this business, as it will contain the debate of Monday last in the House of Lords.[1]

[1] Pitt became first Lord at this date in an administration which lasted (with numerous changes) until his death in 1806.

CHAPTER VII

THE beginning of the year 1784 finds Lady Carlow still in England, and her husband busy in Dublin, trying to defeat a local Protection Bill, by which some of the Irish Members thought they might enrich their country at the sister-island's expense by putting a duty of 2s. 6d. per yard on all imported drapery, and proportionate duties on iron, paper, and other imported articles.   He was also much engaged with the improvements in building and planting which were being carried out at home.   He seems to have left Dublin early in May to join his wife, returning with her in July after a couple of months' stay in London, where Lady Louisa was established as usual with her parents in South Audley Street, having returned from Scotland a few months previously.

LADY CARLOW from LORD CARLOW

Dublin, Thursday Night,
8th April 1784.

I SHOULD have written to you, my love, from Holyhead, but as I found the post did not leave it till this night, I thought I might as well postpone it till I could acquaint you of my arrival here.   I had very pleasant weather for my journey, and although I stopped by the way to see several objects, I got to the Head to dinner on Tuesday. I sailed yesterday at twelve, and after a pleasant passage, in which I was not sick, of twelve hours, anchored last night at twelve in this harbour. I thought it inconvenient coming up in the wherry at that time of night, so lay on board, and got here to breakfast this morning. I find our Parliament have nearly finished their business, and after sitting about three or four days more, will adjourn for a fortnight, then sit for a few days to pass the bills, when it will be prorogued. The populace of this city are very much enraged at the rejection of a favourite Bill for protecting their manufactures by laying a tax on English. They even surrounded the Parliament house last Tuesday and threatened to hang some of the members, when the military were obliged to be called out to disperse them, and the whole garrison remain since in constant readiness for duty. I called on my sister this morning, and finding she had not been well since Christmas, advised her to come with me to the country, which she consented to, so I shall have her and Miss Trevyllian there during my stay, which will be a fortnight. I shall go down next Monday. I hope you will write to me often, and direct to me at Daly's Club-House, Dublin.—Your ever affectionate   CARLOW.

Dawson Court, 14th April 1784.

I HAVE been disappointed this post in not hearing from you, having not received a letter since I left

London. I hope you will write constantly, and which you may do as yet without cost, as letters come free to me.

I left Dublin last Sunday evening, and got here early on Monday. My first business was to survey the havoc made by the storm, which is very considerable in the part of the wood I intended to stand, but which will not materially injure its appearance except in one part among the tall fir-trees, in which there is a very severe chasm. As nobody offered anything to signify for them, they are all lying in confusion where they fell, and would have remained so if I had not come home. I shall have them directly carried off the ground, and the place made clear before your return. All the evergreens have suffered more or less by the frost, but the laurustinus and arbutus entirely destroyed, and among the latter our beautiful one near the old hothouse. This loss vexes me more than any. There is not yet the least sign of vegetation here, and the whole place looks more dismal than ever I saw it We have had continual piercing north winds since I came, which have almost prevented me from looking at the river, which is the only thing that makes a good appearance.

My sister is much better since she came here. She rides every morning before breakfast round the heath. William and Fisher are also with me. The Duchess of Rutland [1] attempted to come over, but was put back to the Head, and has been there for five days past.

---

[1] Lady Mary Somerset, wife of Charles, sixth Duke, Lord-Lieutenant in Ireland from February 1784 until his death in 1787.

The Duke, *en attendant*, pays great attention to the Dublin ladies, and particularly to Lady Anne Hatton,[1] whom, I believe, you saw at Dawson Court with her father, Lord Arran, before she was married. He goes to every one that asks him to their house.

Dawson Court, 20th April 1784.

I HAVE had at last, my love, the pleasure of getting a letter from you, and hearing you were all well. You need not repent not having come over, for the weather has been so bitter, the appearance of the country so dismal, not the least sign of verdure appearing, added to the uncomfortable state of this place, that you would certainly have not been at your ease, and I am glad to have been here before you to make matters a little more pleasant for your reception.

I shall stay here a week longer, and then go to Dublin, and hope to arrange my money matters so as to leave it in a week more. My sister and Miss Trevyllian, Damer, William, and Fisher are all here, so that we have a gay whist party every evening after I have tired myself walking about the grounds. Adieu for the present, my love.—Your ever affectionate

CARLOW.

Dublin, 28th April 1784.

HAVING given all necessary directions in the country, at least more than Meares and Connor[2] will perform, I left home yesterday at twelve, and got time enough into

---

[1] Lady Anne Gore, daughter of the second Earl of Arran, wife of a Mr. Henry Hatton, subsequently Mar- chioness of Abercorn, and Sir Walter Scott's great friend.

[2] Steward and gardener.

town to dress for the Castle. The ball was remarkably full, and people expected the Duchess to dance a minuet, though contrary to etiquette. For that time, however, she observed the usual forms. I played with her afterwards at Commerce, disputed the poole with her and won it. A bad way of paying my court. To-morrow I dine and spend the evening with the Jones's. This evening I go to Lady De Vesci's. I am afraid a letter of yours has been sent to me to the country, so I must wait for it till Friday.

———

In the following letter allusion is made to Lady Anne Rawdon for the first time. She was the eldest daughter of John, first Earl of Moira, by his third wife, Elizabeth Hastings, who succeeded to the barony of Hastings on the death of her brother Francis, tenth Earl of Huntingdon. Lady Anne was one of Lady Louisa's greatest friends, and a few (out of the large number extant) of her letters will be given in this collection, but unluckily none of the answers are forthcoming.

Lady Louisa, writing of her friend in the *Notes* often quoted before, says : " Lady Anne Rawdon came to England in the autumn of that year, 1782, and was several months with her uncle, Lord Huntingdon, her mother, Lady Moira's, brother. We then formed a friendship that made her one of the chief objects of my life till hers ended, and mine must end ere I forget her. She married Lord Ailesbury in February 1788, and died in January 1813. I thought her like Lady Harriet Don, but she might also resemble the first Lady Eglintoun. Without positive beauty, she had the charm of countenance, grace, figure, and altogether something more captivating than beauty itself."

THE SAME from the SAME

Sunday, 2nd May.

I RECEIVED your letter back, as I expected, on Friday, and am very happy to see you amuse yourself so well running about, as it is a sign you are well. I hope to see you and the children very soon. I shall sail the latter end of this week, by which time I shall have arranged my business. My country business, both farming and planting, has been conducted so ill that I find immediate occasion to put it into other hands. I have found a gardener in Dublin, who is, I believe, one of the best in the country, and have engaged him, and have determined to go down for two days and settle him at Dawson Court and dismiss Connor. In regard to a farmer, I have written to Brown at Luton to enquire for a proper person, which if I do not find to my mind in England, I must get one on my return here, as I cannot afford to suffer the loss of keeping Meares in the direction of my business.

I have seen Lady Anne Rawdon since I came up to town. She enquired much after you and Lady Macartney, and told me that she is going this summer abroad with Lord and Lady Granard.[1]

The principal amusement now in Dublin is parading in a part of the circular road which lies between the park and the sea. It is the great scene of pleasure and gallantry. The Duchess of Rutland has her six ponies there every morning, Lady Antrim six more, and the other ladies as many as they can get for love

---

[1] Lord Granard married Lady Anne Rawdon's younger sister, Lady Selina.

or money. The Duke rides, and as soon as he meets Lady Anne Hatton, dismounts and walks with her.

We have a large importation of English Lords. Mount Edgecumbe and Walsingham to qualify as Vice-Treasurers; Lord and Lady Harrington to join their regiment; Lord Muncaster[1] to sue for money owing to him, etc., etc.

I should have sent this letter off to-night, but wait for to-morrow's post to give you an answer about your request to Gandon, whom I have not seen.

Monday Night.

I executed your commission to Gandon this morning, who readily agreed to take your carpenter, and will employ him in the Custom-House as soon as he arrives. When I get to London I can give him a letter to Gandon, with which he may set out when he pleases. I have put off my scheme of going to the country, and shall sail on Thursday or Friday next. I shall bring over so little money with me that we must return here as soon as you find yourself stout enough to travel.— Yours ever,   CARLOW.

LADY CARLOW from LADY LOUISA STUART

Thursday Morning, 24th June 1784.

I THINK it is now time to begin writing, for you will not be sorry to see a letter from hence two or three days after your arrival at Dawson Court, at least I believe so when I judge by myself, for I feel extremely anxious to hear from you. My heart was extremely heavy at

---

[1] John Pennington, M.P. for Westmoreland, created Baron Muncaster in the previous year.

our parting. I will not myself think or talk of how long it may be before we meet again, because I would fain pursue your system of hoping the best. But I hate the idea of your passing years in Ireland. Pray be punctual in writing to me every little occurrence as you used to do. I am quite resolved to keep a constant journal for you, to write something every day, whether I am in a stupid humour or a gay one. But if I hold my present determination, I will never again indulge myself in long lamentations and croaking, as I used to do, but keep all sentiments of discontent to myself. I think you have had tolerable weather for your journey, not very hot, nor, I hope, very dusty. I wish you may think of writing on the road, for it would be a great satisfaction to us all to hear you were got so far safe and well. It gives me a heartache when I think you are probably going to cross the sea at present, though I hope in God your passage will not be dangerous. The Damers talk of setting out on Wednesday next, and I hope I shall get your bundle made time enough to send it with them. Here is a letter directed to Lord Carlow at this house, which I imagine comes from the E.I.[1] I keep it (as it is a double packet) for them to carry; I have been afraid I ought to have despatched it by the post. I have been recollecting what I have done since I saw you; nothing very remarkable, I think — dined twice in Stratford Place. The first time it was a sort of great dinner, the company Lord and Lady William,[2] the

---

[1] Possibly East India Company.
[2] Lord and Lady William Gordon probably, who were intimate at Dalkeith.

Duke of Roxburgh and his friend Mr. Smith, Lord
Graham and a Captain Douglas,[1] *not big Archy*, but a
Sir Something Douglas's son, who is in Parliament for
Roxburghshire in Sir Gilbert Eliot's room.   The
second time we had only Lady Eleanor Dundas and
her husband and Lady Murray, and in the evening
came Lord and Lady Courtown, Lady M. Bowlby,
Miss Herbert for a little while, Miss Brudenell, two
Miss Crawfords, and Lady Brudenell. All the company
except Lady Mary, Lady Brudenell, and Miss Herbert
stayed supper.   We had a great deal of music.   Miss
Crawford sang charmingly, and with either Lady
Brudenell or Lady Eleanor, they made out several
catches.   There was just company enough to divide
into conversation parties of three or four, and, in short,
I never saw anything of the kind pleasanter.   One
day, I think it was Monday, I went with Lady
Frances to a great breakfast and morning ball at
Mrs. Tollemache's,[2] where were all the fine people in
a variety of odd dresses.   Two of Lady Courtney's
daughters appeared to be the beauties of the *fête*.
These sort of entertainments never succeed well when
you cannot go out of doors, but it was very magnificent.
In the evening I stayed at home for Miss Damer
and Miss Herbert.   Last night I was at a very dull
assembly at Bolton House, and afterwards, as my
mother stayed there much later than usual, and it grew
worse and worse, I let Lady Mary drag me to Ranelagh, where we saw all the same company once again.

[1] Captain George Douglas, son of Sir James of Springwood Park.
[2] Probably the wife of Wilbraham Tollemache, afterwards sixth Earl of Dysart.

Friday.

Lady Frances persuaded me to go and see the *Deserter*[1] last night; I was quite charmed with it. Our party consisted of Lady Eleanor and Lady Emily [Macleod] who is come to town for a few days to her (Lady Eleanor's) house. We took possession of the Duchess of Cumberland's box, finding all the house at our discretion, for never was there so miserable an audience, not above twenty people in the pit, and the rest in proportion. I pitied the poor woman whose *disadvantage* it was (that's my Lady Graham's wit) when she came forward curtseying to the empty benches; if she had given us a curtsey apiece it would not have over-fatigued her. I saw Sir James Harris[2] in the room, and made speeches to him for you. By his account Lady Harris is but a little better. I ended the evening by going home to supper with Lady Frances and Mr. Douglas; she seems far from well. Her young thing[3] improved, and for that age is really a pretty child; it continues very fair, and its hair will probably be red. Lady Emily's child[4] (did I say I went to see her on Tuesday?) I found greatly altered for the better, but it has a vast, broad face still. It

[1] A musical drama by Dibdin.

[2] Afterwards first Lord Malmesbury. He married Harriet Amyand, many of whose clever letters are printed by Lady Minto.

[3] Caroline, the first child of Lady Frances and Mr. Douglas. She married Admiral Sir George Scott in 1810.

[4] Lady Emily M'Leod's daughter (born 15th January 1784) lived till 1876, dying on her ninety-second birthday in that year. She married Sir Robert Gardiner, K.C.B., who distinguished himself in the Peninsular and Waterloo campaigns, and was afterwards Governor of Gibraltar. He was appointed Chief Equerry and Comptroller to Prince Leopold on his marriage with Princess Charlotte in 1816, and had a house given him adjoining Claremont Park, where the young couple lived till the sad death of the

had just cut a tooth without any trouble, so she was in great joy. She comes to me to-night, and I have been cross to Miss Herbert, and refused carrying her to Ranelagh, which she wanted me to do, but really I so seldom have an opportunity of seeing Lady Emily in any comfort that I can't give it up. You must know my mother intends going to-morrow to Bulstrode, so I shall not meet Lady Emily any more while she stays in town, and as that will be till Tuesday, Miss Herbert may see her when she pleases. When you see anybody very seldom, going to a public place is quite a different thing from having them at home in quiet, which one does not feel when one lives with them constantly—at least not so much. My mother went to Lady Gower's last night. Miss L. has had a party this week, and Lady Jane's filled up the rest very well. Lady Jane says she is writing to you herself, so gives me no message. Lady Emily is come, her sister, and nieces, so I am forced to conclude in haste. God bless you. I hope I shall hear good news of you and the children. I shall write a little every day.

London, Sunday, 27th [July ?] 1784.

I WAS extremely disappointed not to find a letter when I came home last night. I have been computing days and recollecting winds, and can hardly conceive why I did not get one, but I will have patience, and

Princess. Lady Gardiner was one of the first six bedchamber women appointed by her present Majesty on her accession, which honour she continued to hold on their return from Gibraltar in 1856, until obliged to retire, from age and infirmity. Her son, General Lynedoch Gardiner, with whom she lived till her death, keeps up the family tradition as Equerry to Her Majesty.

hope for better things to-morrow, only one cannot help feeling a little anxious at first. I closed my letter just five minutes too soon on Friday, or else I might have told you for the bonne-bouche that three new Earls kissed hands at the levee—Lord Talbot, Lord Grosvenor, and Lord Beaulieu,[1] the second of whom I think is altogether new, and has not had his dignity spoiled by being talked over beforehand, at least I never heard him named for it. So my Lady Grosvenor is a Countess, and may in all senses be called *the first of her profession,*[2] as I remember Lady M. said of some other famous lame beauty. I wonder her consideration did not cool his Lordship's longings for a higher title. I dined at Richmond yesterday, as I told you I should. We carried nobody but the little girl, and found nobody but themselves, that is to say, the Duke of Montagu, the Duchess [of Buccleuch], and the children, for his Grace is gone upon a fishing party with Mr. Douglas, etc., which must be a most agreeable undertaking in this weather. The sun did not once make its appearance, and we had five or six soaking showers, besides which it was cold enough for a fire. However, you know that company will make up for many evils. Lord and Lady Courtown came in just before we left Richmond. I went home with Lady

[1] John, Lord Talbot, to be Viscount Ingestrie and Earl Talbot. Sir Richard Grosvenor, Bart., elevated to the Peerage as Baron Grosvenor of Eaton in 1761, and advanced to the dignity of Viscount Belgrave and Earl Grosvenor 5th July 1784. Edward, Lord Beaulieu, to be Earl Beaulieu. Lady Louisa does not mention that her brother-in-law, Sir James Lowther, had been created Earl of Lonsdale in the previous month, because Lady Carlow already knew the fact, as she was in England when the honour was conferred.

[2] Alluding to the story of the Duke of Cumberland. See *Lady M. Coke,* iii. pp. 148 and 202

Frances, and we tumbled over drawings, and supped *tête-à-tête*, and had a great deal of comfortable conversation. I am glad to find that Mr. Dundas is *struck* with Lady Jane as a remarkably sensible woman. People always use you the better for having an opinion of your understanding. I am sleepy and tired, you must know, so can only tell you *en gros* that I went to Ran[elagh] to-night according to long engagement with Lady Mary, Mrs., and Miss Cheap, and of course have spent the evening *tête-à-tête* with the latter. She seems a very quiet, well-behaved girl, but I can't say I was highly entertained, and Lady Jane would have *growled* again, at least for my part of the story. I went first for an hour to Lady Brudenell's, where were only Lady Courtown, Mrs. Keene, Lady Frances, two of the Duchess's girls, and the little sylph; so we played at shilling commerce. The sylph is not so pretty as she was, but her beauty may return when she grows up. Lady Courtown was hurried home, her son being just come from abroad. The news of the day is the Dowager Lady Harrington's[1] sudden death.

The following characteristic remarks on Lady Harrington are taken from the MS. *Journals of Lady Mary Coke* :—

" 1st *July* 1783.—I went this evening, at a little before nine, to town. It was the christening at the Duke of Rutland's, and after it was over the Dutchess had a party. Lady Dowager Harrington was the godmother, and I play'd at cribbage with her. Her method is beneficial to herself, but not to others. When she won she took the money, when she lost she said she owed it; nay, more, the gentleman who was

---

[1] Lady Harrington was the widow of the second Earl, and daughter of the second Duke of Grafton.

my partner she asked to put two shillings to the cards for her, and he saying he had only the money for himself, she got up without paying. . . .

" 29th June 1784.—The first news Lady Holdernesse told me was that the Dowager Lady Harrington died yesterday. She was, poor woman, in a great passion with one of her servants, and in coming downstairs fell, but was supported by a servant, and never spoke again ; 'tis supposed to be an apopleptic fit. . . .

"6th July 1784.—This evening I went to Lady Harrington's funeral. Her corps arrived at the church at five minutes after seven o'clock. The herse was drawn by six horses, and accompanied by two black coaches and six horses, with her own coach following ; all the servants in deep mourning ; two of the women cry'd. The clergyman mett the corps at the gate of the churchyard, and went before it into the church, saying ' I am the resurrection and the life, says the Lord, etc.' The coffin was magnificent crimson velvet with numbers of plates of her arms and coronets. She desired to be placed by her daughter, Lady Fortrose, whose coffin was so much decay'd it was fallen in ; yet the people of the church had intended, to save room, to place Lady Harrington's coffin upon it, which must have crucht it intirely, so I interpos'd, and desired the clergyman wou'd order that it shou'd be placed by her daughter, as she had requested, in which I succeeded. Her story is now closed, and I hope she will find mercy. . . ."

THE SAME from the SAME

Tuesday.

I PREVAILED on my mother to go to the play to-night. We carried Miss Bruhl,[1] and Lady Frances

---

[1] Daughter of Lady Egremont and Count Bruhl, afterwards Mrs. Scott of Harden, mother of Lord Polwarth.

and Mr. Douglas joined our party, which was made for the sake of *The Agreeable Surprise*,[1] the farce we have heard so much of and never seen. It is egregious nonsense, and yet makes one laugh more than all the wit in the world. The play was one of their summer pieces, fitter for a fair than a theatre, with everything that could be devised absurd and ridiculous. But for the farce, I believe I shall laugh these three days at the recollection of it. I went home and supped with the Duchess. They don't talk of leaving town yet. I was with Lady Jane for an hour. Miss Herbert came in and described to us a house she is about taking in Edward Street, Portman Square. It would be a very good one, she says, only the kitchen is as high as Westminster Hall, and fit for any use in the world but that of dressing her dinner, and the rooms have all run a race upstairs without any one being able to catch the other, for there are no two exactly upon a floor, and yet no two upon distinct floors. This is her account of it. However, she has it for five and fifty pounds a year. It belongs to an old bachelor with £100,000, and we advised her to take the proprietor along with the house.

Thursday.

At Lady Jane's,[2] *tête-à-tête* except that Mrs. and Miss Cheap came in for a moment to shew themselves dressed for the French Ambassador's ball. The girl looked extremely genteel and beautiful. Lady Jane has asked her to go to Tunbridge, and all the family

---

[1] A comedy by O'Keefe.
[2] Lady Jane Macartney's house was then in Charles Street.

are mightily pleased. My mother told me a pleasant mistake this morning. You know little William Wyndham's match. Lady E. took an opportunity when playing at cards with Lady Galloway, who is deaf, and Cordon, who could not understand her, to open it to Lady Aylesford by saying one of her family was soon to be married. 'Lord,' says the other, thinking of Lord E. or Percy, 'I wish you joy with all my heart; well, I am vastly glad of it.' 'Nay,' returns Lady E., 'you need not be so glad, for I mean William.' 'William! and who is the lady?' 'Why,' says Lady E., 'I believe it is a match your father, the proud Duke of Somerset, would hardly have supposed one of his grandsons to make. 'Tis (in a low voice) Miss Harford.'[1] 'My father!' cries she; 'I believe he would have been the only person who could truly have approved of it. What a strange thing of William! and indeed I am a little amazed at her.' 'At her,' answers Lady E.; 'no, really I wonder *he* should like it, but don't in the least wonder she should.' 'Why, who did you say, and what do you mean?' And so they came to an explanation, and Lady Aylesford, not able to forbear laughing, exclaims, 'Why, ay, I thought you mad when you said my father, who looked upon family as the only thing to be minded, would have disapproved of a Herbert.'

Friday.

My father has not been well to-day—a little sort of a fever, but I hope it is only a cold. William wrote

---

[1] Miss Harford was a natural daughter of Frederick, Lord Baltimore. She married William Frederick Windham, fourth son of Charles, Earl of Egremont. He was sometime Minister at Florence.

word that all the people about Luton have had such illness that he thinks himself well-off to be rid of his so soon.   I went to Ranelagh to-night, *tête-à-tête* with Lady Mary, in obedience to her commands, which I hate of all things.   I have nothing to tell you of it but that I was seized by a very drunken beau and kindly invited to drink coffee—fairly picked up, in short,—a thing I had no notion one could possibly be exposed to there.   Lady Mary chose to be violently frightened, and instead of walking quietly out of the man's way, would whisk backwards and forwards, and run about and stop everybody we met to tell the story.   I could not help muttering that we had better not make people think we were drunk ourselves.   Miss Herbert came to me for an hour this evening.   She is off her bargain for the house because it is next door to a tallow chandler's.

Saturday.

My father is better to-day, and has dined with us. The weather is really growing fine and warm.   Lady Jane has had all her rabble of school-boys with her this week, but she gets rid of them to-day.   And now I believe I must make up my packet, for the coach will be ready presently.   Adieu, and bless you all. Is not this a strange, scrambling, dry sort of letter ? But you must forgive it, for I am *triste* and stupid.

Just come from Lady Courtown's, where we have had two Pelhams, the Duke and Duchess of Buccleuch, who are come to town for to-morrow's drawing-room and the French Ambassador's ball, the Duke of Montagu, Mrs. and Miss Brudenell, Lord

Brudenell, and Lady Frances.   Part of the company
stayed supper, and Lord Stopford[1] was placed at the
head of the table to do the honours.   He is taller, but
otherwise very little altered, and as he used to be very
like the King, Lady Frances tells his mother that many
a poor good woman has lost her reputation upon much
slighter grounds of suspicion than the likeness.   She
wants me to write a paragraph *animadverting* upon
the resemblance of a certain young nobleman, lately
arrived from abroad, to a certain illustrious personage,
which is much the subject of discourse in all polite
circles, and occasions remarks not highly to the
advantage of a certain countess, and so send it to
Lady Courtown as copied out of the newspapers.   It
being the part of a friend, etc., etc.

Lord Macartney had been appointed Governor of Fort
St. George (Madras) in 1781.   When he arrived he found
Sir Eyre Coote in the midst of his victorious career, and
though he held fast the fundamental maxim that the military
should be subordinate to the civil authorities, he appears to
have treated Coote with deference ; but on Coote's retirement
the same allowance was not shown to his successor, General
Stuart, or to Sir John Burgoyne, who were both put under
arrest for alleged insubordination, and the former sent to
England.   See *post* 1786.   Burgoyne's case was brought
before Parliament by his namesake of unfortunate Saratoga
notoriety on 10th August.

[1] Son of the second Earl of Cour-   He married, in 1791, Mary, eldest
town, and Mary, daughter and co-heir   daughter of Henry, third Duke of
of R. Powys, Esq., of Hintlesham.   Buccleuch.

LADY CARLOW from LADY MACARTNEY

2nd August 1784.

I HAVE had the pleasure of receiving your kind letter, my dear sister, and was exceedingly glad to have so good an account of you and the dear children, and also to hear that you and Lord Carlow are so comfortable with Mr. and Mrs. Damer. I wish they may remain some time with you, and could even be cruel enough to Miss Damer to rejoice if I heard that Mrs. Damer was to stay in Ireland till after your confinement. Indeed, I told Miss Damer so when she came to take leave of me the other day for going into the country. Lord Milton and she took their flight on Saturday, and she then entertained good hopes that they certainly should go to Lady Bateman soon.

There is now a ship arrived from Madras, which has brought me a letter of the beginning of last February from Lord Macartney. At that time his health was pretty good, but he complains much of his constitution being in general very much hurt and weakened by all he has gone through. He gives me no reason to hope that he has fixed any time for returning, as he bids me continue to write and send him letters. I have, according to custom, lost some letters in which he says he has given me an account of the arrest of Sir John Burgoyne. If they are not lost they have been suppressed, a circumstance very disagreeable, as the other party have their story to tell, and I have no materials to answer them. I cannot find out yet what was the cause of his arrest, or whether it was by order of General Lang or Lord Macartney. Some people tell me Sir John is coming home immediately; others, that he is going to wait in India to be tried by a court-martial.

I defer my going to Tunbridge till I know what the determination at the India House is with respect to Lord Macartney in consequence of this new Bill; I think they must finally settle in a short time whether he is to be removed or not.

The weather has hitherto been so wet and unpleasant that I have not regretted the country in the least. I am told that the Tunbridge waters are as good in the autumn as now, and there is a probability after so bad a summer that we shall have a fine autumn.

I spent two or three days in visits to the country last week. My brothers Charles and William have been in town, and more sociable than usual; little Charles[1] is now with me, and is, I believe, to set out with his father the end of this week to rejoin Mrs. Stuart. I had a letter from her a few days ago; she seems much better, charged me to remember her very kindly to you, and to tell you she hoped the correspondence between you would not drop again.

The family of South Audley Street are just returned from Luton, all vastly well and in very good spirits. Louisa thinks everything is settled at Luton very much to my mother's wish. They will certainly go to Yorkshire, I imagine in about a fortnight, to remain for the rest of the summer.

Adieu, my dear sister. Pray remember me kindly to

[1] Afterwards Lord Stuart de Rothesay.

Lord Carlow and my dear John. Also my best compliments to Mr. and Mrs. Damer. Your chair is finished, and I have begun again upon the trimming for little Car's Layette. I told Miss Damer that I would inform you she said it was too pretty for Car. —Your most faithful and affectionate   J. M.

I have just heard a piece of news, that Lord St. Asaph [1] has made proposals to Sophia Thynne, and is accepted.

The following letters were written by Elizabeth, wife of Henry, third Duke of Buccleuch, and daughter and heiress of the Duke of Montagu (see *ante*, p. 192), to Lady Louisa, who was staying with her mother at Lady Bute's cottage on her Yorkshire property of Wharncliffe.

LADY LOUISA STUART from the DUCHESS OF BUCCLEUCH

Dalkeith House, 3rd August [1784].

HOWEVER appearances may be against me, I have not forgot, my dear Lady Louisa, that you was so good to say you wished to hear from me, and have every day intended writing to you, but I have been in a continual worry ever since I got out of the coach, never having anything of much consequence to do, but a number of little nothings, which hinder one from settling as effectually as matters of greater importance. The most grievous interruptions I have met with have been from morning visitors, who have relieved one another to torment me every day. We arrived the

----

[1] Afterwards third Earl of Ashburnham. The marriage took place in 1784.

first day of the races (last Monday se'enight), and as they had collected a great number of people more than usual at Edinburgh, and that those people could not be amused by the races, which were very bad (and indeed some days no horses to run), they thought driving six miles into the country to visit me better than doing nothing.

Perhaps you will think me very peevish and ungrateful to my friends for showing so much *empressement* to see me, but as few of them were people I liked very much, and that morning visits are always rather troublesome in the country, I was more inclined to be out of humour with them for coming before I had time to shake off my dust after a long journey, and either had, or fancied I had (which is the same thing), fifty things to do. The bustle is now over in some degree, though Mrs. Siddons is still in Edinburgh, which keeps people together rather longer than usual. She goes away next week. The shooting season begins and the Court of Session rises, when we shall be quiet for some time. I was so stupid, I did not go once to town during the race week; the weather was then extremely hot. It has rained and thundered, and, according to custom, that has produced winter. This day is really piercing cold, and I could not keep myself tolerably comfortable by a pretty hard trot for an hour. I was last night at the play. Mrs. Siddons acted Zara,[1] a character I had never seen her in before. The play I do not like, nor did I ever see her with less pleasure, though she acted as well as ever, but all the other

---

[1] In Congreve's *Mourning Bride*.

performers are so very, very bad, it is quite tiresome.
To-morrow I am to see her in Lady Townley,[1] which
I think she will do well, and the rest cannot be so bad
in comedy as tragedy. I have not yet seen Lady
Betty.[2] Lady Harriet is at Newton, but I hear she
is to be in Edinburgh, in her way to Hamilton
races, which begin on Monday, and where I might
go if I pleased, having had a very civil invitation, but
I could not bring myself to accept. I must now
say a word or two of my journey. To begin with
Luton : nothing ever was so unlucky as the day we
were there ; it rained the whole time, so that we could
not stir out of the house. As much as I could see of
the place, it seems very pretty ; the ground lies beautifully. We were above two hours in the house, and I
admired some of the pictures exceedingly. I did not
omit visiting your apartment, which is very comfortable.
I believe the housekeeper thought me very troublesome, but I would not have missed seeing it upon any
account. We dined at Wooburne, and saw the place,
which I had seen many years ago, and liked it better
than I expected. We lay that night (notwithstanding
your advice to the contrary) at Market Harborough,
and found it very tolerable. Northampton was too
near, and Leicester too far. It was lucky we did not
go there, for the next morning, when we breakfasted
there, the landlord told us he had not a single bed in
his house the night before, it being the Assizes. I do
not know whether you are acquainted with him. I

---

[1] In Vanbrugh's *Provoked Husband*.
[2] Probably Lady Betty Cunningham and her sister Lady Harriet Don.

think him very agreeable, and what surprised me very much, he is a Swiss. We dined at Nottingham, and saw the Castle. There we were again met by a violent thunderstorm, which spoiled the view. I was made some amends by seeing Hardwicke, which fully answered my expectations. I think it is altogether the place most worth seeing of any in England. I was provoked with a stupid woman who showed it, and who had not one anecdote concerning it. I should think much fine timber had been cut down there, for I have so often heard of the fine trees that I looked for them, but though there is much wood, there is nothing remarkably fine, though many picturesque trees. We drove through Welbeck and Worksop parks, and then joined our old road at Doncaster, and from thence plodded on without anything to enliven us except stopping at Lumley Castle to see if there was anything worth bidding for at the auction.[1] I never saw anything so completely melancholy and neglected as the place. The house is a very good one, and many tolerable pictures, but none very good—a great many of the Scarborough family, which will sell for nothing, I daresay. It is quite a melancholy thing to think of a great family place so entirely destroyed; indeed, all his places will be the same, for everything in general is to be sold. Luckily, this Lord Scarborough is a poor creature, and, I suppose, does not feel it much. We found the Duke and his party arrived here about an hour before us, and all our servants, baggage, etc.,

---

[1] There is a fine Holbein, now at Dalkeith, "Sir Nicholas Cary, Master of Horse to Henry VIII.," which was bought at this sale.

etc., both by land and sea, came in the course of the next day, which was very odd, considering we all began our journey at different times. I am so very stupid I forget how to direct, or rather, I believe I was so stupid I never asked, I only know you told me it was to be *turn at Doncaster*. I think it will find you some time or other, at least I hope so; not that it is very valuable, but I should hate to have you think I had been unmindful of you. The sooner, therefore, you relieve me by telling me it is arrived the better. I really wish much to know how Lady Bute does. I hope the journey and change of scene has been of service to her. I beg my best compts. to her, and believe me, dear Lady Louisa, ever yours,   E. B.

The Duchess of Buccleuch from Lady Louisa Stuart

Wharncliff Lodge, 1st September 1784.

I WAS extremely pleased to find you so faithful in fulfilling your promise, my dear Dutchess, but would not set about answering your letter while I staid in town, because I knew Lady Frances had carried you full information of all that concerned me, as well as your other friends there, and I did not care to give you the same news over again. Now, therefore (though I fear the delay has not produced me many more materials), I begin. And in the first place accept a thousand thanks for having writ to me, which I really take as a very great favour, knowing you are not over fond of the imployment itself. In

the second (you must content yourself with this dry
matter of fact) I inform you that we left London on
the 25th in the most comfortless soaking weather it is
possible to conceive, and reached this place the third
day of our journey, which we made a little the longer
by going a few miles out of our way to Matlock, where
we slept the second night. We were so lucky as to see
a few gleams of sun upon it in the morning, and were
both very much delighted with the scene, though we did
not give ourselves quite time enough (at least, not what
I thought so) to be acquainted with all its beauties,
and met besides with a few little *contretemps* that rather
spoiled our frolick; such as being quite in the dark
(contrary to our expectation) before we approached
the valley; when we had gone up hill and down dale
through it, finding no room at the inn; dragging our
tired horses to another; finding that full too; being
then forced to measure our way back for a mile and take
up with a small one, where nothing was in readiness,
and no supper could be got till twelve o'clock at night,
etc., etc., etc., all which made the day very fatiguing to
my mother. But travelling, upon the whole, agrees so
well with her that I flatter myself the journey has done
her a great deal of good, and the air of this country
will not counteract it. We already find we have
amazing appetites, though it is out of our power to
gain them by any exercise except airing in a post-
chaise, for with great grief must I say we have had
but one day in which it was possible to walk; it has
now set in raining cats and dogs as if we never were
to have another, a circumstance which will make

one fret at any time, but which now is seriously alarming and melancholy on account of the harvest.   They
do not complain of their crop in this country, only fear
it will rot before the weather allows them to reap it or
take it in.   I am afraid all these things must go on
ten times worse with you than they do here.

We prudently and wisely imployed one of our worst
rainy days in visiting the Straffords, whom we found
tête-à-tête over their fire, and not in the least sorry to
see two more faces.   There we heard no news but that
Princess Emily had paid a morning visit to Sudbrook,
and Lady G[reenwich] walked about the neighbourhood
with her in her checked apron ; this is very interesting,
and, to be sure, you will hear of it from no other quarter,
so it is ingenious in me to think of telling it you.
It betrays my dulness sadly.   The last thing I was
told before I left town was that Lady Elliot and Lady
Harris were both safely brought to bed, and I believe
nothing else you care to know has happened since Lady
Frances and I parted.   Yes ! a little match published
itself two or three days after, which, I fear, will break
the Duke of Montagu's heart, for I remember he used
to be passionately in love with the lady.   It is our
favourite Miss Hamilton.   I can't very well tell you
whom or what she has got, only the man belongs to
Derbyshire, and has sighed for her, as her friends say,
eight or nine years ; indeed, I believe they say eleven
or twelve, but I am willing to keep within compass,
and not overload your faith, though, perhaps, you may
think whoever had liked her one year might go on the
rest of his life without a wonder.   In the meantime I

rejoice heartily upon Madame de Sévigné's principle, *Le public y gagnera de ne plus voir ce visage là.*

You bid me give you an account of Lady Carlow. I wish I had one to give. She is so bad a correspondent she sometimes makes me uneasy, and I have not heard from her now for almost three weeks. However, I saw a letter she writ to Mrs. Legge two days before I set out, and it was chearful enough to show me she had no disagreeable reason for her silence ; but I fancy she is extremely taken up by entertaining and going parties with the Damers. Mrs. Legge and Lady Macartney have been extraordinarily lucky in getting her a nurse they hope will perfectly suit her, which was a commission so difficult to execute for anybody in Ireland, they hardly flattered themselves they should give her satisfaction. Lady Macartney is still in London, putting off her going to Tunbridge from week to week according to the delays of the E. I. Directors, who are about settling the Government of Madras. I hope it is almost impossible that they should remove, that is to say, disgrace a man who has deserved so well of them as Lord M. ; but still she wishes to be upon the spot and know the event immediately, and since the weather is so bad, perhaps she loses nothing, for I imagine the efficacy of the waters has great dependance upon it. She writes me word she has received a letter from him with an indifferent account of his health, mentioning particularly his being laid up with the rhumatism—no dangerous disorder, but a very painful one. I wish for nothing so much as to hear of his imbarking to return home.

I do agree that you had a right to have your share of Lady Frances, but I should have been very sorry notwithstanding if you had come into possession of it a day sooner, for she was the greatest comfort imaginable to me; and considering all things, I suppose you yourself will think it lucky their journey was delayed so long. I am in great hopes her health and spirits will be much improved this summer. I shall depend upon your goodness and charity more than hers for accounts of them. You are really very kind in telling me how things are going on at Dalkeith, for I always interest myself about places which I have seen enough to like, especially those where I have lived and been happy. I am afraid, indeed, I remember them more affectionately than I do persons, and love your great tree better than my amiable acquaintance Miss Wauchope. However, her tender recollection does me a great deal of honour. I can only say in return that I regret so promising a connection was broken off before it had time to ripen into friendship. And now it is time to conclude my stupid letter. I bad Lady F. forewarn you of the liberty I should take with his Grace by inclosing to him my letters to Lady Betty C[unningham] and Miss Mure, as franks are now at an end. I beg my compliments to him, Lady Mary, etc. Tell Lady F. I will write next post if I can, but think it unnecessary to address myself the same day to two people who are so very near being one, so like one, I mean, the other sounds as if you were going to be married. Adieu, my dear Dutchess; think me ever sincerely and gratefully yours,   L. STUART.

The 3rd.

As we do not send letters every day, this has remained till now in my drawer, so I think I may as well
add a line to say I have heard from my sister, who is
rambling with ye Damers in the neighbourhood of
Dublin, and seems in remarkable spirits. They were
to set sail in two days, and in the meantime are seeing
places and diverting themselves, and she with them.
Our weather is wonderfully changed and improved
since I began writing. My mother's best and kindest
compliments to both of you.

LADY LOUISA STUART from the DUCHESS OF
BUCCLEUCH

September 1784.

MANY thanks to you, my dear Lady Louisa, for
your letter, which I received while I was at Bothwell,
where I staied about ten days. Lady Frances, I
believe, wrote to you during that time, and probably
gave you some account of herself and me. We passed
our time very comfortably, at least, so I thought, and
I was very sorry to leave her, particularly as she gave
me but little hopes of seeing her here before, or rather
until, they go to London, for I hope they will then
make us a visit. I do not think it probable I shall
make her another this year; moving anywhere is
always a serious thing to me, and I expect my father
here every day, which will make it more impossible for
me to stir from home for some time. I suppose Lady
Frances told you what fine things she is doing,
and what great things she is to do. I assisted both
with my advice and also my hands, for I gravelled

many inches of the new walk in a most masterly manner.   The tent is in the old place, and we spent a great deal of our time in it.   There I received your letter, and there we often talked you over, and wished for you as often.   It was the finest weather I ever saw all the time I was there, except now and then a mist about the hills, which I was always scolded for taking notice of.

Saturday, 2nd October.

So far I wrote many days ago, and have never until this minute had time to finish.   My father arrived yesterday while we were at breakfast.   He is vastly well, and not sorry, I believe, to find himself here; he has been doing duty at Windsor almost ever since we left him.

I hope your fine weather continued, and that Lady Bute had no return of the gout.   You will then have enjoyed the beauties of Yorkshire completely.   I conclude you are now returned to Luton—I hope not to London yet, for though the weather (here at least) is become a little winterish, London must be the most melancholy of all places at present, and I believe nobody thinks so more than you do.   I really rejoice most exceedingly for the reason you do that Miss Hamilton has been so fortunate to meet with a man of so very bad a taste.   She is just one of those people whose face is a real nuisance wherever one meets with it.   The Duke of M.[1] will join most heartily with us, for I never saw so determined an aversion as he has always had to her.   You desire I will tell you how things are going on at Dalkeith with regard to the

---

[1] The Duke of Montagu, her father.

inhabitants. Much as you may remember when you was here—one day is as much like another as I can possibly make it ; now and then the arrival of company causes some little variety, and seldom for the better. I think we have not had many sojourners—the Clerks, Miss Pringle, and odd men at different times. Major Scott, whom I believe you do not know, has been here the whole summer, and for ten days we have had a young Stopford, a cousin of Lord Courtown's, who is a midshipman on board the frigate stationed here. Lord Kinnoul is coming next week to spend some days to visit his old friend the Duke of M. This day being Saturday will bring some dinner company, I suppose, but I flatter myself not a great deal, as all the fine people of Edinburgh are now in the country. We met with a very pleasant Frenchman the other day who is travelling through Scotland for his amusement, and whom Lord Morton introduced to us. His name is Le Marquis de Bomballe, or something like it.[1] He is appointed their Minister at Lisbon, and seems sensible, lively, and entertaining, and none of the nonsense and impertinence which generally belongs to a Frenchman, and appears vastly pleased with England and Scotland. He is to return again in May to London and bring his wife with him. I am vastly glad to hear Lady Carlow is so well, as she certainly must be to go about so much in her present situation. Pray always mention her to me when you write, as I have no other chance of ever hearing of her. I hope everything has been settled

[1] Sebastien Jozé di Carvalho e Mallo, Marquis de Pombale, born 1699, died 1782. He was First Minister in Portugal.

to Lady Macartney's satisfaction at the India House. She never can be completely comfortable till he returns to England.   Being at so great a distance from anybody one loves really embitters all the minutes of one's life, and there is not even much comfort in hearing from them, accounts are so long coming.   I had a letter from Lady Frances yesterday.   She is pretty good in writing, but as I know she is in general very idle, I mention her being well, as perhaps you may not hear from her so often as you wish.   She is at this minute (I believe) entertaining the Countess of Dalhousie, who threatened her with a visit of some days.   I forget whether you saw her here.   If you did, I need not add that I pity her exceedingly.   She talked much of making many visits when I left her, but I do not find by her letters that she has yet made one—the Duchess of Hamilton excepted,—and many civilities had passed between them.   The Duke is gone to Inverary to visit his sister Lady Augusta, who is thought in a bad way, and the Duke and Duchess of Argyll talk of spending the winter abroad with her.   The Binnings are gone to live with her sister, who has not been well, but is not thought yet in any danger.   Perhaps you will think me a little mad for writing upon this paper,[1] but Lady Frances gave me a cargo of it.   Winking is good for the eyes. I believe it is better than the white, but it certainly looks very odd.   All here desire to be remembered kindly to you.   Our best compts. to Lady Bute.— Yours ever most sincerely,   E. B.

---

[1] The letter is written on a green-tinted paper.

Lord Macartney was appointed by the East India Company Governor-General in 1784, which post he declined. The following note from Edmund Burke was received by Lady Macartney relating to the appointment :—

Charles Street, 17th February 1785.

MADAM—I take it for granted you are informed that Lord Macartney is chosen Governor-General of Bengal. Permit me to wish your Ladyship joy of this appointment, so pleasant to all your friends and so beneficial to the public. I have the honour to be, with Mrs. Burke's most respectful compliments, and with the highest respects, Madam, your Ladyship's most obedient and most humble servant,   EDMUND BURKE.

———

LADY CARLOW from LADY LOUISA STUART

London, 22nd October 1784.

THANK God a thousand times, my dearest sister, for the good news [1] we had of you yesterday, which Miss D[awson] confirms and adds to in a letter I have just got from her. I fear I must condole with you upon its being a daughter, as I suppose Lord Carlow will not be so well satisfied, but I hope he does not make a disappointment of it, and I own, provided you and the little thing are both safe and well, it signifies very little. They may all grow up and marry off your hands, and if so, daughters are less incumbrance to a family than sons. As for education, to be sure it makes that rather more difficult to have so many near the same age, but the more of either of them the greater the difficulty will be, and so I wish you would

[1] The birth of another daughter, christened Harriet. She married, shortly after her mother's death, the Rev. and Hon. Henry David Erskine, afterwards Dean of Ripon.

stop here. I write to you because, as the letters have
been so long coming, you will be in your third week
before you get this. Pray say something very civil to
Miss Dawson from me. I shall write to thank her in
due form, but as I rather expect another letter from
her, I wait till it is come, that I may do it altogether,
because I should think she would as lieve have one
letter as two, the postage being really a serious thing
now. Both she and Lord Carlow are so concise in
their account that they don't say whether you were a
short time or a long time in labour, or anything else
but the bare fact, and I really could have wished to
hear some particulars, but I hope you despatched
the business with ease as usual.

William came to town yesterday, looking better
than I expected to see him, and very cheerful and
merry. He is going to spend the winter at Bath,
partly for health and partly for economy. I am glad
of it, for it is much better than living by himself at
Luton, not but what I am already so sick of this place
that I would change with him. Really the *ennui* and
melancholy of it is past conception, and when I think
how long our winter is, I could cry. It is certainly
lucky no good, sober farmer comes in my way, for I
might not resist the temptation. I never felt the
change from country to town so sensibly as an animal
before. I have a constant weight on my head, and
hardly feel alive, which, I suppose, is because I come
from a remarkably fine air, and have used myself to be
out all day long. My mother is *ennuyée* enough too,
and there is nobody in town for her but Lady F.

Medows. She was at Court yesterday (not I, for I could not get a hairdresser, and was glad to stay away), and to-day we have been paying a most formal awkward visit where we were not welcome, and I am sure had no business. It was to the Duchess of Argyll,[1] who is going to the south of France in a day or two for her health and Lady Augusta's—both look very ill. The Duchess of Ancaster was there and Lady Derby.

Adieu, my dearest Caroline, and God always bless you and your children. What name will you give the young one?

I forgot to thank you for a letter I got from you since I wrote last, which had been in Yorkshire and was forwarded here. By that you had sent away your man in a wrong time, for I think you must have been brought to bed on the Sunday.

I wish you had made M[iss] D[awson] tell me all these things. My mother is writing to Lord Carlow. My love to him and congratulations.

LORD CARLOW from the HON. MRS. LIONEL DAMER

Came, 5th November 1784.

I RECEIVED your letter, my dear Lord, the beginning of this week on our return from Milton Abbey, and am ashamed not to have answered it immediately, which I should have done had we not been so busy every day with settling and beginning our planting, which, I hope, will plead my excuse with you, and I am less fearful of

---

[1] Elizabeth Gunning, see *ante*, p. 94. Lady Augusta Campbell, her daughter, married General Clavering, and died 1831.

its doing so from being assured that you and Lady Carlow would have no doubts but that I should with pleasure comply with your request of being godmother to your new little visitor, and can have no objection to any name Lady Carlow has the most particular wish for.   I was vastly happy at the good account you gave me of her, and sincerely hope by this time she is quite well and out again.

The Moores are arrived, and promise us with a visit here, as they do not intend returning to Ireland, she writes me word, before January, and most probably they will stay some time longer.   They had a terrible passage of four nights and three days, which must have been dreadful, as she is always so ill on board a ship. I felt delighted, tell Lady Carlow, at being safe here, although I can assure you I always recollect Ireland with pleasure, and more particularly the time I spent at Dawson Court.   Pray tell her, with my kind love, I shall be very happy to have a letter from her, so as to hear all the occurrences she can find time to tell me of.

Mr. Wyatt is not come to us yet, although he fixed the latter end of October, but Mr. Lionel has full employment with his work out of doors, which he desires me to say has prevented him from writing to your Lordship as he proposed before this time.   He hopes to do so very soon.   He sends his kind remembrances to you both, and I am very sincerely, my dear Lord, your most affectionate, humble servant,

WILLIAMSA DAMER.

All the little creatures have my best wishes.

LADY CARLOW from LADY LOUISA STUART

Saturday, 6th November.

I GOT your letter yesterday, and am glad to find you go on so well, but hate to think of your being so solitary and melancholy, without any of us with you. I am sadly afraid it lowers your spirits and hinders you from recovering so fast as usual. But pray take care of yourself, and don't hurry to go out or make any extraordinary exertion. I wonder what became of our letters? I believe my mother wrote to Lord Carlow the very day she received his, and I am sure I did to you the day after, so how Mrs. Legge, who heard of it from us (by Lady Mary), could wish you joy first is past my comprehension. There seem to be nothing but melancholy events round you, but why do they tell you of them at present? It is but a bad amusement to anybody who must be confined to a room. I heard a thing the other day more melancholy than can be conceived, which made me start and shudder as if I had been immediately interested in it. They say poor Lord Herbert [1] is in a very bad state of health, that the leg, of which he has been so long lame, is quite wasted, and the physicians fear it is from weakness and bad constitution, not accident; in short, they talk of him as if the worst were to be very much apprehended, and I fear Lady Egremont, who tells my mother all this, is but too good authority, as his life is as precious to her family upon the account of interest as it is to his own

---

[1] He was now twenty-five years old, and lived to succeed his father in 1794, and died in 1827, aged sixty-eight.

upon all others.   He is now at Bath, and his poor unhappy mother at Paris; they expect her soon in England.   If she must lose him too, I think any friend of hers might rejoice to hear she had perished in the passage.   But I hope in God it won't be so.

Lady Jane has had a letter from Miss Herbert, who is living at Mr. Dalrymple's, and in great distress what to do for a house in London.   She seems to know nothing of all I have told you.

I know no news but that Lord Walgrave [1] has got his father's place of Master of the Horse to the Queen, which almost everybody is glad of.   She has been extremely kind to his sisters, and kept them constantly with her since the poor old man died.   He was so totally failed, and in such a tottering condition, that he had been long lost to them, and therefore I fancy they are not in great affliction.

The Bishop has his regiment, and Lord Percy the Bishop's troop of guards; they talk of Lord Lincoln for the vacant regiment.   I am going to the play to-night with Lady Mary and Lady Mount Edgecumbe. The latter has returned much as she went, only in low spirits, I think, but very full of the French dress, which she says is perfectly plain; so bind your gowns with ribbon, wear no aprons, save your money, and tell your neighbours it is the fashion, and in a morning put on your great coat, with what you will under it, provided you have two handkerchiefs big enough for

---

[1] John, third Earl of Waldegrave, died 22nd October, and his son "kissed hands" on his appointment, 4th November.

the sails of a large pleasure boat. Adieu! for I am writing sad nonsense. God bless you, my love. I hope this will find you and all the children well.

The bishop referred to is Frederick, the second son of George III., who was gazetted Colonel of the Coldstreams in October, and created Duke of York in November 1784. Twenty years earlier, when he was an infant of six months, he was made Bishop of Osnabruck, an office held by the father and brother of George I. Lady Mary Coke, writing from Hanover in 1763, says:—

"Is it yet known in England that he [the King] has recommended him [the infant] to be elected Bishop of Osnabruck? It seems a hardship on his brothers, and may be a loss to the family, as his Majesty has not a second nomination, and the life of a new-born child is very uncertain."—*Journal*, vol. i. p. 6.

Betham, in his great genealogical tables, published in 1795, does not in his list of 'Spiritual Princes of the Empire,' though dedicated to King George, venture to give any date of election or installation. This anomalous appointment can scarcely be accounted for by the curious custom practised in this diocese, since the Peace of Westphalia in 1648, of appointing alternately Protestant and Roman Catholic bishops. It was effectually put an end to by the dissolution of the chapter and the secularisation of the revenues in 1803 during the French Revolutionary war, but in 1857-1859 the Pope reconstituted the diocese, and the Bishop of Osnabruck is now only a Lord Spiritual; the Duke of York was the last Prince Bishop. Burns alludes to this fact in his well-known address to the Royal Family, in which he recommends him, as *Right Reverend Osnaburgh*, to 'get a wife to hug, or troth! ye'll stain the mitre.'

London, 9th November 1784.

I AM very glad to find by your letters to my mother and Lady Jane that you go on so well, and so well pleased with your new *olive branch*. I observe you say nothing about the business of suckling. I suppose if you have taken it upon yourself, you do not mention it for fear Lady Jane should be mortified about the nurse; but don't think she will mind it. She is come to town very well, and continues to walk miles every morning, which she would fain make me do too, but till London is as clean as a green field, and as solitary, and as cheerful with fine sun and fresh air, I believe I shall be deaf to all her lectures. My father returned from High Cliffe yesterday, looking charmingly, and admires to find London in the same fog he left it, for he says the weather has been delightful in Hampshire. So is it not here. I am sure I feel it in my head, and I don't fancy trudging about the dirty streets would remove the weight. I have increased it just now by curling my hair. Do you know poor Monge[1] died last week? I was very sorry for him, and at a great loss what to do. At last his nephew, your man, came to offer his services, and I think I shall fix with him. Those people ought not to wish for my custom, for I always bring them ill-luck. They either die or break as soon as I get used to them, and something of the same fatality attends my acquaintances; whenever anybody takes my fancy, and he begins to be intimate, some unforeseen event settles them, the Lord knows how or where, out of my reach. I don't remember if

[1] Hairdresser.

I said to you last summer that I was *going* to like Lady Murray, and intended trying to see more of her. This autumn, lo and behold, she has taken a sudden resolution to go back and live in Scotland, and decamps with bag and baggage this very week. She will be some time at Dalkeith.

THE SAME from the SAME

November 1784.

I BEGIN upon this large sheet of paper because I reproach myself for doing so little to amuse you, now when you are solitary and (I much fear) melancholy ; and yet I lead so quiet a life, and have so little to say, that the Lord knows how I shall fill half of it. The news of the day will do nothing, for the day has no news, and my day would have none even if the town were fuller and livelier, but I will go back to the date of my last for my stupid insignificant journal. Saturday night I went to the play with Lady Macartney and Lady Mount Edgecumbe. My mother was to have been one of our party, but found another she liked better, and I could have done so too, easily, for I liked mine very ill, and grew heartily tired before a third of the play was over. Mrs. Abington acted, and Lady Macartney saw a number of her acquaintance in the house, which I did not do, according to custom. Lord Barrington, Lord Sefton, and Mr. Dillon were in the box, and I invited them down very kindly as soon as they came in, to secure the row immediately behind us. For you must know the last time we were at the play an officer made his appearance, either half drunk or half mad, sat down almost in my mother's lap, cocked his hat, and whispered first to Lady Mary and then to me. I once heard him utter an oath upon finding us both deaf, and as he had a stick in his hand, I was afraid he would have proceeded to make some use of it. But after pushing us, leaning over us, and playing a few more tricks, a gentleman in the box civilly desiring him to take off his hat, he thought fit to start up and go away. To be sure I need not be under any concern how to fill my paper if I make every foolish story as long as I have done this. There is a knock at the door. Miss Herbert, I suppose. Old Catherine is with Lady Macartney, so she was to lend her to me. It was Miss Herbert. She has sold the lease of her house to her cousin Neville, and has his leave to live in it till Christmas into the bargain, so is no longer upon the *pavé*. Mrs. Dalrymple is in town for her confinement. She seems not to think Lord Herbert in so bad a way as I had heard he was. She is fat, and merry, and thoughtless as ever, has taken an aversion to the Duke of Ancaster[1] and Lady H. Pitt, but made no new friendships at Brighton. She has nothing to do but bathe in the sea to get rid of all cares and vexations. She says I told her I had been bathing in the air, and that was as good. Last

[1] Brownlow, fifth and last Duke, who died in 1809, when the Dukedoms of Ancaster and Kesteven and the Marquisate of Lindsey became extinct : the Earldom of Lindsey reverted to a distant kinsman ; the Barony of Willoughby and the landed property passed into a short abeyance between the sisters, and is now, with the new Earldom of Ancaster, in the descendant of the elder sister. The large personal estate reverted to Brownlow, Earl of Poltimore, son of Viscount Milsington, by his marriage with Lady Mary Bertie, only daughter of the late Duke.

night Fish Crauford[1] came, good-humoured and agreeable.

Friday.

We tumbled last night even into Great Russell Street to visit the Miss Murrays. It rained and blew with such a vengeance as I hardly ever saw. We found them at work, and I was quite sorry for them, for we had not visited them before since Lady Mansfield's death, and the tears came into their eyes. Miss Eliza looked very pretty, but melancholy. I wish that poor girl and Mr. Pelham could marry. I hope he is more constant to her than he was to his former love. This great deed accomplished, we went to a party at Lady G. Cavendish's (it was after her christening), when we found your queen[2] in great beauty, but, according to my observation, not in good spirits. She is really very civil here, and I wonder what has bewitched her to be otherwise amongst you, to whom she should naturally have wished to make herself doubly agreeable. There were several of the fine men, but not many women,—Queen Mary,[3] by the way (who is so disturbed at the fantastical dresses of the young people), the figure of Mad Bess, though perfectly guiltless of being in the fashion. I was *embarrassée de ma personne*, which I always am the first time I find myself in company after the summer retreat, and glad enough to come away early.

I am sick of all the stupid nonsense and good spelling that I write to you.

At Night.—I have been in Charles Street when

Lady Jane had just got your letter.   I am sorry to find
neither you nor the child are quite well.   How I wish
I could fly to you for a month, and stay with you till I
had put you in spirits!   Next to this I wish you had
somebody else you could like and be comfortable with,
for I hate to think of your leading so lonely a life.
Where is Charlotte Cary? and when will Mr. A. bring
his daughter?   You don't talk as if Miss Dawson had
continued with you.   I have had a long letter from the
Duchess this evening to wish me joy of your safety.
She bids me say a thousand kind things to you.   It is
well she makes a tolerable correspondent, for Lady
Frances is quite abominable, so are most of mine, I
think.   I have heard but once this whole season from
Lady Emily, and for Mrs. Alison,[1] I don't know
whether she is dead or alive.

Saturday.

Now I must send my letter.   I am sorry I took
the great sheet of paper, as I have filled it so ill.   It
looks like the French Ambassador's supper—four
plates of oysters in the midst of a huge table.   By
the bye, his Excellence is in his own country, whence
most of our travellers are returned.   Who do you
think have been dancing to Paris and back again
but Mr. and Mrs. Charteris.[2]   They are returned
mighty well pleased with their tour, but abusing

[1] Dorothea, daughter of the distinguished physician, Professor John
Gregory.   She married the Rev. Archibald Alison, Edinburgh, father of the
historian, and grandfather of the gallant
soldier, Sir Archibald, of our own day.

[2] Francis Charteris, eldest son of
the sixth Earl of Wemyss, who married,
in 1771, Susan, daughter of Anthony
Tracy Keck, and became Lord Elcho
in 1787.

France and everything in it like the citizens in Foote's play of *A Trip to Calais*. (I suppose their Hotel Garnie was full of fleas.) They went to Versailles and saw the Court, and swear the ladies were all dressed in washed gauze and tumbled muslin; but they got some of their own dear country folks, the charming Mr. Wraxall[1] amongst others, to comfort them, and made up a mighty pleasant society, and so, *Old England for ever*.

25th November 1784.

I HAVE been lazy all this week, and neglected my journal till your letter came to rouse me. I can't say it pleases me, however, for I am grieved to hear your cold has lasted so long, and appeared in so many disagreeable shapes. I hope in God you are not ill otherwise, but I see it must have hindered you from recovering your strength after your lying in. Besides, it is so melancholy to be wrapped up and confined from one week to another without any company you like, that I hate to think of it. For my part, I go on in the same solemn sadness at Lady Jane's every evening— no variety except that Tuesday I had Lady Emily [Macleod], who was in town for two days *en passant*. She is as big as if she were to have six children and produce them to-morrow, but looks remarkably well, and enquired a good deal after you and your nursery. I observe all you ladies who are often in that way yourselves grow very curious and inquisitive about one another, and desirous to know how such a one was brought to bed, and what sort of a child she has got,

---

[1] Who died as Sir Nathaniel in 1831, and whose Memoirs were so severely criticised in the twenty-fifth number of the *Quarterly Review*.

and whether she suckles it, and how it thrives, etc.,
etc. ; so it was not particular to Lady Mount [Stuart],
whom we used to laugh at in former days for liking to
talk of nothing but of lyings in, but the common infirmity of the sex.   Lady E.[1] has carried her little girl
with her through all her rambles.   They stayed a
month at Bath, where they made a great acquaintance
with Lord Herbert, and are quite charmed with him.
By all I hear, he is not ill, but extremely lame, and they
much fear his leg wastes away, which is a frightful
thing.   He is returned to Bath, and Lord and Lady
Courtown are gone there, so they design to persuade
Lady P.[2] to come there when she has paid her
duty at Windsor.   It is the best thing she can do, as
none of her friends will be in London.   By the way,
not one word from Lady Frances, I don't know why,
but I have taken a fancy into my head that she is with
child again, which I should be very sorry for, and she
too, I believe.   Miss Herbert has charged me over and
over again to tell you that Mrs. Dalrymple was brought
to bed last week of a fine boy, and that she cannot
suckle it, all which she assured me you will think very
interesting news, because of that natural curiosity I
took notice of above.   Ford said, ' Pooh, what does
she care for Mrs. Dalrymple and her child ! '   If it be
so, thank her for it.   Lady Mary has been lamenting
over that lady's fate very seriously for some time, being
sure she would die in the operation, and for a very

[1] Probably Egremont.
[2] The beautiful Lady Pembroke, daughter of the Duke of Marlborough, and high in favour at Windsor. The origin of the Windsor uniform, which has the colours of the Pembroke livery, was in compliment to this lady.

curious reason, which diverted my mother exceedingly, and would you, only I don't think it quite fit to be communicated by the pen of a *spinster*.   Her wisdom was mistaken, however, for Mrs. Dalrymple despatched the affair in as little time as ever you did, and with as little difficulty.   This too Miss Herbert bade me be sure to tell you.   She spent the evening with us yesterday.   Her dear Colonel Cunningham is in town, and she has thoughts of settling at Slanes Castle.   K. U., she says, sat with her for four hours the other morning, and at the end of their conversation told her that he thought he should never marry again, or something to that purpose.   In short, she is persuaded she must be content to lead apes,[1] which she confesses she would rather not do, if it could be helped.   Alas! I desired her to pluck up a spirit and say, as I was determined to do for the future, instead of I *can't* and I *shan't*, I *won't* marry.   But she seems by no means disposed to pronounce that word.   She told me a story I thought good enough.   Lady Caroline was persuading an old friend that had been her sister virgin to marry somebody who, she owned, would not have done for her formerly, but whom she ought to think now a very good match.   'What!' says the other, 'and do you think I have waited so long to take up with *him* at last?'   I like this way of thinking mightily.   To be sure, waiting long in all other cases gives one a right to a better thing than one expected at the beginning, but I doubt one should not get anybody to allow such a claim in this.

---

[1] 'To die an old maid,' *Much Ado about Nothing*, Act ii. Sc. 1.

Sunday, 28th November 1784.

I TOOK a long walk with Lady Jane through the Park and round Kensington Gardens this morning. She has got the better of me at last, and makes me do it almost every day; indeed, I don't dislike it. My aversion is to dawdling backwards and forwards among fine people, or measuring the same ground over and over again in a square. Miss Tryon's party was woefully dull. She had a German harper, whose music was so fine that, to my unpolished ears, it sounded as if he had been tuning the instrument all the time instead of playing upon it. This, with Miss Dayrall's harpsichord and some foreigner's fiddling, made up the concert. Miss Herbert was there, and has been in Charles Street this evening. She desires us all to bewail her ill-luck, for she stayed at home the other day from a presentiment that she should have some agreeable visitor, and, lo! her footman prudently denied Col. Cunningham. This is a very good jest, you understand, but she would rather Col. C. had been let in. 'Were na' her heart light she wad die.' Lady Lucan has an assembly to-morrow, so we shall see the world.

Monday.

Not much of it truly, for my mother was detained at Lady Egremont's, and then in such a hurry to go home that we have not been literally ten minutes in the house. As it happened, I wished to stay longer and see the humours of it. Some of us are glorious figures. Such wings and tails to our caps! Such shelves of plaited gauze under the chin, it puts one in

mind of a Carcau,[1] a Chinese moveable pillory.   The
Duchess of Devonshire and Lady Duncan had their
hair hanging down to their waists, curled in ringlets at
the end.   They were dressed in redingotes—robes
turques, that is to say, with three capes and capells.
But a figaro is the right thing, and that I have not
seen.   I don't think I ever saw new fashions set in
with such a vengeance, except in the year when feathers
and high heads first began, and yours scandalised Lady
Betty [Mackenzie]. Miss Herbert and Col.Cunningham
were there, but at different card tables.   I told her I
hoped she would meet with him, and be as lucky in her
love affairs as the proverb promised her, for she seemed
to be losing all the money she had in the world.

Wednesday.

Yesterday morning was employed in waiting two
hours and a half to see Monsieur Blanchard[2] and his
balloon go off, which it did from a place behind the
Riding House in Green Street.   We had a tolerable
view of it at a window my father secured for us, and a
strange sight it was, rather than a pleasant one.

Charles Street, in the Evening.

What am I saying?   I mean *this* evening, for Miss
Gunning[3] came to me.   I never saw her look so well
since I was acquainted with her, but she is in tribulation

[1] Cangue,see Yule's *Indian Glossary*.
[2] Aërostation was the popular exhibition of the day, Lunardi as well as Blanchard having made previous ascents from Chelsea in September and October.
[3] Sir Robert Gunning of Horton, Bart., the Ambassador, had two daughters, Charlotte, a maid of honour, who married Colonel Hon. Stephen Digby (see Madame D'Arblay's *Diary*), and Barbara,who married General Ross.

about her sister, whom she thinks very ill, consumptive, and I don't know what. Her account of her is more like a stomach complaint than a consumption, and I daresay it will prove so. Lady Mary dined with us yesterday. She was telling us the story of poor Miss Elliot, which I never heard one word of before, did you? She had it from the Cheaps, and they from Sir John Elliot, who attends her. Miss Gunning has been at Lady G.'s to-night. She is in great beauty, and remarkably genteel.

Friday.

We went to Court yesterday, and had a very entertaining drawing-room from a number of presentations, particularly those of the two great Marquises and Marchionesses of Buckingham and Lansdown. (For that, not Wycombe, is Lord Shelburne's title. He has but a far-fetched sort of claim to it, his first wife being related to the Granville family, and his son by her descended from it.) Our sex is commonly reckoned fondest of titles, but I believe the two lords enjoyed their elevation more than the two ladies, who seemed to care very little about the matter. We had also a wedding—a Mr. and Mrs. Carew (pronounced Cary),—Mr. John Yorke's daughter,[1] and all the House of Yorke attended it. And a *second jour de noces*, Mr. and Mrs. Law, son and daughter to the Bishop of Carlisle and Archbishop of York. I suppose you remember the handsome Miss Markham. All relations came with them too. All ministers whatever were there, old and young, and upon the whole it was very full. Lord

---

[1] Elizabeth, daughter of John Yorke, fourth son of Chancellor Hardwicke, married the Rt. Hon. R. Pole Carew.

Campden[1] kissed hands, but my news of the change in the Admiralty is not true, for Lord Howe has it. I doubt your late Lord and Lady-Lieutenant will be ill-pleased to descend to be Lord and Lady Bucks, after having usurped Buckingham so long. They will hardly get people to say that long word, Buckinghamshire.[2] I had not much conversation with anybody but Mr. J. Yorke. I fancy you don't know him. He is a great [friend] of mine.

Saturday.

I got your letter last night, and was much pleased to see it more cheerful than your former ones. I will write 'a single sheet' on my direction for the future, and I hope that will save you the trouble of battling with the Post Office people. You are in the right to make them refund when they cheat you. I hope the dear bairns are all well, as you say nothing of them. Lady Jane has been preaching to you not to like Louisa better than Car—very good advice,—but I wonder how she, who showed so much partiality herself, has the assurance to give it. I have said nothing to answer your questions about Miss Herbert. I doubt she has just now about as much chance of finding a house with such furniture as I have myself. But as you say, her heart breaks and pieces again, and is not much the worse. I never saw her more disposed to be merry, but her way of talking is altogether—what signifies? and who cares? and one lives on somehow or another, let things go on as they will, and so forth; not as if

[1] Lord Camden was Lord President of the Council this year.

[2] Before Lord Temple was made Marquis of Buckingham, Lord Buckinghamshire was generally called Lord Buckingham.

she were in the situation she liked, but as if she found
it necessary to persuade herself that no one situation
could be made better than another.   I have now made
you out a very handsome letter, as far as length goes,
and may leave off with a safe conscience.   My father
has got a bad cold and a sore throat, but I hope nothing worse.   God bless you and yours.   I make no
ending, because I write on.   Adieu.

I find poor Martinnant is just broken and ruined.
It is really ridiculous that this should happen to all the
tradesmen I deal with.   I saw Mary Pelham at Court,
looking very well.   Lady Chatham is at length recovering pretty fast.

8th December 1784.

LADY MARY dined here yesterday, and spent the
evening at Lady Jane's.   She was in a composed
humour, very pleasant and agreeable, just what she was
born to have been always. We have two strange stories,
one about the poor Duke of Rutland being killed by a
fall from his horse, which now gains credit, and if true
is very shocking.   The other my father produced to
us yesterday, and had from Dutens, who heard it told
and discussed at a supper given by his Grace of
Queensberry to the Prince, where a number of
foreigners were assembled.   I will not tell it to you
because I think it wicked to spread scandal, for if
ever so improbable, some good-natured people believe
it.   It relates to a lady and her footman, the former
unsuspected of gallantry, but haughty and impertinent,
therefore likely to have enemies, and it runs strangely

in my head, from certain circumstances I remember, that it must be an Irish invention, saving your presence. The good company at supper, you may be sure, not only gave it full credit, but brought twenty of their own observations to prove it likely. This is the way with these fine gentlemen. His R.H. is said to be abominable in this respect, and as for the Duke of Queensberry, those old worthless rakes always are so. However, even Lady M. hooted at this. Here is the greatest fall of snow I ever saw, with a high wind, after five days' unceasing rain.

Thursday.

All frozen over now, and seemingly set in for a long hard frost. This is very early. I stayed at home last night, and Miss Gunning came to me. She continues very well herself, and I fancy there is nothing seriously alarming in her sister's complaints. I think we have nothing but scandal, and horrible scandal too. I hear Mr. and Mrs. Herbert have arrived, and deny every word of the story of the newspapers, which by the bye those same detestable *Morning Posts* now apply to Lady Glandore. This is a sweet world.

Friday.

One of the most bitter days I ever felt, just as cold, if not colder, than any last winter. Mrs. Stuart[1] came to town on Wednesday with her two girls, whom she left with Lady Jane to stay till to-day. Mary has had her hair dressed and powdered for the first time, and is the happiest of all human creatures. I

---

[1] Mrs. James Stuart and her two daughters.

spent the evening in their company, and what with
laughing, dancing, and romping, was quite worn out.
I like them mightily. They are sensible, and seem
honest, and, as they should be, ready to laugh themselves into fits without any reason but their inward
good spirits. I do love girls of their age, when the
mind is just opening and ripening, and ready to
receive every pleasurable impression, when they begin
to think, but have not learnt to regret and foresee,
and do all that in a few more years makes thinking
uncomfortable. Mrs. Medows called upon us this
morning. The General[1] is in town. I bade her tell him
his friend Lady Jane was at home every evening.
Miss Gunning is gone to the Lodge, and means to
go back with her sister to Horton[2] on Sunday. She
writes me word she is miserable about her, but convinced her disorder is nervous; but you must know
Lady M. and Mrs. S. agree that there is very little
the matter with her, and suspects she is in love. She
certainly looks as well as ever she did in her life, and
grows fat. But Miss Gunning loves affliction as well
as Lady Mary Coke does persecution, and so do they
all, and they are so fond of their fine feelings, that it
is impossible to persuade them out of their imaginary
grievances, because they pique themselves upon the
superiority they think they have over the rest of the
world in being vexed at trifles we vulgar minds overlook.

[1] General William Medows, K.B.,
brother of first Lord Manvers, married
Frances, daughter of R. Hamerton.
He was an old admirer as well as a
cousin of Lady Louisa's. See *ante*,
p. 27.

[2] Seat of the Gunnings of Northamptonshire.

Saturday.

Lady Jane dined here yesterday, and I went home with her, and whom should we find waiting for us but General Medows. He stayed till past ten o'clock—nay, till I had lost my heart. I bid Lady Jane talk no more of Lord Rawdon's heroism or Mr. Erskine's vivacity. The General shall be my beloved. I wonder whether his wife admires him as much as she ought; I am sure some folks do not, or he would be in another situation. He was Lieutenant-Colonel of Lord Percy's regiment, fought at the head of it all the war, and was wounded. This is the very one just given to General Stopford, who lived peaceably in Ireland all the time, and when Medows came to town to ask it, it was already gone, so there he is, likely to remain a half-pay officer till another war. But he seems to have that independent spirit which fortune cannot depress or exalt. He is really a character unlike anything but himself, *au reste*, the most agreeable man I ever met with, and one of the most humorous. We told him if he liked us he would come again. My father continues to have a sad cold and cough, so we are no gayer than the weather at home. I fear he will not easily get rid of it while this snow and frost last, and it appears set in.

END OF VOL. I

Printed by R. & R. Clark, Limited, *Edinburgh.*

Lightning Source UK Ltd.
Milton Keynes UK
UKHW020617070819
347551UK00010B/1560/P

9 781377 084008